SABOTAGE

SABOTAGE

The Mafia, Mao and the Death of the *Queen Elizabeth*

BRIAN IZZARD

AMBERLEY

Dedicated to Tildy

First published 2012

Amberley Publishing
The Hill, Stroud
Gloucestershire, GL5 4EP

www.amberley-books.com

British Library Cataloguing in Publication Data.
A catalogue record for this book is available from the British Library.

ISBN 978 1 4456 0348 3

Typeset in 10pt on 12pt Sabon.
Typesetting and Origination by Amberley Publishing.
Printed in the UK.

Contents

Introduction

The groans and the cries of the giant wreck lasted for weeks, months. The teak decks that had seen royalty, political leaders and Hollywood stars, as well as many hundreds of thousands of other travellers over the years, were gone, as if they never existed. On 12 January 1972 the former Cunard liner *Queen Elizabeth* was lying on her starboard side, blackened and almost unrecognisable. Parts of her superstructure had collapsed and the bridge, from where some of the finest Merchant Navy captains had kept a watchful eye, was a mass of tangled metal. But the last fire appeared to be out. For three days flames and smoke had consumed what many have come to regard as the finest ocean liner of the twentieth century. With her clean lines, the elegant and fast Cunarder had graced the Atlantic for nearly three decades, all 83,000 tons of her. Now she was an object of morbid curiosity for an army of onlookers.

The morning of 9 January, a Sunday, had seemed promising. The ship was anchored in Hong Kong harbour, not far from Tsing Yi Island. It was a fine sunny day, with a cooling breeze, and the sea was moderate. For nearly six months some 2,000 workers had been swarming over the ship, seven days a week, carrying out a hugely expensive refit. The work was nearing completion, and a reception to celebrate the transformation was planned for that afternoon. Some of the guests were so keen to see the ship that they boarded tenders taking workers to the liner at 8 a.m. Shortly before 11.30 a.m. three cabin boys ran along a passageway shouting, 'Fire!' It soon became clear that the ship was doomed.

The cabin boys had spotted one fire but reports of others quickly came in. Nine fires, possibly more, had broken out in different parts of the ship at about the same time. The destruction of the *Queen Elizabeth* made world headlines. In June 1972 a court of inquiry, not surprisingly, came to the conclusion that it had been sabotage. But who carried out the attack? And why? It has been a mystery for forty years.

The liner had been bought at a bizarre auction in Florida in September 1970 by Hong Kong shipping tycoon C. Y. Tung. He did not get the fine ship that was the object of so much admiration during her Cunard days. She was still in the shipping line's colours – black hull and white superstructure, with those two distinctive reddish-orange and black funnels – but she was in poor condition after more than two years of neglect in the Florida sunshine.

In the years following the Second World War Tung built up a huge cargo fleet, making a fortune. Some shipping bosses saw their vessels simply as money-makers. Tung insisted that he did not – he loved ships. And he said that he had always been in love with the *Queen Elizabeth*. When he bought her at auction, there was a plan of action. He would take her to Hong Kong, restore her – though with his own touches – and use her again as a fine passenger ship and floating university.

After a torturous journey from Florida the rusting ship, renamed *Seawise University*, limped into Hong Kong harbour on 15 July 1971 to a warm welcome from small craft, helicopters and sightseers on land. Work on her started soon afterwards.

The *Queen Elizabeth* and her near-sister the *Queen Mary* had been iconic symbols of Britain, and Cunard's decision in 1967 to sell them shocked and saddened the nation. The liners helped to win the Second World War, and in the austere and colourless post-war years they brought glamour to the transatlantic route. Cunard found itself with a licence to print money. However, by the early 1960s the picture had changed dramatically. Jet travel was in vogue and Cunard's profits sank as it struggled to attract passengers with the slogan 'Getting there is half the fun'. In 1967 the company was facing a financial crisis.

The sale of the *Queen Mary* went relatively smoothly. Cunard's board of directors, led by Sir Basil Smallpeice, the unsentimental accountant's accountant, expected to dispose of the *Queen Elizabeth* without fuss. However, a nightmare was about to unfold.

There were more than 100 enquiries but few serious offers. The Cunard board made the mistake of agreeing to sell the liner to three flamboyant American businessmen, who planned to berth the ship in their home city of Philadelphia as a tourist attraction, the 'eighth wonder of the world'. These plans unravelled quickly. The trio, Stanton Miller and his younger brother Robert and Charles Williard, were apparently unaware that the Delaware River was too shallow to take the ship. The *Queen Elizabeth* ended up at Port Everglades, Florida, in December 1968. Cunard had sold the liner for $7.75 million but received only a deposit of $600,000. Problems continued to pile up. It emerged that the Millers and Williard had some unusual friends, two of whom were Angelo Bruno, boss of the Philadelphia Mafia, and Jimmy Hoffa, notorious leader of the Teamsters' Union. Both would end up being murdered. Surprisingly, Cunard persisted in dealing with the Millers and Williard, agreeing to re-financing deals, apparently unaware that south Florida was the holiday home of Mafia leaders from all over the United States.

In August 1970 Smallpeice and the other directors received a shock. The US Department of Justice informed them that it was conducting an investigation into organised crime. It wanted Cunard's deputy chairman, Peter Shirley, who had been mainly responsible for dealing with the Philadelphia trio, to appear before a federal grand jury in Miami to see if the Mafia had been involved in buying the *Queen Elizabeth*.

It was not the only shock. The FBI had been investigating the activities of Jack 'Sonny' Henderson, who resigned as the port manager of Port Everglades shortly after the *Queen Elizabeth*'s arrival. Henderson, a former police chief, was accused of rackets involving the ship. But before his trial – with Peter Shirley as a key prosecution witness – he was found murdered. Henderson had been shot twice in the head in a Mafia-style execution.

The last company running the *Queen Elizabeth* as a tourist attraction in Florida ended up filing for bankruptcy and that led to the auction and C. Y. Tung's purchase of the ship. Tung was originally from Shanghai and a long-time supporter of Chiang Kai-shek, who had been in power in China as leader of the Nationalist Party. When Mao Tse-tung's Communists took over the country in 1949, Chiang fled to Taiwan with his followers, including Tung, who later based himself in Hong Kong. However, Tung always remained loyal to Chiang and Taiwan. He planned to restore the *Queen Elizabeth* as the world's greatest liner – a symbol not of Great Britain and her sea power but of Taiwan and her struggle to remain independent of Communist China.

In 1971 Hong Kong was facing three major problems. The colony was in the grip of a crime wave. There were around fifty triad gangs, with tens of thousands of members. Police corruption was rife, and soon there would be a series of high-profile court cases involving expatriate officers holding senior positions. The third problem for the authorities was spying. China, Taiwan and the Soviet Union found Hong Kong a useful place for espionage. Mao's spies, under the guise of the Xinhua News Agency, always kept a close watch on activities in the colony, and Chinese officials developed links with the triads.

The year 1971, when the *Queen Elizabeth* arrived in Hong Kong, was a crucial one for relations between China and the United States, long-sworn enemies. Suddenly, the climate changed and Mao began wooing President Richard Nixon. US envoy Henry Kissinger's secret visits to Beijing, with Taiwan top of the agenda, coincided with the *Queen Elizabeth*'s arrival in Hong Kong. And Nixon's historic meeting with Mao in Beijing came little more than a month after the *Queen Elizabeth*'s destruction.

Was a political motive behind the sabotage? The case is compelling.

CHAPTER 1

Going to War

The *Queen Elizabeth* began life as order Number 552 at the John Brown shipyard, Clydebank. When she was launched on 27 September 1938, her near-sister, the *Queen Mary*, had been speeding back and forth across the Atlantic for more than two years, establishing a great rivalry with the fine French liner *Normandie*. Both *Queens* had experienced difficult births, surviving the Depression and financial juggling. In September 1938 dark clouds were gathering – another world war was only a year away.

Before launching the new Cunarder, Queen Elizabeth, later the Queen Mother, referred to the dark clouds. King George VI was unable to attend the ceremony, but the Queen told the large crowd:

> He bids the people of this country to be of good cheer in spite of the dark clouds hanging over them and indeed over the whole world. He knows well that, as ever before in critical times, they will keep cool heads and brave hearts. He knows, too, that they will place entire confidence in their leaders who, under God's providence, are striving their utmost to find a just and peaceful solution to the grave problems which confront them.

The Queen also said: 'The launching of a ship is like the inception of all great human enterprises, an act of faith. We cannot foretell the future …'

The ribbon was cut, the bottle of Empire wine – not champagne – smashed against the bow and 'the noblest vessel ever built in Britain' began her journey down the same slipway used by the *Queen Mary*, her speed kept in check by bundles of chains weighing a total of 2,350 tons, which were attached to the hull. Soon she was afloat in the Clyde.

The Times reported:

> She was greeted by the deafening noise of steam whistles from all the craft in the river, which in turn was almost drowned by the roar of the drag chains,

the rising cloud of dust from which almost hid the ship and the river from the launching platform.

Some 30,000 people had gathered at the shipyard, including 8,000 John Brown workers who had been given a day's holiday with pay and free tickets to the ceremony. The number of spectators on both sides of the river was estimated at 250,000.[1]

On the same day it was reported that the Royal Navy had decided to mobilize the fleet, calling up all its reservists.

The plan to have two huge liners conquering the Atlantic with a weekly service in both directions was the dream of Sir Percy Bates, Cunard's chairman from 1930 to 1946. Only four years separated the *Queens*, but he acknowledged in his speech at the launch that there had been important advances in naval architecture and marine engineering. 'The ship you have just seen launched is no slavish copy of her sister,' he said.

> For our schedule we need no more speed than the *Queen Mary* has got. There is no sense in having one-half of a weekly service faster than the other. Yet technical advances made it absurd for us to repeat what we have done. There had to be changes. These changes have cost us little or no money. They can hardly be needed in speed, though I think Number 552 might travel a little faster than Number 534 [the *Queen Mary*'s shipyard designation], but they can be expressed in economy in the weekly job of crossing the Atlantic.

Bates did not mention the *Normandie*, but she had played a part in the design of the *Queen Elizabeth*. The French ship had attracted praise from the outset for her pleasing lines. By contrast the upper decks of the *Queen Mary*, which had large ventilators, were seen as rather cluttered. The *Queen Mary* and the *Normandie*, which entered service in 1935, both had three funnels, and it was decided that the *Queen Elizabeth* needed only two. Along with other improvements, this helped to give her a cleaner look. It has since emerged that Cunard booked a voyage on the *Normandie* for one its designers so that he could get a better idea of the competition. To throw the French Line off the scent he apparently listed his occupation as 'grocer'.[2] Sadly, the *Queen Elizabeth* and the *Normandie* would suffer a similar fate.

Three days after the *Queen Elizabeth*'s launch, Prime Minister Neville Chamberlain returned to Britain following talks with Hitler in Munich. Waving a piece of paper at Heston airport in west London, he made his famous 'peace in our time' claim. Later that day, outside 10 Downing Street, he said: 'My good friends … I recommend you go home and sleep quietly in your beds.'

Fortunately a lot of people were not sleeping. Being built alongside the *Queen Elizabeth* was a King George V class battleship, which would become HMS *Duke of York* and play a role in helping to destroy the German battlecruiser *Scharnhorst* in 1943.

By the time war was declared, on 3 September 1939, the *Queen Elizabeth* was still in her Clydebank fitting-out basin. The following day the *Queen Mary* arrived in New York and there she stayed. What should wartime Britain do with these liners? In the case of the *Queen Elizabeth*, suggestions ranged from hiding the ship in a loch to converting her to an aircraft carrier. Winston Churchill, so long a political outcast, had returned to government as First Lord of the Admiralty, and he expressed concern that German bombers might attack her at Clydebank. Work on the ship was speeded up so that she would be able to sail. There was another reason for urgency – the fitting-out basin was needed for the *Duke of York*.

The liner would be ready early in 1940, but it turned out that for the entire year there were only two days when the ship could sail and the tide was high enough for her to negotiate the Clyde, and they were six months apart. On 26 February, with the aid of tugs, she slipped slowly away, a grey ghost. Her black hull and white superstructure had been repainted.

The departure date had been kept a secret, and more subterfuge was planned. Five hours later she stopped at a Clyde anchorage called the Tail o' the Bank, and the following day John Brown officially handed over the ship to Cunard. It was highly unusual – there had been no sea trials.

The *Queen Elizabeth* remained there for a few days as some 400 crew joined her. Shipyard workers finished off some of the many jobs and tests were carried out on machinery. Passenger areas had been completed and luxurious décor contrasted sharply with many other parts of the ship that still needed work, including some of the crew's quarters. Electrical cables were strewn around and steel decks were bare. This was a ship that had left in a hurry.

It was suggested that the *Queen Elizabeth* would be heading for Southampton, which had a dry dock large enough to take her. Crates apparently containing parts and fittings for the ship were sent to the port, and the port authority was told to expect her. Across the Channel, the German air force was waiting for her to arrive. Southampton would be badly bombed during the war. Fifty-seven attacks, some involving more than fifty bombers, left 630 civilians dead and 898 seriously injured. Nearly 500 tons of high explosives were dropped, as well as 30,000 incendiary devices, and 45,000 buildings were destroyed or damaged. On 6 November 1940 a bomb fell on the city's civic centre, where an art class was being held, and fourteen children were killed. Clydebank did not escape either. On two nights in March 1941 the town was largely destroyed, with the loss of 528 lives. Some 48,000 civilians lost their homes, many of them shipyard workers.[3]

It was never intended, however, to send the *Queen Elizabeth* to Southampton. Churchill wanted her to leave Britain as soon as possible. On 27 February the crew were told they would be leaving home waters but they were given the option of staying behind. Some decided they did not want to sail and they were taken off but kept on a tender in a nearby loch until the ship left. The remaining crew were given a pay rise. The *Queen Elizabeth* weighed anchor on 2 March for the strangest of maiden voyages. She was given an escort of four destroyers until she reached the Atlantic. Her master, Captain Jack Townley, opened his sealed orders. They were going to New York.

The *Queen Elizabeth* was unarmed and she would be relying on her speed to beat the U-boats. Cunard's superintendent engineer had assured Sir Percy Bates that even without a proper working up the liner could do about 25 knots or, at a push, 32 knots. The start of the German navy's wolf-pack strategy for U-boats was only a few months away, and from July until October 1940 more than 220 Allied ships were sunk.

One person who had not expected to make the trip was Captain Duncan Cameron, the pilot who had taken the ship down the Clyde, as he had done with the *Queen Mary*. At the Tail o' the Bank he left the *Queen Elizabeth* but was asked by Cunard to rejoin her so that she could continue the voyage to Southampton – all part of the ruse for the benefit of German spies and the Luftwaffe. He had no luggage, of course, and members of the crew donated items of clothing.

Radio silence was broken once to tell the ship to alter course to avoid a convoy in case the enemy was watching. The liner had been ordered to zig-zag to make it more difficult for submarines to attack. During the wartime years this would be a familiar routine, but on one occasion, involving the *Queen Mary*, it would lead to a high loss of life.

On 7 March an airliner flew over the ship as she neared the east coast of the United States. The American plane was carrying reporters and, despite the secrecy, New York knew the liner was about to arrive. The *Queen Elizabeth* berthed on one side of Pier 90. On the other side was the *Queen Mary*, which had also been painted grey. Occupying the next berth was the *Normandie*, glowing in her peacetime colours. The world's three greatest liners were lying side by side.

The Queen sent a special message:

I send you my heartfelt congratulations on the safe arrival in New York of the *Queen Elizabeth*. Ever since I launched her in the fateful days of 1938, I have watched her progress with interest and admiration. Please convey to Captain Townley my compliments on the safe conclusion of her hazardous maiden voyage.

Churchill's reaction: 'Splendid!'

Of the 'strangest maiden voyage of any ocean queen', *The New York Times* reported on its front page:

> Contrasting with the gala first arrivals of other passenger liners that have preceded her into one of the world's busiest harbors, she was greeted with no rousing cheers, and at the dock no gay groups of passengers trooped down the gangway to a crowded pier.
>
> Her arrival and docking at Pier 90, after a few scattered blasts from the whistles of wandering harbor craft in the outer bay, took place in a quiet that seemed to have in it some essence of the trouble that sent her here, unfinished, unready for service, a half-manned ghost ship that was to be barred permanently to all visitors.

Captain Townley was obviously under orders to say as little as possible. 'It was a lovely voyage,' the master volunteered as he was almost mobbed by reporters and photographers in the Cunard lounge on Pier 90.

A leader column in *The New York Times* was enthusiastic about the new arrival:

> Those lucky New Yorkers who went to the waterfront yesterday afternoon will have a thrilling memory to pass on to their children and grandchildren. Many sagas of the sea have begun and ended in our harbor; but can the old-timers remember anything to compare with the unheralded arrival of the biggest and fastest liner in the world, after the most daring of all maiden crossings? It did not matter that the *Queen Elizabeth* wore a drab coat of gray on her first visit to New York, or that no brass bands went down the Bay to meet her. The interest of New Yorkers was echoed by admiration of Americans everywhere for those who built her, sailed her, and sent her on her way.
>
> She was due for launching on that terrible September day in 1938 when the Munich crisis reached its height. The British fleet was mobilized, and peace hung in the balance, but no crisis could keep this sea *Queen* from her schedule. For the past six months British shipyards have been crammed with war orders, and workers have been pressed relentlessly into war industries; yet war was not enough to prevent or delay her being made ready to sail. Neither could the threat of submarines and mines keep her from her first voyage, and now she lies safely in a harbor where German bombers cannot harm her.
>
> Any landlubber can see that the *Queen Elizabeth* is a fine ship, as sleek and graceful as a yacht, a credit to the British merchant marine. Her distinction is not only in being the largest ship in the world; she is also new in design,

as the *Queen Mary* was not. The *Queen Mary* was planned before the first crossings of the *Bremen*, the *Rex* and the *Normandie*. The *Queen Elizabeth* is the first British super-liner to embody the lessons of these maritime pioneers of our streamlined era. The British were right in not leaving such a ship at the mercy of air attack at home. Their luxury liners will have a job to do when the war is over. The dramatic maiden voyage of the *Queen Elizabeth* proves that the British are looking ahead to the days of peace, and to the laurels of peace which must be won.[4]

But the *Queens* were not going to sit out the war in New York. That month Churchill decided they could play a vital role in the war effort as troopships, moving many thousands of men at a time. The *Queen Mary* was the first to be called up and she sailed for Sydney, Australia, on 21 March to be converted. She made her first voyage as a troopship in May, sailing from Sydney to Scotland. November saw the *Queen Elizabeth* on the move. She needed to enter a dry dock for work – part of her launch gear was still attached to the hull – and she headed for Singapore via Cape Town. She could not use a dry dock in the United States because the country was still neutral and would not enter the war until the attack on Pearl Harbor on 7 December 1941.

Three weeks after leaving New York the liner arrived in Singapore, where her accommodation was expanded to carry 5,000 troops. Guns were fitted to her upper decks and she was repainted. Her next destination was Sydney and she arrived in February 1941 to an ecstatic welcome. Also there was the *Queen Mary*. Two months later the ships set off with nearly 12,000 troops from Australia and New Zealand for the campaign in North Africa – 5,600 on the *Queen Elizabeth* and 6,000 on the *Queen Mary*. It was the first time the ships had sailed together and they joined a remarkable convoy which included four well-known liners, Cunard's *Aquitania* and *Mauretania*, the *Ile de France* of the French Line and Holland America's *Nieuw Amsterdam*.

That year the *Queens* shuttled between Sydney and Port Tewfik at the southern end of the Suez Canal, carrying nearly 80,000 troops to the war zone and bringing prisoners of war, many of them wounded, on the return trips. But the liners, designed for the cold North Atlantic, became floating ovens in the tropics. On the return from Suez, with the decks overcrowded, the wounded were particularly vulnerable and it was not unusual to have a burial service every four hours.

Even the healthy Australians and New Zealanders found the heat intolerable and on one of the *Queen Elizabeth*'s voyages in July 1941, as troops headed for Suez, a near-riot broke out on a mess deck. Fists flew and so did crockery. This started off some of the crew, who had grievances of their own – poor quarters, indifferent food and little leave. They hurled kitchen utensils and pans of boiling water at each other, and a cook was forced into a heated oven and severely burned. Order was only restored when a party of Royal Marines was put on board from the cruiser HMS *Cornwall*. The ringleaders were sent to Britain for trial and jailed.[5]

When Japan went to war at the end of 1941, Australia decided it could no longer send troops for overseas campaigns. Men were needed at home to defend in case of an invasion by the Japanese, who would quickly conquer Malaya and Singapore. The *Queen Elizabeth* went to Canada for dry-dock work and later sailed to San Francisco to pick up US troops for Australia's defence. At that stage it was easier to use American soldiers than to return Australians from the Middle East. Senior US officers were surprised to learn that the liner had been transporting 5,000 troops at a time. Too few, they said – and drew up plans to accommodate 8,000. The Australian bunks were replaced by 'standee' beds of tubular steel and canvas, which could be arranged in tiers. The work took only five days, and the ship headed back to Sydney with 8,000 GIs.

By April 1942 British and American military planners were already looking at a build-up of forces in Britain with the aim of launching an invasion across the Channel. The two *Queens* would play a crucial role in ferrying huge numbers of troops across the Atlantic, the GI shuttle.

The *Queen Elizabeth* was sent to New York and on 5 June 1942 she headed for Gourock, not that far from her birthplace, Clydebank. There had been another rethink about accommodation, and she was transporting 10,000 troops. That figure would soon increase to 12,000 – and keep rising to more than 15,000. Standee beds appeared all over the ship. The swimming pool? The order went out: stack the beds seven high. The *Queen Elizabeth* had been designed to carry around 2,300 passengers.

From Scotland she took reinforcements to Suez to try to halt the progress of Erwin Rommel's Afrika Korps in North Africa. She returned to New York on 19 August and, with the *Queen Mary*, the regular five-day shuttle of troops to Gourock was established. Gourock, at the mouth of the Clyde, was considered just beyond the range of German bombers.

Hitler was aware of the importance of the *Queens* in taking American and Canadian troops to Britain, and he offered a reward equivalent to $250,000 to any U-boat captain who could sink either ship. One November day in 1942 Harry Grattidge, staff captain of the *Queen Mary*, which was berthed in New York, heard shocking news. It was reported that the *Queen Elizabeth* had been sunk. That morning he had a visitor to his ship, the Secretary to the US Treasury, Henry Morgenthau, whom he met at the head of the gangway. Morgenthau said: 'I have come to see where most of the money from the US Treasury seems to be going. Would you be kind enough to show me round this expensive military unit?'

Grattidge would recall: 'We began the tour of inspection. In truth, neither of us had too much heart for the job. The news was all over New York that morning that the *Queen Elizabeth* had been torpedoed and lost with all hands.'

Morgenthau said: 'I know it's unconfirmed as yet, but if it is true we have to accept it as a great military defeat.' Grattidge continued: 'I agreed, for, I knew, when I dared to think about it, that if either *Queen* was lost, the chance of saving 15,000 lives was pretty remote.'

After the tour they went to Grattidge's cabin where another guest joined them. 'But the gloom was so great that lunch hour that none of us had the heart to take a drink,' Grattidge recalled. 'Soon it became obvious there was no point in prolonging the party. We were just making our farewells when the phone rang. It was the girl at the Cunard exchange on the Pier Head [the shipping line's Liverpool headquarters].

'"Captain," she gulped, "Oh, captain – the *Queen Elizabeth* …"'

'"I know," I said patiently. "It's terrible news."'

'She almost squawked in her excitement. "No, no, you don't understand. Oh, captain, it was all a rumour … She's here. She's just anchored at Quarantine …"'

'"Gentlemen," I said, replacing the receiver, "will anyone refuse a glass of wine when I tell them that the *Queen Elizabeth* is with us now, safe and sound?"'

'There was not a dissenting voice. We charged our glasses. It was Henry Morgenthau who raised his first: "To the two great ladies of the Atlantic – the *Queens*".'[6]

It was Joseph Goebbels, Germany's propaganda chief, who claimed that the *Queen Elizabeth* had been sunk after a report from a U-boat captain was passed to him. Horst Kessler of *U-707* said he had spotted a large ship about 200 miles west of Ireland, which he identified as the *Queen Elizabeth*. A spread of four torpedoes was fired, and Kessler claimed one hit. On November 9 the *Queen Elizabeth* was travelling to New York and members of the crew did report hearing an explosion. But the ship had not been hit. It is believed that three of the torpedoes ran too deep and the fourth exploded after hitting a large wave. The ship was carrying several thousand women and children who were being evacuated, as well as British government officials and army officers who were on their way to a meeting on Allied strategy.

The previous month another U-boat captain, Ernst-Ulrich Bruller, had claimed to have attacked the *Queen Mary* in mid-Atlantic. *U-407* also fired four torpedoes, all of them missing. In March 1945, as the *Queen Elizabeth* neared the coast of Ireland on her way to Gourock, escorting destroyers warned that they had picked up the sounds of U-boats. The *Queen Elizabeth* ploughed on at speed, with depth charges exploding around her.

Churchill, who had replaced Chamberlain as prime minister in May 1940, and the Americans had recognised early on that they were running a massive risk with the overcrowded troopships. In December 1941, soon after Japan went to war, Churchill travelled to the United States in the new battleship *Duke of York* (he would also make similar trips in the *Queen Mary*) for talks with President Franklin Roosevelt. At one meeting the president told the prime minister he was willing, if necessary, to send 50,000 American troops for the defence of Australia and outlying islands. The attack on Pearl Harbor also led to the United States declaring war on Germany. At the White House one evening General George Marshall, Chief of Staff of the US Army, went to see Churchill and said that in addition there had been an agreement to send nearly 30,000 troops to Northern Ireland. The *Queens* had already been offered as troopships, and the general was concerned about the high numbers they would carry. Lifeboats and rafts could cope with 8,000, assuming they were all used to capacity and conditions were favourable, but 16,000?

Churchill said: 'You must judge for yourself the risks you will run. If it were a direct part of an actual operation, we should put all on board they could carry. If it were only a question of moving troops in a reasonable time, we should not go beyond the limits of lifeboats, rafts. It is for you to decide.'

This answer was received in silence. Churchill acknowledged that later on in the war the ships were 'filled to the brim'. He wrote: 'As it happened, fortune stood our friend.'[7]

In May 1941 Churchill had complained to navy and army chiefs that the *Queens* were carrying too few troops. He discovered that a War Office directive meant that eight gallons of water had to be provided for each man every day on a troopship. In a message to his chief military assistant, General Hastings Ismay, and the Admiralty, he commented:

I was much surprised to learn that only about 3,500 men were taken in the *Queen Elizabeth* and the *Queen Mary* each. This is hardly more than the numbers they carry when engaged in luxury passenger service. If I remember rightly, over 8,000 men were sent in the *Aquitania* or *Mauretania* to the Dardanelles in May 1915.[8]

The GI shuttle was involved in one disaster. On the morning of 2 October 1942 the *Queen Mary*, with more than 10,000 American soldiers on board, was zig-zagging her way towards the north-west coast of Ireland. She had an escort of five destroyers and the light cruiser HMS *Curacoa*. Visibility was good, and the captains of the *Queen Mary* and the *Curacoa* were aware of each other's speed and course. But somehow both ships ended up on a converging path and the 81,000-ton *Queen Mary* sliced completely through the 4,400-ton *Curacoa* at 28.5 knots. The collision was hardly felt by the men on *Queen*

Mary's bridge, but hundreds of GIs on the open decks saw it and many tossed their lifebelts into the water. *Curacoa*'s stern section sank quickly. The *Queen Mary*, under orders never to stop, steamed on. Four of the destroyers were given the task of picking up survivors – there were only 101 out of a crew of 439. The tragedy was kept secret until after the war. A court of inquiry ruled that the collision was the fault of the captain and officers of the *Curacoa*. The Admiralty lodged an appeal and the House of Lords decided the cruiser was two-thirds to blame.

Most of the service personnel carried by the *Queens* were infantrymen, but a significant number of air force ground staff boarded the ships in New York. Crates of fighter planes were also taken – sometimes a complete fighter wing. Twenty-six Allied divisions were assembled for the D-Day invasion in June 1944, and more than half of them were brought over by the *Queens*. Heading west, the ships also transported wounded GIs and thousands of German and Italian prisoners destined for camps in the United States and Canada. In March 1945 the *Queen Elizabeth* made her last visit to Gourock to disembark troops. Between April 1941 and March 1945 she had steamed 492,635 miles with 811,324 passengers. The highest number of people on a single voyage was 15,932, including the crew, but the *Queen Mary* could top that with 16,683.

The *Queens* probably shortened the war by a year. Churchill paid the ultimate tribute:

> The *Queens* challenged the fury of Hitlerism in the Battle of the Atlantic. At a speed never before realised in war, they carried over a million men to defend the liberties of civilisation. Often whole divisions at a time were moved by each ship. Vital decisions depended upon their ability continuously to elude the enemy, and without their aid the day of final victory must unquestionably have been postponed. To the men who contributed to the success of our operations in the years of peril, and to those who brought these two great ships into existence, the world owes a debt that will not be easy to measure.

The *Queen Elizabeth* happened to be in New York on both VE Day and VJ Day and her whistle joined in the celebrations. New Yorkers were in joyous mood. The liner had known only war and now she was about to experience peacetime and visit Southampton, her new home port, for the first time. In contrast to New York, she arrived there on 20 August to find a small, muted crowd, the local police band and the city's mayor. Perhaps the badly bombed port, with its skeletal buildings and rubble everywhere, could be forgiven for feeling a little weary.

The liner soon returned to duty. Another massive job had to be carried out – taking all those GIs back. The *Queen Elizabeth* left for New York with nearly

15,000 of them. She had a new master, Commodore Sir James Bisset, who had been in command of the *Queen Mary* for most of her wartime voyages. This time there was more of a celebration, and eight Meteor jets of the Royal Air Force flew over the ship in salute.

She made three such trips and then she was switched to the task of repatriating Canadian soldiers. On the journey home she brought British servicemen who had been prisoners in the Far East. Her hull and superstructure were still wartime grey, but on one trip Commodore Bisset had her funnels painted reddish orange and black so that she would start to look like a Cunarder.

There had not been a general election in Britain since 1935 and one was held in July 1945 in the wake of victory. The result was a shock for Churchill, who had been inspirational during the war years. The Labour Party, led by Clement Attlee, inflicted a heavy defeat on his Conservatives. The khaki vote believed that Labour would be better at rebuilding Britain in peacetime.

On her first voyage of 1946 the *Queen Elizabeth* sailed with 12,314 passengers, most of them Canadians. Among them was Churchill. Out of office, he was taking a well-earned break, a three-month holiday in Florida. A day before arriving in New York, the orator decided to make a broadcast to the ship and he was soon in full flow:

What a strange fearful yet glittering chapter this war has been. What changes it has brought throughout the world and in the fortunes of so many families. What an interruption in all the plans each of us has made. What a surrender of the liberties we prized. What a casting away of comfort and safety. What a pride in peril. What a glory shines on the brave and true. The good cause has not been overthrown. Tyrants have been hurled from their place of power, and those who have sought to enslave the future of mankind have paid, or will pay, the final penalty.

You Canadians, many of whom served in the Canadian 5th Division, no doubt have your minds filled with the victorious war scenes of Italy and the Rhine. But we Englishmen always think of the days of 1940, when the Canadian Army Corps stood almost alone in Kent and Sussex, and the Germans had 25 divisions ready to leap across the Channel and wipe Great Britain out of life and history. I think about those days, too, sometimes, and how fine it was to see everyone, at home and throughout the empire, moved by the same impulse, so simple, so sublime – conquer or die.

Victory in arms, or in any walk of life, is only the opportunity of doing better on a large scale and at a higher level. Do not be anxious about the future. Be vigilant, be strong, be clear-sighted, but do not be worried. Our future is in our hands. Our lives are what we choose to make them. The great British Commonwealth and empire, emerging from the fire once again, glorious and free, will form a structure and an organisation within which there will be room for all, and a fair chance for all.

He added: 'Let us therefore have purpose, both in our national and imperial policy, and in our own private lives. Thus the future will be fruitful for each and for all, and the reward of the warriors will not be unworthy of the deeds they have done.'[9]

For someone who had experienced a crushing general election defeat, Churchill was in a remarkably optimistic mood. Perhaps he sensed he would become prime minister again.

On 6 March 1946 the British government announced that the *Queen Elizabeth* would no longer be needed as a troopship. A golden era of Atlantic travel was about to unfold.

CHAPTER 2

Glamour and Profits

Cunard bosses were in a hurry to get their flagship into service as a luxury liner plying the Atlantic. Despite carrying all those people and steaming all that distance, she had yet to make a proper commercial voyage, unlike the *Queen Mary*. A lot of work needed to be done on the *Queen Elizabeth* in 1946 to return the ship to her original design, with particular emphasis on the interior. First she had to shed many tons of troopship fittings, including 10,000 standee beds. And there was still work that had been left unfinished when the liner eased from her fitting-out basin at Clydebank all those years ago.

It was agreed that the *Queen Elizabeth* would return to the Clyde so that John Brown's workers could once again swarm over her. She could not reach Clydebank and instead would anchor off Gourock, the arrival point for so many GIs. The timescale was twelve weeks. John Brown would have liked longer, but Cunard insisted on a tight schedule. The ship would then return to Southampton for further work lasting ten weeks.

The *Queen Elizabeth* survived the Second World War, but she was lucky to remain intact in peacetime Southampton. On 8 March 1946, two days before she was released from government duty, a serious fire broke out. Smoke was seen pouring from an area that was being used to store medical supplies, some of them highly inflammable. The former isolation hospital was one of the few parts of the ship that had not been fitted with automatic sprinklers. The smoke spread through the ventilation system, hampering efforts to fight the blaze. When firefighters from Southampton and surrounding towns arrived, it was discovered that their ladders were not long enough. The resourceful Commodore Bisset came up with a solution – the lifeboats were lowered, firemen climbed in and they were hoisted high enough so that hoses could be trained on the fire, which was on Promenade Deck. It took three hours to put out the blaze. An investigation concluded that a workman's discarded cigarette was the likely cause.

On 30 March, with a reduced crew, the ship sailed for Scotland. There were numerous jobs: machinery had been worked hard during the war years, the main areas and cabins needed restoring, decks had to be replaced, fine wooden panelling, one of the ship's features, required attention. The grey ghost also had to be transformed into Cunard's colours. That job needed 30 tons of paint.

On 16 June the *Queen Elizabeth* returned to Southampton carrying 1,000 Clydebank workers who would help with the second phase of the task. Fittings deemed unnecessary in wartime, from beds and settees to carpets and works of art, had been removed in New York and Sydney. They were collected and ended up in two aircraft hangars outside Southampton. The liner needed more than 21,000 pieces of furniture, much of it fitted. Finally, she entered the King George V dry dock for checks on her hull, rudder and propellers.

On 6 October she was heading back to the Clyde for speed trials. Before setting off, Cunard's chairman, Sir Percy Bates, told Commodore Bisset he would have a special visitor when the ship arrived – the Queen. Bates also cautioned the master against racing the *Queen Elizabeth*. The *Queen Mary* was the holder of the prestigious Blue Riband for the fastest crossing of the Atlantic, based on average speed because routes varied (in 1938 she made the eastbound crossing at 31.69 knots). The Blue Riband had caught the imagination of the British public and many people hoped to see competition from the *Queen Elizabeth*. But as Bates had made clear at the launch of the *Queen Elizabeth*, he was not keen on his *Queens* racing each other.

A few days later the Queen and her daughters, Princess Elizabeth and Princess Margaret, boarded the ship. Bates introduced the Queen to the commodore and she told him: 'I have been looking forward to this moment so much. I have been watching the ship with great interest throughout the war.'

The royal party were taken to the bridge during the afternoon and the two princesses were given stopwatches so that they could check the ship's speed over a measured mile in the Firth of Clyde. Two speeds were recorded – 29.71 knots and 29.75 knots. Commodore Bisset knew his ship could easily do more than 30 knots but any temptation to go faster must have been tempered by the knowledge that the boss was on board. The speed trials were deemed a success and the *Queen Elizabeth* returned to Southampton on 10 October. Strangely, this veteran of some half a million miles was about to have a maiden voyage. This was set for 16 October 1946, Southampton to New York.

There were three classes for passengers, first, cabin and tourist. The ship could accommodate 850 first-class passengers and, naturally, they had the best-designed and best-placed cabins and public areas. The first-class restaurant and the Observation Lounge's cocktail bar were probably the most impressive areas. The huge restaurant, the height of two decks, was panelled in fine wood and displayed carvings and sculptures. A superb tapestry with a nautical theme dominated one end of the restaurant.

The voyage should have been one of the highlights of Sir Percy Bates's career. He was due to sail with the ship but the day before her departure, he suffered a heart attack at Cunard's Liverpool headquarters and died aged 67. Flags at the company's Southampton's offices and on many vessels flew at half-mast, but the *Queen Elizabeth* remained dressed overall. Commodore Bisset said: 'Percy would have wished it that way. We shall pay tribute to him on the day of his funeral in an appropriate way.'

At sea, Bisset did indeed pay tribute during a memorial service:

Sir Percy Bates was mainly responsible for the building of these two great vessels, *Queen Mary* and *Queen Elizabeth*. He watched them grow, from masses of steel girders and plates, into the magnificent structures they are today. They were the children of his brain. He lived for them, he worked for them, he wore himself out with anxieties for them, and he has died for them.

We who knew him, admired him, and loved him, have felt a shock of intense sorrow at his untimely passing – untimely for he was to have been with us on this maiden voyage, and like all of us in any way connected with this ship, he had looked forward with high hopes to its accomplishment. He loved the sea, he loved the ships, and he loved those who do business in the great waters.

Here, in this ship, in mid-ocean, we remember him, with grief in our hearts and profound sympathy in our thoughts for Lady Bates and his sorrowing family and all the loved ones he has left behind.

Sir Percy's brother Frederick took over as chairman.

The maiden voyage attracted 2,228 passengers, some of whom had booked years earlier when they thought it would take place in 1940. Many eminent people were on the passenger list, but the person who attracted the most attention, despite efforts to shield him from publicity, was Vyacheslav Molotov, the Soviet foreign minister, who was heading for a session of the United Nations. Comrade Molotov, apparently, did not have any objections to his luxurious surroundings or the extensive menus (Britain was still living with ration books although Cunard pointed out that it obtained most of its food from the United States and Canada). Churchill had met Molotov during the war and regarded him as a 'man of outstanding ability and cold-blooded ruthlessness'. Lenin had not been so impressed, describing Molotov as 'mediocrity personified'. Certainly the old-guard Stalinist had a reputation for dullness. Ironically, he is probably best remembered for having a firebomb named after him, the Molotov cocktail. But in 1946 he was one of the most important characters on the world's political stage.

Because of Sir Percy's death there were no bands on the quayside when the *Queen Elizabeth* set sail, but tens of thousands of people cheered as she made her way down Southampton Water towards the Solent. At Spithead, off

Portsmouth, she exchanged signals with the battleship HMS *Queen Elizabeth*. The liner arrived in New York on 21 October, Trafalgar Day. A flotilla of small craft added to the city's enthusiastic welcome as the ship negotiated the Hudson River and berthed. An unsmiling Molotov was one of the first passengers to disembark.

The *Queen Mary* had been on government duty until September 1946, carrying American and Canadian servicemen home. She was also given another important job – transporting thousands of GI brides, and babies, across the Atlantic to a new life. After being demobbed, work was urgently carried out to restore the *Queen Mary* to the iconic status she had enjoyed before the war.

In 1947 the two *Queens* began the Atlantic shuttle service that had been the dream of Sir Percy Bates. In July of that year the liners, in their newly acquired Cunard colours, passed each other near the Isle of Wight. The *Queen Elizabeth* was heading for New York and the *Queen Mary* was returning to Southampton. In the years to come the ships would often pass in mid-Atlantic, to the delight of passengers. First-class passengers in the *Queen Mary* had the added advantage of a superb artwork map, 24 feet by 15 feet, at one end of their restaurant, which showed the course and position of the ship, represented by a liner in crystal.

The next ten years were a prosperous time for Cunard. Profits were high and bookings were sometimes made six months in advance. For many famous and wealthy people, including Hollywood stars, the *Queens* were the first choice when it came to Atlantic travel. The Duke and Duchess of Windsor boarded the *Queen Elizabeth* for her second voyage from Southampton. They became frequent passengers, and on one occasion seventy-five suitcases were delivered to their suite, with a further seventy trunks labelled for the hold. It must have been a large suite.

Humphrey Bogart, Rita Hayworth, Joan Crawford, Bing Crosby, Laurel and Hardy, and David Niven were among the stars who chose Cunard. The shipping line had a well-deserved reputation for serving food and wine that could match the world's best restaurants. Its chefs were also noted for being able to satisfy unusual requests. But not all the stars wanted haute cuisine. Richard Burton and Elizabeth Taylor favoured steak and kidney pie, and Noel Coward often ordered sausages and mashed potatoes.

For nearly five years, from 1947 to 1952, the *Queens* did not have any serious competition on the Atlantic run. The French liner *Normandie* had been scrapped after a fire at her berth in New York in 1942. However, in July 1952 a new liner appeared, the *United States*. US government officials had long been impressed by the troopship capabilities of the two *Queens* during the Second World War. It was decided to build a liner that could be converted quickly into a troopship – and the emphasis was on speed. The ship's construction was heavily subsidised by the US government. The *United States* of the United States Lines made her maiden voyage on 4 July 1952 and broke the transatlantic speed record that had been held by the *Queen Mary* for the past fourteen years by more than ten hours. She did the eastbound crossing in 3 days, 10 hours and 40 minutes at an average speed of 35.59 knots. The *United States* also broke the record for the westbound crossing – 3 days, 12 hours and 12 minutes. But she lacked the glamour of the *Queens*. At 53,330 tons, she weighed in at a lot less than her rivals, although a great deal of aluminium had been used in her superstructure to make her lighter. Her interior was more functional than decorative, largely because the focus had been on using fire-resistant materials. The liner was withdrawn from service in 1969, and over the ensuing years various plans to relaunch her as passenger ship failed to materialise. In 2012 she was a forlorn sight at a berth in south Philadelphia, but at least she had avoided the breaker's yard. She still holds the Blue Riband for the fastest Atlantic crossing by a passenger ship.

Such was the impact of the *Queens* in the early days after the war that the airlines were soon running scared. At the end of 1946 Pan American World Airways admitted that it could not compete. On a single Atlantic crossing the *Queen Elizabeth* could carry enough passengers for fifty-six Pan Am flights. A plane could take only forty passengers. The airline cut the number of flights and announced job losses at its offices in London and New York. In the late 1950s the picture would start to reverse and it would be Cunard finding the competition too much – because of the age of the jet-setter.

Cunard's bosses had seen only good times ahead on the financial front. As Commodore Geoffrey Marr noted:

For ten glorious years, until 1957, the Cunard Line had passengers clamouring to be able to sail in its ships, some of them quite willing to put down a deposit six months before they wanted to sail, in order to secure the cabin of their choice. Indeed to the directors sitting around that oak table on the fifth floor of the very solid Cunard Building at Liverpool's pierhead it must have looked as though they had found the secret of eternal prosperity.

When the two *Queens* got into their stride each ship was showing a gross profit of over £100,000 per round voyage, and in 1949 the chairman, in his annual statement, was able to announce a gross profit of about £7,000,000, of which half had to be paid to the government as excess profits and other taxes. In 1957, with a magnificent fleet of 12 passenger liners, we were to carry the greatest number of passengers across the Atlantic and on luxury cruises than in any year of the company's 117-year history.

But also in 1957, the first of the big jets went streaking across the Atlantic in less than six hours, and although to us at the time it seemed like the proverbial 'cloud no bigger than a man's hand', this was to prove the start of a new era in travel history.[1]

The golden age, however, was not without incident. In January 1947 Commodore Bisset handed over command of the *Queen Elizabeth* to Captain Charles Ford, who was nicknamed 'Foggy' because his vessels frequently encountered fog. On 14 April he was about to live up to his nickname. The liner was sailing towards the Isle of Wight and Southampton with 2,246 passengers on board when she encountered thick fog. Fortunately this cleared and a pilot was picked up to guide the ship on the final stretch. Usually, Cunard insisted on using pilots from an approved list, but on this occasion none was available and a new face joined the ship. Unfortunately, it was the first time that this pilot had handled a ship as large as the *Queen Elizabeth*.

Off Cowes the ship turned to enter a channel between two sandbanks so that she could make her way to the entrance of Southampton Water. Geoffrey Marr was on board as senior first officer. He was not on the bridge but he sensed that something was wrong. The ship was not turning quickly enough. 'Suddenly everything began to shake,' he reported.

> The four big propellers started to thresh up the water as they checked her headway; but it was already too late. The ship must have been making about six knots through the water as she slid past Bourne Gap's red flashing buoy on the wrong side and buried her bows, almost up to the bridge, in the mud, sand and shingle bank.[2]

Moments earlier on the bridge, Captain Ford expressed concern that the ship was turning too slowly, but the pilot replied that everything was fine and continued to navigate. Instinct took over. The captain shouted: 'Half astern on the starboard engines.' It was not enough. The *Queen Elizabeth* was aground.

The captain gave the order to reverse engines but the ship was stuck. A tender took Cunard, port and salvage officials to the *Queen Elizabeth*, where long meetings were held in the captain's cabin. Early the next morning thirteen tugs arrived at the scene and an attempt was made to pull her free at high tide. It took three attempts and many hours, with tugs pulling first to port and then to starboard, to free the liner. Big crowds had gathered on shore to see the spectacle. There were cheers when the ship's whistle sounded to indicate that she was under way once again. And then the fog descended. The *Queen Elizabeth* berthed in Southampton 50 hours late. A diving inspection showed that the ship was undamaged, and Captain Ford was later absolved of blame.

According to another captain of the *Queen Elizabeth*, Commodore Robert Thelwell, the ship came close to disaster one day when two tankers appeared in the wrong place. The liner, with a pilot called Holt navigating, was heading down Southampton Water within sight of the jetty at the Fawley oil refinery. Thelwell gave this dramatic account:

Near the jetty a black blob of a tanker lay at anchor, almost athwart of the channel and heading westerly into the path of the *Queen Elizabeth*. Further south, a second tanker was attempting to make fast to buoys and sheering easterly in the process.

Holt snapped out an order at once: 'Reduce speed.' He waited for a moment until the order was transmitted. 'They told me before we sailed that the tankers would be safely berthed and out of our path,' said Holt in his quiet voice.

Those who have served under me in the big ships will concede, I think, that whatever my defects, a tendency to panic is not one. But I confess that at that moment I was near to panic. Holt was navigating the ship but the responsibility for the safety of the ship itself, was mine alone.

And I knew, as Holt did, that we were heading for certain disaster with hardly any cards in our hands to play and little to do except wait and pray that our luck would hold. For the tankers were loaded with oil. The slightest collision would generate sparks and the tankers would become more lethal than a torpedo discharged into the unprotected belly of the ship I commanded.

I began to think of the orders I would give when the searing explosion took place – assuming that I was still alive to give orders and that there were any officers and seamen left to carry them out. My war experience had not, fortunately, included the sight of a tanker attacked by enemy aircraft, but friends had told me how terrible it could be and I had a picture in my mind of broken bodies, a smashed ship and a sea of blazing oil. It was quite possible that the explosion would be so violent that my gigantic ship would be sent to the bottom of Southampton Water before we could lower any of the boats.

Whilst these fearful thoughts raced through my mind, I glanced away from the tanker for a few moments. The white, tense faces of the staff captain and chief officer showed that they had seen what the pilot and I had seen. Below us on the decks the passengers strolled about in the sunlight or leaned over the starboard side to gaze in awe at the refinery. The ship was gliding to almost certain destruction yet only a handful of us, of all the souls on board, knew it.

A quiet voice interrupted my thoughts. 'You know, captain,' said Holt, 'this is the sort of situation that can cause considerable danger.' I could not and cannot recall ever hearing such an understatement in my lifetime. We both stared ahead, unable to take our eyes away from the two tankers as we bore down on them. I knew as well as Holt that we dared not reduce speed any more or the rudder would be useless and the ship hopelessly out of control. We had gone to the limit of what we could do in the matter of speed. 'Ease the helm.' Only superb steering and luck – especially luck – could now save the ship. 'Port easy. Port more.' We had sailed at high water, and the tide was behind us and a still freshening wind would have made it hard to keep the ship on course at the best of times without additional hazard. Yet Holt's voice contained no hint of nervousness.

A hundred yards and we should know our fate. Fifty yards. Now we were within twenty yards of the leading tanker and we could see her cable across the bow and apparently leading somewhere astern. The two tugs which had been berthing her stood off. The wind blew harder and, in spite of all the pilot could do, caused the ship to drift nearer the tanker.

Fifteen yards to go – fifteen agonising yards which could just as end in death as in life. I could scarcely breathe as the gap between the tanker and the track we were taking narrowed inexorably. Ten yards. The crisis was on us and over almost at the same time. The *Queen* was holding to her course. 'I think we're in luck's way this morning,' said Holt.

A few more moments and we were safe, though with no more than ten feet to spare. The passengers on the rails, cheering and waving to the tanker's frightened crew, would never know why there was not a wave in return or how close they had been to a terrible death.[3]

The *Queen Elizabeth* also missed the second tanker.

However, most of the publicity that the *Queens* attracted was good, stoked largely by the Cunard publicity machine. Take this advertisement to woo the American market:

The biggest shows on earth aren't on earth at all – they're Cunard's *Queen Elizabeth* and *Queen Mary* plying the sparkling Atlantic. The *Queens* reign as the biggest liners afloat by far, affording you more room for pleasure. And it's all in the fare. Peerless international gourmet cuisine. Meticulous British service. Sports and games. Dancing. Nightclubbing. Rejuvenating and refreshing you as only the grand resort life at sea can do. Begin your vacation with a vacation. Sail. Soon. Big.

CHAPTER 3

A Rival Called Boeing

It all began with one Samuel Cunard, the son of a dockyard carpenter from Halifax, Nova Scotia, and a 1,145-ton paddle-steamer named *Britannia*. The ship set off on her maiden voyage, Liverpool to Nova Scotia, on 4 July 1840. Samuel Cunard, who was on board, had secured a lucrative British government contract to carry mail, and he never looked back. His shipping line grew quickly, though not all his passengers were impressed with their voyage across the Atlantic.

The Cunard publicity machine of the twentieth century, which was never reticent when it came to the use of adjectives, would have been keen to promote the fact that Charles Dickens had been a passenger, but not his thoughts on coping with a stormy time at sea.

The giant of English literature, who sailed to the United States in *Britannia* in January 1842, wrote this amusing account:

> I am awakened out of my sleep by a dismal shriek from my wife, who demands to know whether there's any danger. I rouse myself, and look out of bed. The water-jug is plunging and leaping like a lively dolphin; all the smaller articles are afloat except my shoes, which are stranded on a carpet-bag, high and dry, like a couple of coal-barges. Suddenly I see them spring into the air, and behold the looking-glass, which is nailed to the wall, sticking fast upon the ceiling. At the same time the door entirely disappears, and a new one is opened in the floor. Then I begin to comprehend that the state-room is standing on its head.
>
> Before it is possible to make any arrangements at all compatible with this novel state of things, the ship rights. Before one can say, 'Thank Heaven!' she wrongs again. Before one can cry she is wrong, she seems to have started forward, and to be a creature actually running of its own accord, with broken knees and failing legs, through every variety of hole and pitfall, and stumbling constantly. Before one can so much as wonder, she takes a

high leap into the air. Before she has well done that, she takes a deep dive into the water. Before she has gained the surface, she throws a summersault. The instant she is on her legs, she rushes backward. And so she goes on, staggering, heaving, wrestling, leaping, diving, jumping, pitching, throbbing, rolling, and rocking: and going through all these movements, sometimes by turns, and sometimes all together: until one feels disposed to roar for mercy.

A steward passes. 'Steward!' 'Sir?' 'What *is* the matter? What *do* you call this?' 'Rather a heavy sea on, sir, and a head-wind.'

A head-wind! Imagine a human face upon the vessel's prow, with fifteen thousand Sampsons in one bent upon driving her back, and hitting her exactly between the eyes whenever she attempts to advance an inch. Imagine the ship herself, with every pulse and artery of her huge body swollen and bursting under this maltreatment, sworn to go on or die. Imagine the wind howling, the sea roaring, the rain beating: all in furious array against her. Picture the sky both dark and wild, and the clouds, in fearful sympathy with the waves, making another ocean in the air. Add to all this, the clattering on deck and down below: the tread of hurried feet; the loud hoarse shouts of seamen; the gurgling in and out of water through the scuppers; with, every now and then, the striking of a heavy sea upon the planks above, with the deep, dead, heavy sound of thunder heard within a vault – and there is the head-wind of that January morning.

Dickens also noted 'the breaking of glass and crockery, the tumbling down of stewards … and the very remarkable and far from exhilarating sounds raised in their various state-rooms by the seventy passengers who were too ill to get up to breakfast'. The author was 'excessively sea-sick'.[1]

But still the passengers flocked to Samuel Cunard, travelling in bigger and better ships, decade after decade … until 1957, when warning signs emerged. Air travel was growing rapidly. No longer did Cunard's directors possess 'the secret of eternal prosperity', as Commodore Geoffrey Marr had put it.

At a shareholders' meeting in May 1957, Cunard's chairman, Colonel Denis Bates, who had replaced his brother Frederick, reported a healthy surplus for the previous year, despite rising costs. More passengers had been carried across the Atlantic, and the cruise and cargo sides of the business were doing well. He told his shareholders he did not consider air travel to be a direct threat:

From time to time I have been asked what effect the air has had on our passenger business. In my view, sea and air passenger traffic have been complementary rather than competitive; so far Atlantic travel has largely promoted its own traffic and total numbers by sea and air have continued to increase.

The colonel was, however, unhappy about the amount of public money that Britain's state-owned airlines, the British Overseas Airline Corporation (BOAC) and British European Airways (BEA), were swallowing – £126 million, with losses of nearly £40 million. 'We ourselves can fairly ask why people who want the speed of air travel should not pay the economic price for it and why they should expect to be subsidised by their fellow taxpayers,' he complained.

But he remained optimistic:

> Last year a record number of passengers crossed the Atlantic by sea and we are convinced that for the foreseeable future the demand for Cunard travel will be well sustained.

The following year he could look with pride on a fleet of twelve liners on routes between Britain and the United States and Canada. And the total number of Atlantic passengers for 1958 was a record 1,036,000. However, October of that year saw a significant development for air travellers – a regular jet service between New York and Paris. While Cunard would continue to insist that 'getting there is half the fun', Boeing advised there were 'only seven hours to brush up on your French'.

The shipping line did try to hedge its bets. Why not offer ships and planes? In May 1960 Cunard took a majority stake in an independent airline, Eagle Airways, which had been formed in 1948 by an ex-wartime pilot, Harold Bamberg. The airline was renamed Cunard Eagle, and the Air Transport Licensing Board was asked for permission to operate services between Britain and the United States. After a three-day hearing in London a licence was granted, much to the annoyance of BOAC's managing director, Basil Smallpeice – Cunard's future boss.

Smallpeice – he would be knighted the following year – recalled:

> The timing could not have been worse from our point of view. If Cunard were allowed on to the North Atlantic with additional aircraft, it could only be at the cost of traffic that we badly needed in the recession then beginning.

Cunard Eagle had already ordered two Boeing 707s. BOAC appealed and another hearing was held, this time conducted by a retired judge. Smallpeice was again a leading witness. BOAC won and the licence was revoked. 'The outcome was very gratifying,' Smallpeice noted.

But BOAC and Cunard did not remain enemies for long. Smallpeice:

> Glad as I was that we had prevented Cunard Eagle from coming on the transatlantic route and taking much needed traffic away from us, it did seem

to me that there was a good chance of strengthening British aviation on the North Atlantic if Cunard Eagle were prepared to enter into a genuine association with BOAC.

There were obvious advantages. Cunard's name was 'magic', the company had an excellent network of sales offices in the United States – and there were those new Boeing 707s. BOAC's idea was to form a subsidiary company, with Cunard taking a minority holding. Secret talks were held and agreement was reached quickly. A deal to form BOAC-Cunard was signed on 6 June 1962.[2] It was a difficult time for the world's airlines, with major players, including Pan American Airways, Trans World Airlines and Lufthansa, experiencing financial difficulty.

Cunard, too, was making a loss – £1.9 million on its passenger ships in 1962. And it would get worse. Losses were set to mount during the 1960s, and much of the fleet would disappear. With one or two exceptions, the *Queens* attracted fewer and fewer passengers in the years from 1956 to 1967. In 1956 the *Queen Elizabeth* carried a total of 73,875 passengers on 44 Atlantic crossings, averaging 1,679 passengers on each trip. By 1967 the total number of passengers had dropped to 36,858, averaging 1,084 on each of just 34 crossings. At full capacity the liner could, of course, carry around 2,300 passengers. The figures for the *Queen Mary* were even worse. In 1967 she carried a total of 28,774 passengers on 30 trips, with an average passenger list of 959.

In 1963 Smallpeice, noted for his integrity and not a man skilled at playing political games, was experiencing a bumpy ride in charge of BOAC. There had always been an uneasy relationship with government over the airline's finances, and the aviation minister, Julian Amery, decided on a change at the top of the nationalised industry, despite the fact that it was heading back towards profit. He gave Smallpeice and BOAC's chairman, Sir Matthew Slattery, an ultimatum – resign or be sacked. 'I simply hated having to leave BOAC and all the fine people in it, and all that I had worked for in the past fourteen years,' said Smallpeice, who left at the end of December. 'My last seven weeks as managing director were a mixture of sadness and anger.'

But the man who had helped to shoot down Cunard Eagle was soon invited to join the Cunard board, and after taking a three-month break he became a director in April 1964. Smallpeice was not impressed with what he saw. The top management appeared to have been put in place by 'Buggins's turn' and there had been little attempt to bring in new talent. The malaise in the company could be traced back to the 1930s and the all-powerful Sir Percy Bates, the inspiration behind the *Queens*. When he died, a vacuum was left, even though his brothers carried on the family tradition. Managers still ran the company from Liverpool even though many of their ships operated from

Southampton. Subsidiary companies were left largely to their own devices. Smallpeice saw the top management as 'weak and inbred'.

He was not the only person to come to that conclusion. Colonel Bates had died in September 1959 and he was succeeded as chairman – reluctantly – by Sir John Brocklebank. Commodore Marr met a shipping correspondent who was about to interview Sir John on his new appointment, and he asked him how he saw Cunard's future.

The correspondent, unnamed, did not mince his words:

> I think Cunard still has a future, but things are in a hell of a mess and it could take at least five years to get rid of the dead hand of Colonel Bates. He boasted that he had never set foot in America, yet hoped to get 60 per cent of his business from there, and had only twice been on board the *Queen Elizabeth*, the largest unit in the fleet. His idea was that he and a couple of cronies could run a worldwide shipping company from his fifth-floor office in Liverpool.[3]

The eccentricities of the colonel were noted by the *Daily Mail* after his death:

> He gave gracious living to millions aboard his ships, yet he lived a spartan, almost a recluse's life. He persuaded the same millions that cruises and business trips by sea were just the thing. Yet he went to sea only twice during his six years as chairman.
>
> He had to see that his company was at the forefront. Yet his aversion to self-advertisement was so strong that he refused to have his name in *Who's Who*. 'Tell them to mind their own business,' he said.
>
> Bates, the Spartan, was horrified at the thought of a chauffeur and an imposing Rolls, so he drove himself in a Morris Minor from his home, Chorlton Hall, near Malpas, Cheshire, 34 miles to his Liverpool office every morning. Each evening he drove home to more work. He and his wife had no servants, took no part in the town's life, entertained only relatives and close friends.

Cunard's inefficiency had not escaped the attention of Commodore Marr:

> Increasing concern to those of us on the sea staff was caused by the size of the Cunard shore organization, with more than 600 people employed in our Liverpool office alone. During 1965 the company's recently retired chief accountant was a passenger on one voyage, and I asked him to break down the figures in the latest balance sheet. I was amazed to find that out of the revenue earned by the fleet in that year nearly £6 million went to maintain the company's shore establishments, with another £2 million for advertising and promotion.

In spite of reductions in the size of the fleet, there never seemed to be any reduction in the size of the shore staff, and the gulf dividing the sea staff from the shore staff seemed to grow wider. During the early part of 1965 I was relieving captain for two voyages on the *Queen Elizabeth* when I was asked to attend a meeting on time and motion study, to see if this method could be used to improve efficiency and cut costs.

I felt that, although some of these new ideas might be tried in a new ship with new equipment, they could do little for us on board the *Queen Elizabeth*. When I was asked to open the discussion session at the end of the meeting, I said this; and then I added: 'In my opinion there is only one way in which the efficiency of the Cunard Line can be improved – that is, by finding some way of breaking down the barriers that have built up over the years between the sea staff and the shore staff, between those of us who go to sea and do the job, and the people who sit in office chairs and try to tell us how it should be done, often without having any clear knowledge of the problems involved.'

Much of this was, I fear, not very well received at the time. But later, when Sir John Brocklebank called in business efficiency experts to look into the company's organization, one of the first things they said was that it was like investigating two entirely separate organizations.[4]

As one of the directors, in a largely non-executive role, Smallpeice was not in a position to push through change. The picture altered on 8 November 1965 when Brocklebank resigned on health grounds and Smallpeice was appointed chairman and chief executive. He was under no illusions. Cunard's business had been static for at least ten years, with annual revenue of about £60 million. The passenger business had lost £16 million between 1961 and 1964. The company was living off its capital, with little prospect of growth.

Outwardly, Cunard was putting a brave face on its business:

A total of 178,296 passengers crossed the Atlantic in Cunard liners in 1963, the largest number carried by any Atlantic steamship line during the year and an increase of 3,978 on the 1962 Cunard total of 174,318.

Carryings by the *Queen Elizabeth* and the *Queen Mary* in 1963 totalled 107,430, an increase of 5,878 on their 1962 total, despite the fact that the two ships made seven fewer transatlantic sailings in 1963 than in 1962 as a consequence of their cruising programmes.[5]

In October 1965, the month before Smallpeice took over as chairman and chief executive, an internal memo spelled out the difficulty in attracting passengers:

First Class – October sailings of the *Queens* are not doing as well as expected and space is available on all departures.

Cabin Class – In general the forward estimates for October departures do not make encouraging reading and a maximum effort will be required to produce final figures which are even comparable with last year.[6]

At 59, Smallpeice relished the challenge although he knew it would be 'a daunting prospect'. Behind the uneasy smile was a person who could display grim determination. How many people would launch their career by working for five years without pay?

He had been born in Brazil, the son of a senior clerk at the Rio de Janeiro branch of the London & River Plate Bank. The young Smallpeice was sent to England to be educated, knowing that he would not see his parents for five years because his father had to wait that long for leave. He ended up at Shrewsbury School, where he shone on the games field, particularly in cricket and football – 'scholastically I wasn't much good'. A plan to go to Oxford failed to materialise when it emerged that his father had lost all his money after a revolution in Brazil. Before leaving school at 18, a housemaster pointed out that he was good at maths and that perhaps he could become an accountant. 'I have never regretted the decision to embark on accountancy as a career, even if it was made for no good reason,' Smallpeice reflected.

He was articled to a firm of chartered accountants for five years. This was the 1920s, and the firm was seen as doing him a huge favour. There were no wages during training. Initially, Smallpeice received help from his father, who had returned to Britain and taken a job with foreign exchange brokers in London to supplement his pension.

The training was tedious but eventually he settled down to a life of figures. Qualified, he hoped to enter the relatively new and exciting world of aviation, but reality was a job with the vacuum cleaner company Hoover in west London. He went on to jobs at Doulton's and the British Transport Commission, and later, in 1950, the quiet, reserved accountant was recruited by the more glamorous BOAC.[7]

When he took over at Cunard, Smallpeice decided that he had to act quickly. There was a management shake-up, and moves were made to run down the Liverpool headquarters and base operations in Southampton. New directors were recruited to the board, and meetings were switched from Liverpool to London.

He also looked at merging Cunard with another shipping company. P&O and Ocean Steamship were approached, and they carried out a secret study. In May 1966 Smallpeice received their answer and it was not the one he expected:

They had concluded that Cunard was nothing better than a break-up situation. Accordingly neither saw any benefit in any part of Cunard's business. This was a shattering judgement. While I was rather relieved that P&O didn't want to gobble us up, I was sorry that nothing had come of a merger with Ocean Steamship, shipowners whom I had long admired and whose cargo trades were complementary to ours.[8]

May was not a good month. The National Union of Seamen called an all-out strike on 16 May over pay and a demand to cut the working week from 56 hours to 40 hours. A week later the prime minister, Harold Wilson, declared a state of emergency and claimed that Communists were behind the action, which disrupted the entire shipping industry. Berths at the major ports, Southampton, London and Liverpool, quickly filled up. The *Queens* did not sail, and it was another blow to Cunard's finances. The strike carried on until 1 July, costing the company about £4 million.

Cunard still had its 30 per cent stake in BOAC-Cunard and it decided to sever its ties with the airline business to help balance the books. Two months after the strike ended it sold its stake to BOAC for £11.5 million, making a profit of £3 million.

There was more bad news early in 1967. The US Coast Guard wanted to introduce costly fire regulations that would force Cunard to withdraw the *Queen Elizabeth*, *Queen Mary* and *Caronia* from the American market.

The company's directors were warned:

This in turn could mean the abandonment of the entire passenger operation and there would then be no organisation capable of putting the Q4 [*Queen Elizabeth* 2] into service, which would jeopardise the whole project.

The chairman had left the Board of Trade in no doubt as to the seriousness of the Coast Guard's proposals and the prime minister had also been informed. Every possible effort would be made through the highest government and diplomatic channels to secure the re-drafting of the regulations in a form not damaging to Cunard.[9]

The cost of the Q4 project was another headache. It would be £28.5 million, £3 million more than the original estimate. Queen Elizabeth II was due to launch the *Queen Elizabeth* 2 on 20 September 1967. Cunard's finances were so critical that the ceremony was on the verge of being cancelled on 15 September unless the government agreed to loan more money. The shipping line might even have to go into liquidation. At the last moment the government guarantee arrived. And just to add to the financial headache – the loss on the passenger business for 1967 was estimated at £3.5 million.

It had been planned to retire the *Queen Mary* in October 1968, but that decision was brought forward by a year. The shock decision to withdraw the *Queen Elizabeth* from service had been taken at a board meeting in April 1967:

It was now apparent that, contrary to previous expectations, the *Queen Elizabeth* could not be successfully marketed as a cruise ship during the winter season once the Q4 [*Queen Elizabeth* 2] was in service. Operational problems, the necessity to charge high rates and the diminishing public appeal of the ship due to her age made her uncompetitive in the limited long cruise market. The ship was only marketable for short cruises at holiday periods and this would necessitate a reversion of unprofitable North Atlantic employment for some part of the winter months.

The board considered the possibility of improving the profitably of *Queen Elizabeth* by re-rating and more effective sales techniques but concluded that this action although desirable in 1968 could not overcome the long-term difficulties. Concern was expressed at the proposal to withdraw *Queen Elizabeth* in view of the conversion of the ship carried out in 1965/66 but it was recognised that this had been proved to be ineffective. The fact that this expenditure had been incurred did not justify the retention of the ship in service if further continuing losses would result.

It was recognised that the proposal would be a shock to morale in the organisation. On the other hand, nothing would erode morale more than continuing losses coupled with external pressures and criticisms. Such losses were jeopardising the whole future of the company – they must be faced realistically as there was no time or money for further experiments. Long-term profitably from 1968 onwards was more likely to be achieved with one large ship than with two.

The proposal that the *Queen Mary* should be withdrawn from service in the autumn of 1967 and the *Queen Elizabeth* in the autumn of 1968 was therefore agreed. While a simultaneous announcement might give rise to certain marketing problems, a positive statement of our future intentions should be made as soon as possible in order that an early start could be made in evaluating the complex personnel and organisational problems involved without the inhibitions imposed by security requirements. The chairman would therefore make an announcement at the earliest opportunity.

The board were told of the need for complete secrecy before the announcement. The group secretary would keep a list of those 'privy to the decision and no others were to be informed of it without major clearance with him'.[10]

CHAPTER 4

Three 'Bouncy' Americans

Cunard announced on 8 May 1967 that it would withdraw the *Queens* from service. The decision to dispose of the *Queen Elizabeth* particularly shocked and saddened many employees and former passengers. Commodore Marr was one of the critics, viewing the move as hasty and unnecessary. He had been appointed commodore of the Cunard Line on 1 January 1966, flying his flag in the *Queen Elizabeth*, and he was given the news by the managing director, Philip Bates, who telephoned him during a spell of leave at his home in Wiltshire. Bates said the seamen's strike and the new American fire regulations were the main factors.

Marr would reflect:

This was a very sad blow as far as the *Queen Elizabeth* was concerned because she was only just feeling the full effect of her big refit, which had cost the company £1.75 million, and although her first season of winter cruising had not produced good financial results, it being a new role for her, I felt that she was only just getting into her stride.

I thought that if the management would consult the ship's people about the selection of cruise ports where we knew that the ship could operate efficiently, she could do well, for I had received so many appreciative letters from passengers.

I felt that it was a mistake, too, to announce the end of her useful life so long before it was to happen. It seemed to me that they could have put in that little word 'if' somewhere in their announcement; it would have done so much for my crew's morale, and it would have stopped all the passengers who came to my cabin for cocktails saying, 'We feel so sad to think of your beautiful ship being scrapped, commodore.'[1]

At about this time Marr was asked to write the foreword to a book about a voyage in the *Queen Elizabeth*, written by an admirer of the ship, Professor Leonard Stevens.[2] Naturally, the commodore lamented the death sentence. He submitted his piece to the managing director for approval. It was heavily edited. Marr was told that he had expressed his personal feelings too strongly and that readers might think he was reflecting company policy. These are some of the sentences that were cut:

> When construction of the *Queen Mary's* replacement [*Queen Elizabeth 2*] started on Clydebank, I realized that her days were numbered and this announcement has only brought forward the sad day of her final voyage by about a year. But I felt that the *Queen Elizabeth* ... was still in great heart – having during her extensive overhaul on the Clyde in the winter of 1965-6 been fully air conditioned and fitted with lido decks and an outdoor swimming pool to enable her to operate as a cruise liner in those periods when the number of passengers crossing the North Atlantic by sea was insufficient to sustain a ship of her size.
>
> I was convinced that she still had several years of useful life ahead of her – both as a cruise ship and as a running mate for the new Cunarder in maintaining the two-ship weekly transatlantic express service that had been the dream of her creator, the late Sir Percy Bates. Unfortunately, the stern laws of economics – which we are told must be obeyed, if any commercial enterprise is to survive – leave no place for sentiment. Within the year, this magnificent ship has to follow her older sister into retirement, leaving many sad hearts among those who have sailed in her and grown to love her sea-kindly qualities and her atmosphere of solid comfort and luxury.[3]

Prime Minister Harold Wilson was concerned about the future of the *Queens*, and two days after Cunard's announcement on 8 May his private secretary, Roger Dawe, sent a letter to the Board of Trade.

Dawe wrote:

> He [Wilson] understands that it is likely that the *Queen Mary* will be sold for scrap and that the *Queen Elizabeth* will be sold to another user if there is a bid above the scrap value provided she would not be used in direct competition with the remaining Cunard passenger fleet.
>
> The prime minister has suggested that a group of ministers should consider the future of both ships including the various suggestions which have been made such as Mr Ben Whitaker's [a Labour MP] proposal that they might be used as temporary housing accommodation. Other possibilities that occur to the prime minister are for their possible use as floating hotels, floating exhibition centres or for carrying troops.[4]

Copies of the letter were sent to the Department of Economic Affairs, the Chancellor's Office, the Ministry of Defence, the Ministry of Housing, the Ministry of Technology and the Cabinet Office.

On 22 May a meeting was held at the Board of Trade with representatives from Cunard. Officials from the Ministry of Housing and the Ministry of Health also attended. The Cunard representatives said enquiries for the *Queens* had been 'quite numerous but not many of them could be taken seriously since they showed no conception of operating costs'.

The meeting was given details of the accommodation on both ships, and it was pointed out that neither liner had air conditioning, though the *Queen Elizabeth* was equipped with a 'cool air' system – 'but there is no denying that the ships are hot, particularly the *Queen Mary*, and the *Queen Elizabeth* is not entirely comfortable when berthed on a hot day'. The only places where the *Queens* could be berthed permanently were Southampton, Liverpool and Tilbury, but even then there would be problems with tides.[5]

The other ministries were consulted and by 19 June the Board of Trade had come up with a report considering all the options. 'The cost of acquiring either ship would depend upon what offers Cunard may receive for them,' said the report.

> The basic price will be the scrap value which is believed to be about £650,000 each and which, it is reasonable to assume, could be recovered if and when the ships were subsequently disposed of. Most of the existing cabins in the ships would be too small for family accommodation. Before the ships could be used for permanent housing many of them would have to be run together and arrangements for cooking installed in each accommodation unit. The cost of such conversion in a ship is very high and might reach £1 million.

General running costs, excluding berthing charges, would be about £4,000 a day or £1.46 million a year.

The *Queens* had helped to win the Second World War, but in 1967 the Ministry of Defence did not see a role for them as troopships:

> The defence requirement is for the swift, often unexpected movement of relatively small numbers of men over long distances and, administratively, at frequent intervals. Accordingly air trooping is favoured since it is cheaper, quicker, more flexible and more economical in manpower. Apart from the cost of conversion and maintenance as operational troops carriers there are other formidable objections to using the *Queens* – their size imposes restrictions on the routes and ports which could be used; it would not be possible to fill them with men and, even if it were, too many men would be non-operational in transit.

What would Churchill have made of that? Fifteen years later the liners *Queen Elizabeth 2* and *Canberra*, the big ships, played crucial roles as troopships in the Falklands conflict.

Using the ships as temporary accommodation for homeless families was seen as too expensive. Floating hotels were a possibility but 'most prospective visitors would require an attractive location and to obtain that in Great Britain would involve off-shore mooring with all the consequential difficulties including those of access and weather hazards'. The report noted: 'No reliable reports have been heard that hotel concerns in this country are interested in the *Queens.*'

A floating exhibition was also ruled out. For many years the Board of Trade had been prepared to consider assistance, but there was not enough support from industry.

And so the report recommended that 'ministers should agree that no practical or economic use can be found for either of these ships after their withdrawal from service'.[6]

The sale of the *Queen Mary* went ahead relatively smoothly. In July the Cunard Board decided to accept the highest offer – $3.45 million, which had come from the city of Long Beach, California. The Board of Trade told Cunard that the government saw the sale as a 'purely commercial transaction without political element'.[7] A contract was signed the following month, and on 31 October the liner left Southampton for the last time after 31 years of Cunard service, heading for California round Cape Horn.

August saw the first 'serious' negotiations to buy the *Queen Elizabeth*. An approach had been made by the Airport Boatel Corporation of Philadelphia, which was offering $5.85 million for delivery in October or November 1968, but 'it would be an absolute condition of sale that at the time of signing the contract the buyers would open an irrevocable letter of credit in favour of Cunard and in a form acceptable to Cunard for the balance of the purchase price'. Smallpeice and his fellow directors were right to be concerned about payment, and they would soon wish that they had never heard of the Airport Boatel Corporation.[8]

There was some good news, however. It seemed the *Queen Elizabeth 2* was capturing the public's imagination, perhaps partly due to the sadness over the departing *Queens*. There had been more than 4,000 applications for her maiden voyage.

In October the Cunard directors heard that negotiations with the Airport Boatel Corporation had ceased. But the following month talks resumed, and Cunard's group secretary told the board that 'if the requisite letter of credit materialised then we had a contract prepared and ready for signature'. And it was noted that 'because of devaluation the proceeds could yield more sterling than originally expected'.[9]

No contract was signed and the Airport Boatel Corporation was out of the picture once more.

January 1968 saw Cunard agreeing to sell the *Queen Elizabeth* to Japanese buyers who wanted to turn her into a museum of oceanography or a science foundation. The price was £2,695,000 and a contract would be ready for signing in February, with a deposit of 10 per cent and a letter of credit from the Bank of Tokyo securing the balance. The deal was subject to the approval of the Japanese government.

Because of 'national currency problems' the Japanese government would not give the go-ahead and the sale fell through. Cunard was now pinning its hopes on 'Brazilian interests' who wished to use the ship as a hotel in Rio de Janeiro and were offering $7.5 million. But it turned out that the Brazilians had 'too many financial uncertainties as revealed by information obtained confidentially through the Bank of London and South America'.[10]

If at first you don't succeed ... the Airport Boatel Corporation returned to the negotiating table, offering $7.75 million, with a deposit of $600,000 and the balance being paid 105 days later. Cunard agreed and was offered a 60-day option to take a 15 per cent interest in the equity of the proposed convention centre/leisure 'boatel' of which the ship would form the major part, in lieu of $1.9 million of the purchase price. The directors felt that 'this could well be a worthwhile diversification in the form of an investment in a growth business and might represent a good commercial risk'. A contract was signed in London on 5 April but Cunard asked for an extension on the share option in case it proved impossible to 'complete investigations'.[11]

So who were the buyers? The Airport Boatel Corporation had been set up by Stanton Miller and his brother Robert and Charles Williard, who were owners of the Drake Hotel in Philadelpia. They joined forces with a real estate developer, Philip Klein, who was leasing 30 acres of marshland in Tinicum Township, outside Philadelphia. The original plan was to build a 'boatel' – a motel for boat owners – on the marshland, situated between Philadelphia's international airport and the Delaware River. Then the Miller brothers and Williard, who were all directors of their corporation, decided to scrap the 'boatel' scheme and buy the *Queen Elizabeth*, berthing her next to the marshland, which would be developed as a Disney-style attraction. And the liner would be advertised as the 'eighth wonder of the world'.

The Miller brothers and Williard liked to be known as CBS – Charlie, Bob and Stan. During negotiations to buy the ship Williard, small and plump, took to wearing a bowler hat, giving him 'the appearance of a cherubic London barrister'. CBS and Klein flew to London for the signing of the contract at the Savoy Hotel. They had persuaded Philadelphia's mayor, James Tate, and the city council's president, Paul D'Ortona, to support the purchase.[12]

The London *Evening Standard* described CBS as 'three US millionaires'. The *Daily Mirror* said:

> They are tanned, bouncy guys who intend squeezing a bundle of fun out of the old Lizzie ... Now they're taking over the captain's stateroom on the

Elizabeth for their own personal high jinks. There's a panache, a heedless zest about the three which makes success boringly inevitable ...

Malcolm Finister of H. E. Moss & Company, Cunard's ship brokerage firm, told *Philadelphia* magazine:

> After the *Mary*'s sale the Philadelphia group came to us and asked if we would consider a private deal on the *Elizabeth*. They seemed to know quite a bit about the problems they were going to run into at the airport site. They told us they'd made tests on noise levels from the jets, obtained clearance from your air authorities as to the height of the stacks and masts, said they'd have river surveys done and, in short, knew what they were about.
>
> We grew rather to like them and to tell you the truth we rather held back on dealings with other parties. It was important for us not only to get the best price for the ship but also to know that she would have a good home. Finally, we decided we could hold off no further.[13]

A month after the signing of the contract cracks began to appear. Philadelphia's mayor and council president had assumed that the *Queen Elizabeth* would be berthed on the Delaware River at a city site, giving a huge boost to tourism. But officials had not bothered to check with CBS that this would be the case. D'Ortona discovered by accident that the ship was destined for Tinicum Township during a conversation with a restaurateur at a club on the second floor of the Drake Hotel one evening.

According to *Philadelphia* magazine, D'Ortona, to put it mildly, was livid.

> He marched downstairs to the Drake's Sir Francis Room and confronted the Miller brothers with what he'd just learned. There followed a finger-shaking half hour in which the Millers were their usual glib selves.[14]

It then emerged that CBS wanted to acquire 90 acres of public land near the airport for parking. There was no access to the marshland and a six-lane highway would be needed, although the state highways department had yet to be approached. An official of the Federal Aviation Administration said it had never been contacted about a possible hazard to planes. Most important – a survey of the river to check if the *Queen Elizabeth* could be berthed there had not been carried out. The US Army Corps of Engineers said it was asked about the possibility of doing a survey on 25 April, nearly three weeks after the sale of the ship. It seemed that a major dredging operation would be necessary to accommodate the liner.

Stanton Miller said a 'top design firm' had been hired to shape the marshland complex into a Disney-style resort. The 'top design firm' turned out to be two men operating from the Drake Hotel, Gus Flamos, a former used car salesman, and Vic Potamkin, who had worked for a carpet company.

Philadelphia magazine noted:

> The proposed site at the old Gulf Oil Hog Island dock may not be the ugliest section of the Delaware Valley but it comes close. The land is flat and marshy, the river smells combine with the odours of nearby refineries and the oil-unloading docks a few hundred feet away. When the prevailing west wind is blowing the air is torn with the thunder of commercial jets which need no measuring on a decibel meter.

The magazine had headlined its article 'What's a nice Queen like you doing in a place like this?'

A proposal to berth the ship near the city's Independence Hall was turned down because she was too big and would become a navigational hazard.

The magazine asked:

> Why, if Cunard was so deeply concerned with the *Elizabeth*'s final resting place, did it not send a representative to look over proposed sites? It has shown that it is extremely sensitive to the reaction of the British people to the sale of a national heritage.

Soon after the magazine's publication CBS announced that the *Queen Elizabeth* would not be going to Philadelphia, or rather the marshland at Tinicum Township, after all. Her final destination probably would be Fort Lauderdale, Florida.

The newspaper *Philadelphia Inquirer* quoted Stanton and Robert Miller as saying that the plan to bring the *Queen Elizabeth* to the city 'has been threatened seriously by a local magazine article …'

In its July issue, *Philadelphia* magazine pointed out:

> No one at the *Inquirer*, Stanton Milller knew, had yet read the *Philadelphia* magazine article. Stanton read part of it to a rewrite man the night before as he sat fuming at the bar of the Sir Francis Room in the Drake Hotel.
>
> The ease with which Stanton Miller got his charges into print is remarkable, especially in light of the fact that Miller was able to assure a close friend that night that the next day's paper would carry 'a real blast against the magazine'.[15]

The magazine went on to claim that since April the Miller brothers and Williard had been dealing with a Florida group interested in having the ship in

Fort Lauderdale. The first contact, Fort Lauderdale promoter William Skillings revealed, was made 'a couple of days' after CBS bought the ship.

According to Fort Lauderdale's press office, Florida's governor, Claude Kirk, had made a special trip to the port in May to discuss final arrangements with CBS.

Philadelphia magazine quoted Skillings as saying:

> It's a great thing for us. As a matter of fact, I was part of a south Florida group that bid on the *Elizabeth* last year. But old Charlie, Bob and Stan outbid us by a quarter of a million dollars. Once they'd signed on the dotted line in April, I got hold of them right away and said we were interested in getting the ship. They hired me as their representative down here and I put together a proposal.

The July article in *Philadelphia* magazine was headed 'God save the Queen' and sub-titled 'Dept of utter confusion'.

That month the Cunard directors learned of the 'revised' plans for the *Queen Elizabeth*. A 30-day extension on an 'irrevocable letter of credit' was granted, but the purchasers were warned that no further extension would be considered 'unless a further substantial cash payment was made'. Peter Shirley, the deputy chairman, planned to fly to Miami on 12 August to meet the various interests to make an assessment of the position.[16]

Shirley returned with bad news. The Airport Boatel Corporation or CBS – it was no longer clear who exactly was buying the ship – were unable to come up with the rest of the money. But there was a new plan ... a corporation would be set up in Florida. Cunard would lease the *Queen Elizabeth* to the new company for $2 million dollars a year for 10 years – and it would still own the ship.

It was clear that at least one of Cunard's directors, the hotelier Maxwell Joseph, was fast running out of patience. He said the purchasers could only be regarded as unreliable and that the plan was unacceptable because it involved Cunard investing money in the ship.

But the board agreed on a modified plan because the *Queen Elizabeth* had to be delivered by the end of November for technical reasons. It was decided that the company would not spend any money on modifications to the ship, $4 million dollars – two years' rent – would be paid to Cunard on signing the agreement, and the company would pay $1 million for 40 per cent of the equity of the new corporation.

In September the Miller brothers telephoned Cunard's finance department to say that the bank facilities to pay the two years' rent had been arranged. The following month Smallpeice told his board that the Millers, in fact, had been unable to raise the money. Maxwell Joseph again expressed his concern and was further annoyed to discover that an option to sue for damages had been allowed to lapse.

But Cunard went ahead with a yet another plan to send the *Queen Elizabeth* to Florida. The board agreed that the project was still viable and could be profitable if properly run. Cunard would have an 85 per cent share in The Elizabeth (Cunard) Corporation, with the remaining 15 per cent going to CBS. The ship would leave Southampton on 29 November and arrive at Port Everglades on 8 December. She was expected to start earning money before Christmas and it was anticipated 'that revenue would exceed all costs', apart from a bill for dredging at her berth. On 4 December the Cunard directors were told that 'the Millers were continuing to be co-operative and had admitted that they now thought the project would have proved beyond their scope'.[17]

November was a bleak month for Cunard's employees. There was 'the night of the long knives', as Commodore Marr put it. On board the *Queen Elizabeth* he assembled his ship's company and read a statement from Smallpeice. In addition to the *Queens*, three other liners, *Caronia*, *Sylvania* and *Carinthia*, were to be taken out of service and sold. Cunard's great passenger fleet of 1957 was being reduced to just three ships.

Marr reflected:

> But it was what this meant in terms of human lives that was important, because within the space of a couple of months 2,700 men and women, many of them with a lifetime of service, were to lose their means of livelihood. It was certainly a grim time and, as the ships came into their home port, those on whom the axe was to fall were called in and told that it was a case of being given redundancy pay or taking early retirement.
>
> However one looks at it, the choice was bitter, and it seemed a poor reward to those who had in many cases devoted the whole of their working lives to the service of the once great Cunard Line.

The last year of the *Queen Elizabeth*'s life as a Cunarder saw a sharp rise in passenger numbers, especially on cruises. This may have been due partly to nostalgia, but the company had heeded advice to send the ship only to suitable ports. Smallpeice joined the liner for five days on one of the cruises, travelling from Barbados to New York. Marr had been told that he faced retirement when the *Queen Elizabeth* was taken out of service, and he felt he had nothing to lose in having a frank discussion with the chairman. He said the board was making a mistake, especially in view of the ship's expensive refit. The commodore was convinced that she could be profitable on cruises and Atlantic crossings, even though more money would have to be spent to comply with the new American regulations.

Marr noted:

I must say that he listened politely to this and to many other suggestions I made about other aspects of the company's business, but I believed that the 1967 decisions had to stand, because once the board had made a decision, it would be unlikely to reverse it, if for no other reason than that it might lose face. The most I got out of these discussions was an admission that some mistakes had been made by the 'new boys', and with this I had to be content; but I couldn't help reflecting that, working under the same difficulties of the seamen's strike, rising costs and so on, other shipping companies appeared to be doing well. Surely it could not be by accident?[18]

The *Queen Elizabeth* sailed from New York for the last time on 30 October 1968. Before she left the pier the city's mayor, John Lindsay, came on board and made 'a very fine speech'. He presented a plaque from the US government in tribute to the liner's war service and a bronze medallion to mark the close links between the ship and New York. Many boats, crowded with sightseers, saluted the *Queen* as she headed downriver towards the Verrazano Bridge, linking Staten Island and Brooklyn.

In Southampton on 6 November, the Queen Mother boarded the *Queen Elizabeth* to say goodbye to the liner she had launched in 1938. Lunch was served in the Verandah Grill and she sat between Marr and Smallpeice. Marr would write:

> With Her Majesty's wonderful capacity for making everyone feel completely at ease, lunch was a very pleasant affair, and she asked many searching questions about what would happen to the ship when she arrived in Florida at the beginning of December, and expressed the hope that the end of her life would be in line with the same proud tradition that she had maintained in both war and peace. I kept my forebodings to myself.

How comfortable was Smallpeice during the lunch? The Queen Mother's visit merited only once sentence in his memoirs.

On 8 November the *Queen Elizabeth* sailed on an eight-day farewell cruise to Las Palmas and Gibraltar, with a full passenger list. As she left Gibraltar, Royal Navy ships, led by the destroyer HMS *Cambrian*, gave her an escort as Royal Air Force jets roared overhead.

'It was a wonderful farewell,' said Commodore Marr. 'The dreadful thought behind it was that it was a farewell.'

CHAPTER 5

Turmoil in Florida

The *Queen Elizabeth* left Southampton for the last time on 29 November 1968. It was a cold and dreary day, and only a few people on the quayside braved her early departure for Florida. Surprisingly, she left without fanfare, slinking away as if her presence had become an embarrassment. There were no passengers, only a skeleton crew, a reminder of her first voyage when she made that secret dash across the Atlantic in wartime.

Commodore Marr was not impressed:

> Compared with all the glamour of the *Queen Mary*'s departure from Southampton the previous year, with a full load of cruise passengers, flags flying, bands playing and aircraft flying overhead in salute, the *Queen Elizabeth* almost folded her tents like the Arabs and silently stole away. It compared ill with the farewells in New York and Gibraltar, a British understatement with a vengeance, as though the British world of ships and ship lovers looked the other way until she had gone.

Marr's wife described it as a 'shameful departure'.[1]

But there were tributes. As the liner neared the Nab Tower, east of the Isle of Wight, the guided missile destroyer HMS *Hampshire* came alongside, with her crew lining the rails and cheering. That evening the *Carmania*, returning from a Mediterranean cruise, saluted the *Queen Elizabeth*, and there was a message wishing the liner success in Florida from Cunard's new great hope, the *Queen Elizabeth 2*, which was undergoing trials off the Isle of Arran. The *QE2*'s message 'made some of us smile wrily', Marr recorded.

The voyage across the Atlantic was uneventful, apart from a crisis when the ship ran out of beer. The skeleton crew of some 200 had been particularly thirsty. The *Queen Elizabeth* arrived off the east coast of Florida on 7 December, and her warm reception could not have been in sharper contrast to the miserable send-off from Southampton. She was greeted by an armada of small craft, as well as planes and helicopters. One helicopter charter company said it had been 'besieged' by callers happy to pay $175 for an hour over the water. But the Federal Aviation Administration was forced to impose restrictions on flights, banning planes without special clearance from going below 3,000 feet and within two miles of the ship. Thousands of people lined the shore, and Fort Lauderdale faced the worst traffic jams in its history.

Marr could not berth his ship at Port Everglades because dredging was still going on. He was asked to sail slowly along the coast until the following day. Squeezing the *Queen Elizabeth* through the port's narrow entrance was the toughest job that the pilot, Captain Irving Shuman, had ever taken on. At some points only a gap of about six inches separated the bottom of the ship and the harbour mud. Shuman manoeuvred the liner using her four engines and helped by six tugs, cutting the speed from six to three knots with these final commands: 'One half ahead on two engines ... slow ahead on two engines ... dead slow on two engines ... stop all engines ... two engines slow astern ... four engines slow astern ... stop all engines.' The operation took three hours. Even Marr was impressed. The liner had arrived without a scratch. One report said: 'The stately *Queen Elizabeth*, monarch of the high seas for three decades, gave up her reign without a murmur as she was prodded inch by inch into her new home.' Marr commented: 'The ship behaved like the perfect lady she is until the very end. It's a very sad moment when the end of a ship has to come.' Shuman agreed: 'The ship behaved beautifully.'

As Marr spoke of 'this speed-crazy age', a large jet flew overhead towards Miami International Airport. Reporter Morris McLemore noted:

> Even the sky giant took notice of the *Queen Elizabeth*, for it banked gently to the left and one could almost hear its captain tell his passengers about the awesome ship with two orange and black stacks below and how she will spend the rest of her enormously eventful life in south Florida. [2]

However, her time in Florida was about to become more eventful than anyone would have wished. Contrary to appearances, she had not moved to a permanent home in the sunshine state. Over the next two years problems would come thick and fast. The Millers and Williard had grand plans bearing a price tag of around $50 million. They wanted to transform the ship into a floating hotel, convention centre and general tourist attraction, with developments on 135 acres of land surrounding the berth, which included a golf course, tennis courts and an 'international village'. The trio were wildly optimistic about their attraction, estimating that it would bring in three million visitors a year who would generate $50 million in annual revenue. Businesses in Fort Lauderdale and nearby Hollywood were also expecting to reap riches.

The first problem emerged in January 1969. A local fire chief, John Gerkin, suggested that the liner might need extensive renovation to meet fire regulations if she became a hotel and conference centre. There was less concern on the question of guided tours of the ship. A few days later another fire chief, W. T. Burkhart, took a softer liner, saying the *Queen Elizabeth* would have little trouble complying with the state's fire regulations. Burkhart was compiling a special report. 'The ship is in excellent shape as far as we're concerned, but certain revisions will have to be made,' he said.

> For one thing, on a ship at sea, passengers scramble to the upper decks and the lifeboats in case of fire or other emergency. When the ship is permanently based on land as a hotel escape routes will have to be reversed. It would be kind of stupid for people in a hotel to go up to the lifeboats.

But Gerkin's fears would prevail eventually, although they cost him his job.

There were also rumblings about the generosity of the port authorities. Such was the enthusiasm, '*Queen* fever', for Florida's new star that the port authority agreed on a 50-year lease for the 135 acres of 'choice real estate' adjoining the berth – with the first four years free. And the authority waived berthing charges – thousands of dollars a day – for the duration of the ship's conversion. A new port commissioner, Phil McConaghey, began questioning the deals but quickly found enemies. 'If you criticised the *Queen Elizabeth* at that time it was like being against the flag, motherhood and apple pie,' said McConaghey.[3]

Eyebrows were raised when it emerged that the father of Claude Kirk, Florida's governor, had been put on the payroll of the Philadelphia businessmen, 'duties unspecified'. Soon afterwards it was revealed that a company set up by the governor's campaign manager, Robert Lee, and a key fundraiser, Charles Whitfield, had been involved in a $136,000 deal covering 'public relations' for the liner.[4]

On 14 February 1969 the ship opened to the public for tours. Cunard insisted that she should be promoted as the '*Elizabeth*', in deference to the Queen Mother and to avoid confusion with the *Queen Elizabeth 2*. It looked promising at first, with visitors averaging 2,000 a day and paying $2.50 for an adult ticket. But it soon became apparent that not enough money was coming in to cover the expenses, despite those lucrative deals with the port authority. The ship needed 40 tons of fuel a day, and Marr and a crew of around 150 were still on board to keep things running. As well as looking after the ship and the crew, Marr was busy entertaining VIPs in the hope that they would join the project. He 'felt more like a used-ship salesman than a ship's captain', and he would come to recognise that the 'wheeling and dealing' over the liner's sale was 'sometimes sordid'.[5]

As for her appearance, Miami journalist John Pennekamp painted this picture:

> The old girl doesn't look so good. We first saw her from a mile or so away
> ... As we got closer it became evident that distance had lent enchantment
> because she looked old and tired. What she needs, as the ladies say when
> they retire to the rest room, is 'to put on her face'. *QE*, as she was called in
> her prime, and later *The Lizzie* could do with a paint job on the outside at
> least. Matter of fact, we got the impression that she was showing a rust spot
> or two.[6]

Alarm bells at Cunard had started ringing soon after the *Queen Elizabeth*'s arrival. There were serious doubts about the hotel and convention centre plans. The shipping line, of course, still owned the vessel but it could not afford mounting losses. In April Smallpeice and his directors decided once again to put the liner up for sale, severing ties with The Elizabeth (Cunard) Corporation. A number of potential buyers came forward, including Hong Kong tycoon C. Y. Tung, who offered $7.5 million.[7]

Cunard was unlikely to have a problem getting the money from Tung, but it decided to go for the highest bidder, a new American company called The Queen Ltd, which dangled $8.6 million, with $2 million as a down payment and the remainder to be paid within a year. The sale was agreed in July 1969. Cunard no longer owned the *Queen Elizabeth*. Smallpeice and his directors no doubt breathed a sigh of relief, but the saga was far from over. The Queen Ltd was backed by a Philadelphia company, Utilities Leasing Corporation, and involved ... Stanton and Robert Miller and Charles Williard. Yes, those three 'bouncy Americans' had bounced back yet again. It was claimed that their stake was only 15 per cent but it turned out to be 42 per cent. They had the ship, which would be kept at Port Everglades, and those 135 acres of 'choice real estate'. There were even bolder plans to promote the liner and her surroundings. Questions, however, continued to be raised about financial arrangements. Why did an associate of the Miller brothers receive a 'finder's fee' of $258,000 for involving The Queen Ltd in the purchase of the *Queen Elizabeth*?[8]

Marr and his crew flew home after a team of American engineers were recruited to keep the ship operational. That August several fires broke out, and an investigation revealed that a security guard had started them. Two months later there was another blaze. This time, fire chief John Gerkin decided to pay a further visit. He came to the conclusion that staff would not be able to cope with a major emergency – and he closed the ship to visitors. He insisted on new safety rules, with limits on visitor numbers, before any reopening – and shortly afterwards lost his job.

Backers of The Queen Ltd had planned to make a killing by offering shares in the company to the public, which would bring in more than $13 million and clear all debts. But the economic climate was not good, and the Securities and Exchange Commission had its suspicions and thought the proposal needed scrutiny.

The debts continued to pile up, and even the port authority made threatening noises over unpaid bills, with commissioner Phil McConagney trying to close the ship. An exasperated McConaghey said getting money from The Queen Ltd was like 'prodding a mule'. What the company needed was 'not more specialists and consultants but someone who could sign a check – a good check'. His complaint resulted in the payment of bills totalling $18,380.[9] In May 1970 a federal marshal, Cecil Miller, announced that he had seized the *Queen Elizabeth* after an engineering firm in California, Rados Western Corporation, claimed it was owed $200,000. Two weeks later there was a bizarre scene at the quayside, when six children paraded with placards saying 'Give our dad his pay check'. Willard Turnpaugh, an employee of The Queen Ltd, who actually had ten children, complained that his cheque had been marked 'returned for insufficient funds'. He was not the only worker to lose out. A spokesman for the company promised that 'everyone will be paid'. But by the end of May 1970 the game was up. The Queen Ltd filed for bankruptcy in Philadelphia, with debts totalling $12 million, at least $5 million of which was still owed to Cunard. There were 146 creditors in Florida and more than $600,000 was owed in local, state and federal taxes. Respected Florida politician Jack Eckerd said the failure was 'a public scandal of major significance'.[10]

In September the *Queen Elizabeth* was up for sale again, this time at a public auction held in a Fort Lauderdale hotel. The auctioneer, one Abraham Plone, who was more used to dealing with factories, said he would try to sell the ship as one lot, otherwise she would go piece by piece 'right down to the doorknobs'.

The Greek shipping magnate Aristotle Onassis and Hugh Hefner of Playboy fame were among those rumoured to be interested. But the *Queen Elizabeth* was sold to C. Y. Tung for $3.2 million – $4.3 million less than he had offered Cunard the previous year.

McConaghey, the port commissioner, perhaps summed it all up: 'The *Queen Elizabeth* came to south Florida only because a lot of influential people were bribed legally or illegally.'

And Cunard would remain millions of dollars out of pocket.

CHAPTER 6

Enter the Mafia

If a shipping line needed to produce a guide on how not to dispose of the world's greatest liner, Cunard would have been in an ideal position in 1970. The sale of the *Queen Elizabeth*, with all the setbacks, was a painful and embarrassing experience for Smallpeice and his directors, though they would never acknowledge that publicly. In August 1970 Cunard's bosses received probably their biggest shock. The US Department of Justice was in touch. It wanted Peter Shirley, the deputy chairman, who had played a major part in negotiations for the liner's sale to the Philadelphia businessmen and then The Queen Ltd, to appear before a federal grand jury in Miami, which was investigating organised crime. Specifically, the jury wanted to know 'whether a prima facie case existed of Mafia influence in the negotiations for the purchase of *Queen Elizabeth*'. Shirley was asked to appear on 3 September, one week before the liner's public auction at the beachfront Galt Ocean Mile Hotel in Fort Lauderdale.[1]

Were Smallpeice and his directors aware when they sent over the *Queen Elizabeth* that south Florida was home to the highest number of Mafia members and their associates in the United States, gangsters who represented fifteen of the country's twenty-four mob families?

The Cunard bosses, who included Lord Mancroft, no doubt saw themselves as gentlemen, but they may well have been naïve in their dealings with the three flashy businessmen from Philadelphia. Huge question marks over Stanton and Robert Miller and Charles Williard appeared as early as June 1968.

It emerged that Stanton Miller had been involved in two companies that went bankrupt and that there were controversial business deals involving his brother Robert. The Millers bought a significant stake in the Drake Hotel in Philadelphia, a landmark building, in 1964. The hotel was rundown but there were ambitious plans to renovate it. The brothers paid $2.5 million for the business. It transpired that the money came from the pension fund of the

Teamsters' Union, which was being run by the notorious Jimmy Hoffa, who frequently stayed at the Drake.[2]

In 1964 Hoffa went on trial in Chattanooga, Tennessee, accused of jury tampering. The Millers visited him during the case. The union leader was found guilty and received an eight-year jail sentence. Hoffa also faced a trial in Chicago later that year. He was given five years for improper use of the Teamsters' pension fund. But he remained free until 1967, unsuccessfully appealing against his convictions. Four years later he was released from a prison in Pennsylvania after President Richard Nixon commuted his sentences. On 30 July 1975 Hoffa disappeared after going to a restaurant in a Detroit suburb, apparently to meet two Mafia leaders. He was almost certainly murdered. According to one claim, he was shot twice behind the right ear. No one was charged with his murder, and his body has never been found.

Charles Williard acquired a share in the Drake in 1966. Angelo Bruno, the head of the Mafia in Philadelphia for twenty years, often went to the hotel. *Philadelphia* magazine reported that he had 'frequent' meetings with Stanton Miller. 'What specific mutual interests they have is not known,' said the report.

> The Millers don't talk about their meetings with Bruno. In fact, C, B and S seem somewhat resentful that anyone would question where they're going to get the money to buy the world's biggest ocean liner. Charlie Williard, especially, resents the questioning. Where the financing will come from is nobody's damn business.[3]

Life magazine said of Stanton Miller: 'He was once indicted for embezzlement, although the case was later dropped, and he has been known to inform his enemies that they might soon find themselves wearing "cement shoes".'[4]

The businessman was also friendly with a lawyer who acted for Bruno, Salvatore Avena. Avena's father, John 'Big Nose' Avena, had been boss of the Philadelphia mob in the 1930s until his death in a gunfight. Salvatore Avena also represented the boxer Sonny 'The Big Bear' Liston, who gained fame after knocking out world heavyweight champion Floyd Patterson in the first round of their encounter in 1962. Liston had a criminal record, and it was well known that he had connections with the mob. He adopted Philadelphia as his home city but left after complaining of police harassment, going to Denver, where he declared: 'I'd rather be a lamppost in Denver than the mayor of Philadelphia.' He was controlled by racketeer Blinky Palermo. Liston had two famous defeats at the hands of Cassius Clay/Muhammad Ali. The Big Bear was found dead at his home in Las Vegas in January 1971 in mysterious circumstances. There were rumours that he had been killed by some of his underworld contacts.

Salvatore Avena acted as a lawyer for Mafia figures for several decades. In 1994 he was charged with racketeering and obstruction of justice after the FBI bugged his office. Avena was accused of being involved in murder. He was found not guilty.

Angelo Bruno was known as The Gentle Don because he disliked widespread violence and preferred not to draw attention to his activities, though with humour, intentional or otherwise, he did own a company called Atlas Extermination. He once served a two-year jail sentence for refusing to give evidence to a federal grand jury. It was the astute mob leader's longest spell in prison. Bruno was killed by a shotgun blast to the head as he sat in his car in Philadelphia on 12 March 1980. Another local Mafia figure, Antonio Caponigro, also known as Tony Bananas, who opposed Bruno's 'quiet way', ordered the murder. Mob leaders in New York were appalled and sanctioned Caponigro's killing. The murder of Bruno set off a chain of mob killings in Philadelphia, violence so great that the local gangsters acquired the unenviable reputation of being the most dysfunctional Mafia family in the United States.

It is certain that in 1968 the Philadelphia Mafia knew about the purchase of the *Queen Elizabeth* by the Miller brothers and Charles Williard. Angelo Bruno made it his business to be aware of everything that went on in his territory. He was careful with his money and invested wisely. Whether he bankrolled the project initially or later – or not at all – remains open to debate. But he usually went for good investments, which the *Queen Elizabeth* seemed to be, at first examination.

If the Philadelphia Mafia knew about the activities of CBS early on, then many mob families in the United States were certainly aware of them when the *Queen Elizabeth* arrived at Port Everglades. Rumours would persist that 'Mafia interests' wanted to convert the ship into a floating casino. Whenever the Miller brothers and Williard visited Port Everglades, the Fort Lauderdale police intelligence unit had them under surveillance. The Florida Bureau of Law Enforcement and the FBI opened dossiers on the Philadelphia trio and the 'coming of the *Queen Elizabeth*'. A state lawyer said:

> We know the Millers are not members of the Mafia, and we know they are not criminals, but they have apparently had a close enough relationship with certain Teamster Union officials and underworld characters to arouse our curiosity.[5]

Miami and the surrounding area had an unusual status as far as the Mafia was concerned. No one family was in control. It was 'open' territory. Since the 1920s south Florida had drawn gangsters from all over the United States. The older Mafia men, with creaking bones, those who had endured damp and cold prison cells, the harsh winters of Philadelphia, New York or Chicago, found the mild climate of south Florida particularly attractive. And when they were taking their breaks in the sunshine there were still plenty of business opportunities. Land development, hotels and restaurants were favourites. In fact, any business that made money could be a target, even garbage collection. Fort Lauderdale was a 'haven' for experts in stock and bond manipulation. The Organized Crime Strike Force, based in Miami and working with the FBI, was a busy outfit. One police estimate suggested that at least 2,000 'mob-connected' people, representing most of the country's Mafia families, were living permanently or seasonally in south Florida.

Angelo Bruno was a frequent visitor, and he owned an aluminium products company at Hialeah in the metropolitan area of Miami. It was also discovered that his wife paid taxes on a large piece of land west of Hollywood, Florida, and not far from the *Queen Elizabeth*'s berth. The land was held in the names of Bruno's lieutenant, Peter Maggio, and Carlo Gambino, the powerful boss of the New York Mafia, who liked winter breaks in south Florida.[6]

Alfred Felice, one of Bruno aides, had a home at North Bay Village, near Miami Beach. In evidence to a Senate hearing, he was accused of being one of the top heroin dealers in the country. Felice was a 'friend' of the singers Frank Sinatra, Dean Martin and Sammy Davis Jr. Martin was the godfather of Felice's first-born son. When Felice phoned one day and said he wanted to name a North Bay Village restaurant after the singer, Martin readily agreed and there was no fee. Martin told an Internal Revenue Service intelligence agent, Tom Harrison: 'I know he is not a baker or grocer, but what he did or does for a living, I don't know, but all I know he has been sweet and nice to my family and nice to me.' Sammy Davis Jr denied that Felice ever received a regular cut of his showbusiness earnings. 'I don't want to know nothing,' said the singer. 'It ain't none of my business to know.'[7]

Anthony 'Big Tony' Ricci lived at Hollywood. According to Miami police intelligence agents, he was 'a living legend' in the Mafia's 'hall of fame'. Ricci was credited with setting up Al Capone in Chicago. He was also friendly with Meyer Lansky, a major organised crime figure in the United States. Lansky did not belong to the Mafia but he had many dealings with the mob. He lived at Miami Beach.

Another local resident was Anthony Giacalone, identified in Senate testimony as a 'big man' in the Detroit Mafia. Giacalone was questioned over the disappearance of the Teamsters' Union leader Jimmy Hoffa, who just happened to have a luxurious apartment at Miami Beach.

The links that the Miller brothers and Charles Williard had with Hoffa and Bruno raised a lot of questions. How many of those questions were answered at the federal grand jury hearing that Cunard's deputy chairman attended is not known. The report of the investigation was sealed – something not unusual – and it has remained secret ever since.[8]

Federal grand juries investigating organised crime have often encountered problems over lack of evidence. Mafia figures simply refuse to answer questions on the grounds that their answers might incriminate them, citing the Fifth Amendment. Other witnesses often feel intimidated. Nicodemo 'Little Nicky' Scarfo, who took over the Philadephia family in 1981 and unleashed a reign of terror, was eventually convicted on major charges only because mob members feared they were on his hit list and went to the police and FBI for protection. The authorities usually end up trying to get convictions on tax offences. Scarfo, incidentally, knew the Miami area well. He had a home in Fort Lauderdale, where he threw lavish parties for mob members.

In November 1969, when the controversy over the future of the *Queen Elizabeth* at Port Everglades was at its height, Florida's Attorney General, Earl Faircloth, filed twenty-one lawsuits aimed at businesses, including hotels and restaurants, operated by the Mafia in the Miami area. Faircloth declared it was 'the opening shot in a war against the Mafia in Florida'. But no one was talking. In January 1971 it was announced that all the lawsuits would be dropped ... for lack of evidence.

In December 1984 Stanton and Robert Miller were sentenced to eighteen months in jail after being convicted by a Philadelphia court of federal conspiracy, gambling and tax charges.

CHAPTER 7

Corruption and Murder

The Mafia's suspected involvement in the purchase of the *Queen Elizabeth* was not the only criminal investigation that gave Cunard serious concern. As well as being asked to appear before the federal grand jury in Miami investigating organised crime, the company's deputy chairman, Peter Shirley, was needed as a prosecution witness in a case against Jack 'Sonny' Henderson.

Henderson was the port manager of Port Everglades when the liner arrived in December 1968. Less than two months later he resigned amid allegations of corruption. Henderson had long been a controversial figure in south Florida, and over the next four years he would face a number of accusations.

Soon after his resignation, it emerged that the Airport Boatel Corporation, run by Stanton and Robert Miller and Charles Williard, had awarded a lucrative contract for parking at the ship's berth to a company registered in the Bahamas, Heatherstone Enterprises. This company was set up in July 1968 – and the owners were Henderson and one of the port's commissioners. A second port commissioner also acquired shares in Heatherstone.[1]

In 1971 Henderson went before a Broward County grand jury accused of rigging a $56,000 bid for equipment when he was port manager. He claimed he had been forced to take the action by one of the port commissioners – who died before the trial. Henderson was cleared.

But he admitted that he had set up secret companies to profit from the tourist trade generated by the *Queen Elizabeth*. 'I was just trying to arrange some income for myself after I left the port,' he said. 'Hundreds of local businessmen were getting contracts.'[2] It was not just the Fort Lauderdale police who were looking at his activities. The FBI was showing an interest too. Soon after being cleared by the Broward jury, Henderson was charged with the federal offence of soliciting illegal payoffs from Cunard. This trial should have been held in Miami in 1972, but deputy chairman Peter Shirley was unable to attend as a witness. It was postponed until early the following year, when Shirley said he would be available.

However, the short and balding Henderson would never appear in court again. On 21 November 1972 he was found murdered on his large 'plush' houseboat, which was moored in a marina at North Miami Beach. He had been shot twice in the head in a Mafia-style execution. There were no signs of a struggle and nothing had been stolen, and divers who searched the marina did not find the murder weapon. Police said the body had been found by 'an associate' of 59-year-old Henderson, whom they refused to name. The associate turned out to be Fort Lauderdale businessman William Skillings, who had helped in the campaign to bring the *Queen Elizabeth* to Port Everglades.

A detective assigned to the case said: 'We think Henderson knew the killer and had no warning he was about to be shot.' Another officer commented: 'The number of people involved in this thing is unbelievable. He had so many acquaintances and friends. We're trying to talk to all of them. Everybody is a suspect at this point.' Police were working on the theory that 'the murder sprang from one of Henderson's varied and international business interests'. A British woman friend was apparently the last person to speak to Henderson before he opened the door of his home to the killer. The woman, a yacht broker in Miami, said she had a phone conversation on the night he was shot, and he referred to a dispute without giving details.

It was revealed later that Henderson had been a member of a business syndicate planning to invest in a hotel and casino at the resort of Santa Marta on the northern coast of Colombia. He was in the process of raising funds for the project. Skillings, 'a long-time Henderson associate', was also involved.

Henderson, married three times, had been living alone on his houseboat. With some irony he came to prominence in public life in south Florida after being appointed the sheriff of Dade County in 1951, vowing to take on racketeers. He was not reappointed sheriff and over the years filled various public posts, generating 'rumours of payoffs and misconduct', before becoming the port manager of Port Everglades in 1964.[3]

In February 1973 one Patrick Delaney was cleared of murdering Henderson. The jury took only seventy minutes to reach its verdict. Delaney was the captain of a charter fishing boat owned by Henderson, and the prosecution claimed that the motive was fear of losing his job if the former port manager sold up and moved to South America. Describing Henderson as 'notorious', Delaney's lawyer pointed out that 'a lot of other people' could have carried out the murder. After the not guilty verdict Delaney said: 'I knew all the time I was innocent.'[4]

Cunard's Peter Shirley did not have to make that trip to a Miami courtroom. No one else has been charged with Henderson's murder. The case remains unsolved.

CHAPTER 8

Will She Ever Get There?

When C. Y. Tung bought the *Queen Elizabeth* at auction in Fort Lauderdale, he knew that the liner was not in the condition that Cunard had kept her during the years she graced the Atlantic run. But he did not realise quite how badly she had been neglected in Florida after a comparatively short stay. On the outside she was still impressive, a giant displaying some blemishes. Within, however, there were problems. The engines could not propel her a few yards, let alone take her on a long journey in sometimes unforgiving seas. The plan was to sail to Hong Kong via the Cape of Good Hope for an extensive refit, which would give the *Queen Elizabeth* a new lease of life, not as a static tourist attraction but as a great liner travelling the world. She would have wealthy passengers and she would also be a floating university, an ambassador. Tung was passionate about education. She would be called the *Seawise University*, a play on his initials, C. Y.

Tung paid a lot less for the ship than he had offered Cunard, but he still needed to dig deep into his pockets – $900,000 – to get her seaworthy. He flew in nearly 300 of his own workmen and a skeleton crew. These men were familiar with tankers, freighters and small passenger ships, but not a liner of the size and complexity of the *Queen Elizabeth*. Tung approached Cunard's technical services in London. Would Commodore Geoffrey Marr be willing to come out of retirement to help with the voyage to Hong Kong? Marr was finding nothing more challenging than the garden of his village home in Hampshire. He had thought that the voyage to Port Everglades, with the final order 'Stop all engines', signalled the last chapter. Marr did not need much persuading, nor did Ted Philip, who was the ship's last chief engineer under Cunard. The two men were invited to meet Tung at a Chinese restaurant in London, where the tycoon 'bubbled over with enthusiasm and good humour'. Marr was 'elated' when Tung outlined his plans for the liner, especially as he believed that the *Queen Elizabeth* had been given a raw deal. He remained critical of Cunard's decision to take her out of service so soon after the costly refit on the Clyde.

Then, because Cunard had sold her to the highest bidders without making a very close investigation into their financial or personal backgrounds, she had become a pawn in some rather shady Florida politics, which seemed to me a sad end for a ship with such an unblemished record in both war and peace.

Marr also reflected:

It was wonderful to think of her being restored to her natural element once more, with the great engines that are her heart throbbing as they drive her across the ocean, instead of just lying rotting away in a Florida creek at the mercy of men whose only real interest was trying to use her as a means of making a fast buck.[1]

Marr and Philip flew out in November 1970. When Marr saw the liner again, she still looked 'most imposing', but he was shocked at the 'scene of utter desolation' he found when he stepped off the gangway leading to C Deck. Rubbish was everywhere, mostly from the engine and boiler rooms. Lighting was limited and supplied by an emergency generator. He was reduced to creeping around with the aid of a torch, and 'everything looked drab, dirty and depressing'. It had been planned to sail the ship in December, but Marr knew that idea was wildly optimistic. With luck, they were looking at February 1971. The ship, already renamed *Seawise University*, had a Chinese captain, Commodore William Hsuan, who faced problems on a daily basis, largely because the liner was overwhelming his scratch crew. Marr felt some sympathy. He had always enjoyed the benefit of a highly trained and efficient crew. Two of the biggest problems were the state of the boilers and the accumulation of about 4,000 tons of water in the oil tanks and holds. Just six of the twelve boilers could be used but only after hundreds of boiler tubes had been replaced. At one point it was suggested that it might be better to tow the ship to Hong Kong. But enough work was carried out to make Marr reasonably confident that the ship could sail away under her own steam on the morning of 10 February 1971, a cold and windy day, though clear. Getting the *Queen Elizabeth* to her berth at Port Everglades had been a difficult manoeuvre because of the narrowness of the harbour entrance and leaving would be just as tricky. The job fell once again to the port's chief pilot, Captain Irving Shuman, helped by six tugs.

Among the people on the bridge was port commissioner Phil McConaghey, arch critic of the deals covering the ship's stay at Port Everglades. His presence baffled some of those on board. Don Clark, who had managed the ship during bankruptcy, shouted up at McConaghey: 'Why don't you just jump off the bridge?' Another man yelled: 'You've got some nerve, McConaghey.' The commissioner waved a big cigar and shouted back: 'The devil made me do it.'[2]

There had been bad news during the night. One of the operational boilers was shut down because of leaky tubes. As the liner headed for the harbour entrance, needing as much speed as possible, another boiler was put out of action. Marr had already warned that the *Queen Elizabeth* could end up as 'a cork' in the harbour entrance. He noted:

> Fortunately, the ship had already built up sufficient way to carry her clear of the dredged channel, with a maximum effort on the part of the tugs to keep her on course in spite of the pressure of the beam wind. But had this boiler gone ten or even five minutes earlier, it could have been a very different story: without sufficient headway the tugs would have been powerless to prevent the ship grounding in the approach channel and perhaps breaking her back as the tide fell, thus becoming the cork that would have most effectively bottled up the harbour of Port Everglades for many weeks.[3]

She got through. The seas were choppy, however, and when it was time for the pilot to leave, Captain Shuman made a dangerous leap onto the heaving deck of one of the tugs. McConaghey also had to jump, and Marr recorded:

> As he had been the man who had had more uncomplimentary things to say about the ship than anyone else in Florida, one can only assume that he had come along to see the last of the ship he had worked to get rid of. His last few minutes on board her must have been extremely anxious ones as he stood in the shell door and watched the gyrations of the wildly plunging tug on whose deck he had to jump; and a lot of people would have thought it no more than poetic justice had he missed his footing and the Old Lady dunked him into the sea as a farewell gesture. However, he made it safely.[4]

The Miami Herald probably summed it all up with the first two paragraphs of its front-page story on the departure:

> After two years, two months and two days of being touted, exploited and finally bankrupted, the retired luxury liner *Queen Elizabeth* limped out of Port Everglades.
>
> She left trailing clouds of black smoke, and carrying scars of rust and political battle deeper than any wound received when she carried troops during World War II.

The departure was in sharp contrast to her colourful welcome. A handful of people watched the *Queen Elizabeth* sail away. Her treatment had turned out to be a huge embarrassment for the Sunshine State. The liner pressed on towards the Caribbean at about eight knots, relying on just four boilers, which would soon be reduced to three. On 13 February a serious fire broke out in one of those boiler rooms. It was eventually brought under control, but it left the ship without power. 'All our spirits slumped again,' Marr reported. The ship was left drifting between Cuba and Haiti. At night she was in darkness apart from 'a dim white oil light at the bow and stern, and two dim red "not under command" lights on the foremast'. There was further humiliation. A Norwegian cruise ship, *Starward*, came into view, fully illuminated. Hundreds of passengers lined her decks to witness 'a sad and desolate sight'. Marr recorded:

> After steaming in close up and down both sides of the ship, with her searchlights playing on us and the flashbulbs from dozens of cameras making bright pinpoints of light, she asked us through her loudhailers if there was anything she could do for us. We replied 'No, thank you' and she veered away, increased to full speed and resumed her course to Port au Prince – leaving many of us old Cunard hands feeling very dashed, and wondering what the hell we were doing there.

On board were four women and one of them, Mrs Peter DeLisle, wife of a British crewman, wrote a letter home telling of the ship's woes. Soon after sailing from Port Everglades her husband came off watch and went to his cabin to find that all his clothes had been stolen. Of Friday, 12 February, Mrs DeLisle wrote: 'Well, I am certainly glad today is not Friday the 13th. We have a small problem. We have lost all water and are standing still.' The next day she 'awoke to a fire alarm ... everyone said it was the worst fire they had seen'. For Sunday, 14 February she reported:

> Happy Valentine's Day. One of the funniest things happened today. Mr Philip [the ship's former chief engineer] informed us that since water is so short the girls could share a toilet and the crew would build outside commodes over the side, in fact right below our porthole. They are three-seaters. You have never seen anything like it ... the world's largest luxury liner with bottoms down over the side.

Three days later there was a special treat: 'Water – enough to take a shower. I know this must sound silly but water is like gold around here.'[5]

As well as Philip, there were several other British engineers. They found themselves in conflict with their Chinese counterparts over solutions to the boiler problems. As the captain was Chinese, his views prevailed. On 16 February, after three days of 'utter frustration', a tug, aptly named *Rescue*, arrived on the scene. Strong winds made towing difficult and the ship ended up taking a 'crab-like course'. A second tug came to her aid. The original destination for repairs was Kingston, Jamaica, but this changed to Curacao and then the island of Aruba, off the northern coast of Venezuela, where the *Queen Elizabeth* arrived on 24 February, two weeks after leaving Port Everglades. The average speed had been about three knots. Further problems were encountered when the ship was taken to the wrong anchorage. In strong winds she dragged her anchor and drifted into deep water. It took until 4 March to tow her back to Aruba. Various experts were flown to the island, and it was decided to carry out extensive repairs on the boilers. More than 600 boiler tubes and other spares were sent from the United States and England. The ship remained at Aruba for nearly eleven weeks. The climate was pleasant but monotony set in, and Marr and Philip were pleased when they were offered the chance to take a two-week break in a cold and damp Britain. Tung visited the ship, boosting the spirits of his men. Marr returned to find that all engine and boiler rooms in use had been cleaned and painted

> so that down below she not only looked but really was a very different ship from the one which had staggered out of Port Everglades in such a shocking condition. She was indeed beginning to look so much more like she used to do in her Cunard days that for the first time one could really feel she was being given a new lease of life.[6]

On 10 May – three months after leaving Port Everglades – the *Queen Elizabeth* sailed from Aruba, going the short distance to Curacao to pick up fuel and fresh water. After a brief stop at Port of Spain, Trinidad, the ship headed for Rio de Janeiro, arriving on 30 May and 'attracting considerable attention'. The Atlantic run to Cape Town, 3,343 miles, was achieved without incident and she docked on 13 June, once again receiving a lot of publicity. The next stop was Singapore, almost the end of the journey. There were still tensions between the British and Chinese engineers. Philip and his men believed the Chinese were restricting the ship's speed unnecessarily, and the language barrier did not help. In the busy Strait of Malacca cargo vessels kept overtaking the *Queen Elizabeth*, which was restricted to about eight knots (her average speed on Atlantic crossings had been 28.5 knots). But she finally arrived in Singapore on 8 July to be greeted by six Royal Air Force fighters and six Royal Navy helicopters. Tung's company had decided not to hold a press conference because it wanted to show off the ship after her refit in Hong Kong. However, they could not deter newspaper, TV and radio interest, even though the ship was berthed 14 miles from the city centre. A party of journalists boarded her after Commodore Hsuan and his senior officers had gone ashore, and Marr found himself back in his old role of 'doing the honours'. He had mixed feelings, however. 'Once more I said to myself, "What is she doing here? What am I doing here? Why couldn't she have stayed in Britain?"'

Finally, the big day came – her entrance to Hong Kong harbour. Like her arrival at Port Everglades, she did not steam straight in. Bizarrely, despite her slow speed, she arrived early and spent 24 hours cruising around 'rather like a nervous prima donna waiting apprehensively in the wings'. When she did sail between the colony's many islands towards her anchorage on 15 July, small craft and helicopters gave her an enthusiastic reception. The fireboat *Alexander Grantham* put up 'a much finer display of water fountains than I had ever seen in New York', Marr recorded. The irony of this display would not be lost in January 1972. Marr also noted:

> Everyone seemed delighted to see the ship safely here at last, but in spite of her new name nearly everyone seemed to think of her as the *Queen Elizabeth*, and one got the feeling it was as this that she was being welcomed.

A voyage that should have taken about 45 days had lasted more than five months.

One day after her arrival the families of the Chinese crew and about 100 local and foreign journalists were invited on board for a welcome party. 'We want you to inspect the ship today and then come back in a few months' time to compare how she looks after the conversion,' said M. H. Liang, an executive of Tung's Island Navigation Corporation. Another executive said the 'outstanding features' of the *Queen* would be preserved but she would be modernised to 'combine the best of the cultures of the East and West'. He promised: 'She will be more beautiful than ever.' The ship would accommodate 800 first-class passengers and 800 students. A reporter observed:

> Although the upholstered chairs were soiled and frayed, the light wood panelling, tall columnar lamps, grand piano, parquet flooring and other marks of her 1930s glamorous elegance were still there.

But something was missing from the ballroom:

> Gone since her last Atlantic crossing in 1968 were the gowned, bejewelled women and tall, grey-haired men in tuxedos dancing and drinking to the music of a smooth band.[7]

Days later, work began on the ship's extensive refit. Changes would ensure that she met the requirements of the 1948 SOLAS (Safety of Life at Sea) agreement and the 1966 IMCO (International Maritime Consultative Organisation) agreement, fire precautions that Cunard had decided it could not afford.

Marr did not doubt Tung's commitment to the ambitious project or his financial clout, but he wondered if the ship would turn out to be a success when she entered service again. He pointed out:

> I have always held that any ship, no matter how large or expensively fitted out, is just another piece of hardware until you get the right crew for her; and it has to be a crew who like the ship, and who are prepared to stay with her and help to build up her reputation with the travelling public for excellent service and safety. And that is even more important, with the travel agents, upon whom every shipping company has to depend if it is going to survive. It was going to be a fantastically difficult task for Mr Tung's organisation to find, and in a few short months to train, nearly 1,000 men and women to operate a ship as complex as this, and to give that very high standard of service which the wealthy American cruise passengers, upon whom he would have to depend for the bulk of his revenue, demand. Having not been very favourably impressed with the standard of discipline I had seen on board, I found it hard to believe that he could, because a well-run ship requires a lot of organisation, and my experience of the Chinese generally was that were hard workers but poor organisers.[8]

The *South China Morning Post* also had reservations:

> There is no more fitting symbol of the pre-eminent position of Chinese businessmen in the world of shipping than the presence of the *Seawise University* now in Hong Kong, the proud possession of Mr C Y Tung. His grandiose plans for this vessel are another matter: there is no reason to believe that Mr Tung is going to succeed where Cunard failed in making this great ship pay her way.[9]

Soon after the ship's arrival, Hong Kong's Director of Marine, Kenneth Milburn, warned that he was unhappy about the lack of fire precautions. This followed a visit by officers from his department and the Fire Services Department. Assistant Chief Fire Officer Leonard Worrallo had quickly come to the conclusion that there was 'an extremely dangerous fire and life risk'. An inspection revealed, among other things, that the sprinkler systems and fire main were not working, watertight doors were being left open with cables running through them, the electrical systems were in poor condition, the condition of fire equipment was 'suspect', and there were no experienced fire crews on board. The ship presented a 'very serious fire risk', which would increase when the refit began if measures were not taken. Milburn made a staggering twenty-one recommendations.[10]

The following month, August, Milburn complained about the lack of safety for workmen on board. He stated:

It appears there are no life buoys or buoyant apparatus available for use in case of fire by any person who may have to escape over the ship's side. Moreover, of the lifeboats apparently intended for use none are turned out and no boarding ladders are available.

There were other concerns, including fire hoses without nozzles and widespread smoking.[11]

Milburn gave a further warning in September. He called for the removal of quantities of combustible material on C Deck, and stressed the need for firewatchers whenever burning operations were being carried out.[12]

The *Queen Elizabeth* and Tung were featured in one of Alan Whicker's television documentaries as part of the *Whicker's Orient* series. Whicker and Tung took a small boat out to the liner two months before her refit was due to be completed. The interviewer was incredulous after seeing her poor condition and surveying open decks strewn with tons of rubbish. Would the ship really be ready in time? A relaxed Tung insisted that the work was on schedule and that the liner would sail to Japan for dry-docking in January 1972 before beginning her first cruise as the *Seawise University*.

'She's cost him a packet,' Whicker pointed out in his commentary. Tung admitted that the bill so far stood at US$12 million – after buying the ship he had spent $3 million to bring her to Hong Kong and then a further $6 million on the conversion work, which was well over budget 'but not beyond my expectations'.

Whicker said he had been told there were labour problems. Tung replied:

Yes, for a short period – three or five days. It was something beyond our control. They (workers) wanted to play poker or Chinese dice. People reported to police that they were gambling. One or two men were arrested. They said we did it but we never said a word to the police department. It was a storm in a teacup.

Whicker referred to the men's Communist-led union and the practice of going ashore for lunch, which meant that they spent five hours sailing to and from work. It was a 'big problem', Tung acknowledged because it meant that the working day was reduced to three hours. 'We offered them some Cantonese opera to stay on board but they wanted to go back to shore for lunch.'

K. T. Woo, a Hong Kong newspaper editor, was interviewed by Wicker about Tung's purchase of the *Queen Elizabeth*. 'I think it is foolish but I'm sure I'm wrong,' he said. 'If I didn't think it was wrong I would be C. Y. Tung and not K. T. Woo. The whole business is completely fantastic.' Woo added: 'Shipping is a very scary business. If I was in the business I'd be scared to death. I'd have sleepless nights, a nervous breakdown.'

Finally, Whicker spoke to one of the tycoon's sons, C. H. Tung. He began by saying: 'The *Queen Elizabeth* was a dream of your father but an old man's dreams are not always economic.' Sitting at his desk in an impressive office, a smiling C. H. Tung replied: 'We feel that in our market research there is a tremendous requirement and interest in passenger cruising. We think we can make a go of it.' Whicker pointed out that there was a shipping recession and asked: 'Is this a good time to take over 83,000 tons of rusty *Queen Elizabeth*?' Back came the reply: '*Queen Elizabeth* is by no means a rusty old ship. She is a beautiful ship. She was run down because of negligence by the previous owner. These are problems we can easily overcome.' Whicker observed: 'The whole thing seems like a mad fantasy. Your skipper is from a tanker, the crew is from goodness knows where, stewards are being trained in a Hong Kong hotel, you've got a chef from a hotel – it doesn't really sound professionally nautical.' C. H. Tung insisted it would 'work out'.

Whicker's documentary appeared on British TV screens on 15 February 1972, little more than a month after C. Y. Tung's dream had been destroyed.[13]

CHAPTER 9

The Onassis of the Far East

When C. Y. Tung bought the *Queen Elizabeth*, he was widely known as the Aristotle Onassis of the Far East. But about the only things that the two men had in common were huge fleets of merchant ships and a passion for business. The private life of the Greek tycoon attracted a great deal of publicity – an affair with opera singer Maria Callas and a marriage to US President John Kennedy's widow Jacqueline – while Tung enjoyed a solid family life and the relative calm of the Peking opera.

Tung had arrived in Hong Kong from Shanghai in 1949 after the Communists swept to victory in China. Two other men who would go on to become great ship owners also turned up in the colony at about the same time, Sir Yue-kong Pao and T. Y. Chao. They all saw themselves as Shanghainese, though Pao came from Ningbo, some 100 miles south of Shanghai. Tung's parents were also from Ningbo, once an important port that was eclipsed by Shanghai in the late nineteenth century.

Tung, son of a 'modest businessman', developed an interest in transport during his youth. He joined the Tientsin Navigation Company in 1930 when he was 18 and quickly gained a reputation for hard work. Later he would happily tell friends: 'I've been working seven days a week for the past 40 years.' Friends described him as 'soft spoken and ambitious with a good sense of judgement'. His industry had been noted early on by a shipping boss, C. S. Koo, who thought he would make a good husband for his daughter, Koo Lee-ching. They were duly married. Tung's reputation grew, and in 1936 Chiang Kia-shek's Nationalist government asked him to come up with a master plan for the Chinese shipping industry, which had been hit by recession. Tung would develop strong ties with the Nationalists, support that would continue after Chiang and his followers fled to Taiwan. And the Nationalist leader helped him to build up his fleet. Tung preferred to have Chinese crews, with officers from Taiwan, 'a reflection of national pride'. A Tung company, the China Maritime Trust, was relocated from Shanghai to Taiwan. But his first company, the Island Navigation Corporation, had been registered in Delaware in 1940 so that his ships could sail under non-Chinese flags and avoid being seized by the Japanese. In the years ahead, many of his ships would fly flags of convenience.

By the end of the Second World War he owned ships totalling about 100,000 tons. He made a fortune in the early post-war years when a shipping shortage saw his vessels heading to ports in North and South America.

Tung loved ships, unlike most ship owners, who saw them as commodities. Over four decades his fleet grew to 150 vessels totalling more than 11 million tons.[1]

And he never wavered in his support of Taiwan.

CHAPTER 10

The Triads

In 1971, the year of the *Queen Elizabeth*'s arrival, Hong Kong was facing three major problems: criminal activity by triad gangs; corruption in public services; and spying by China, Taiwan and the Soviet Union.

Secret societies had existed in China for centuries before the triads emerged. The Triad Society was formed in Fuijan province during the seventeenth century with the aim of overthrowing the Manchu Ch'ing dynasty and restoring the Chinese Ming dynasty. According to legend, Shaolin monks were behind the movement, but that has been disputed – as has the idea that it was one co-ordinated body from the outset. But certainly the Triad Society did play a significant role in resistance, right up until the end of the Ch'ing, or Qing, dynasty in 1912.

Triad is a western term stemming from the society's emblem, a triangle whose sides represent heaven, earth and man. Chinese in Hong Kong have various names for the society, including the Sam Hop Wui (Three United Association). Elaborate ceremonies, colourful costumes, complicated arm and hand movements and lists of oaths have been features of triad recruitment. In the twentieth century political aspirations were jettisoned in favour of criminal activity. Triads remain a challenge for police forces in many countries.

When Britain was handed Hong Kong in 1842 under the Treaty of Nanking, triads were already established, and resentment against the new foreign power helped recruitment. Less than three years later the authorities decided to ban triad membership. The proposed penalties were severe – up to three years' jail, branding on the left cheek and deportation. This was amended to branding under the left arm and deportation. The Triad Society flourished.

Laws declaring the society illegal were revised over the years, up until 1949, but membership in the former colony remains an offence. The society has spawned many groups, but unlike the Mafia there is no controlling 'godfather'. Each group usually acts independently, with its own territory.

Traditionally, there has been a hierarchy. At the top is Shan Chu (Mountain Master) and at the bottom are the 49 Chai, the ordinary members. In between, depending on how seriously a group takes tradition, are Fu Shan Chu (Deputy Mountain Master), Heung Chu (Incense Master), Sin Fung (Vanguard), Hung Kwan (Red Pole), Pak Tsz Sin (White Paper Fan) and Choi Hai (Straw Sandal). The titles always come with code numbers. For example, Shan Chu is 489 and Heung Chu is 438. Ordinary members are 49.

A traditional initiation ceremony is held at a lodge decorated with banners and containing paraphernalia, with an altar at one end. There are eighteen steps, including 'passing through the fiery pit' and 'chopping off the chicken's head'. The Red Club, the Sword of Loyalty and Righteousness, the Grass Sandal and the Yellow Umbrella are other features, as well as thirty-six oaths. The ceremony could take up to three days.

But a modern ceremony will probably last an hour, greatly reducing the risk of a police raid. A recruit is warned of the fate of traitors and swears loyalty. The ceremony usually involves the drinking of blood.[1]

Yan Sui Kuen, forty-two, claimed that he took part in a triad ceremony when he was only ten years old. It was held on a Hong Kong rooftop on a hot summer night. He was one of eleven youngsters.

'The ceremony was very long,' he said. 'They read many lessons and made us swear to many things.'

Forty adults wearing white headbands watched as each recruit pricked his middle finger and squeezed blood into a cup. The blood was mixed with water and the youngsters drank from the cup in turn.[2] Apparently, only death can release someone from membership.

Fighting between triad groups was relatively rare before 1941. A major split appeared shortly before the Japanese invaded Hong Kong. The Triad Society roughly formed three camps. Some supported China's Nationalist government and wanted to fight the invaders, others were prepared to join the Japanese, and the third camp decided to wait and see who emerged victorious.

In the event, the Japanese did use triads t   help maintain order in some of the occupied districts and even allowed them to carry on their activities in prostitution, drugs and gambling. The triads were given a new title, Hing Ah Kee Kwan (Asia Flourishing Organisation). Some even joined the police force set up by the Japanese.

After Japan's surrender in 1945 the triads continued to flourish. As the British struggled to set up an effective administration, looting and crimes of violence rose. The black market was lucrative and, ironically, the triads also found a source of revenue by threatening to expose people who had been collaborators. When the military administration banned opium, which had been legal before the war – if bought from a government supplier – the drugs trade increased.[3]

One of the biggest triad groups in Hong Kong is the 14K, which expanded greatly in China from 1945 with the blessing of the Nationalist government. The group was seen as another weapon in the fight against Communists.

The man in charge of recruiting was an army general, Kot Siu Wong, who also happened to be a leading triad figure. Many thousands of soldiers and civilians joined, and the focus was on saving the Nationalist regime, not crime. When the Communists secured victory in 1949, there was a crackdown on organised crime in China. Many triads fled to Hong Kong, including a significant number of 14K members. The '14' in the title refers to the address of their former headquarters in Canton. The 'K' stands for 'karat' gold and is a form of battle honour following victory over a rival group.

Another group that arrived with the influx of refugees was the Green Pang, an out-and-out criminal organisation. These triads were responsible for supplying heroin in large quantities in Hong Kong for the first time. Protection rackets, prostitution and daring armed robberies were the gang's other main activities. The police were forced to set up a special squad to deal with the Green Pang and success only came when their leader, 'a solid and respected businessman', was deported in 1952.

Four years later, Hong Kong faced a crisis when rioting broke out among Nationalist supporters and Communist sympathisers. Triads exploited the troubles with widespread looting. A public outcry led to the police rounding up 10,000 suspects, and some 600 triad members were deported. There was also tougher enforcement of the law banning triad membership. In the year before the riots there had been seventy-nine arrests but by 1959/60 that figure had risen to 3,521.

Even so, it was a small number compared to the total. In 1960 Commissioner of Police Henry Heath said it was estimated that one in six of the population of three million was a triad member, which works out at a staggering half a million, though many would have allowed themselves to be recruited simply as a form of job insurance.

Heath pointed out:

The vast majority are, of course, inactive members, but it should always be borne in mind that all organisations, however large, are normally controlled by small groups of active officials. The rank and file follow, willingly or otherwise, as directed by their leaders.

Legal enactments alone cannot destroy an organisation of this magnitude. Haphazard arrests of individual members cannot seriously weaken the societies which are continually recruiting new members. All available resources must be concentrated on curbing its potential for evil and assisting to speed up its own process of self-destruction. In particular, it is necessary that action must be directed against the controlling officials and pressure maintained until such time that organised triad activity collapses from lack of members willing to accept positions of responsibility that will automatically expose them to personal attention by the forces of law and order.

He made one thing clear:

> In earlier centuries the Triad Society might well have been a massive and
> fearful organisation, but it cannot be too strongly emphasised that in present
> day Hong Kong the triad member is nothing more than a run-of-the-mill
> hoodlum masquerading in the name of a long-dead giant. Today, the word
> triad should not engender fear, but contempt ...[4]

That view was shared by Commissioner of Police Brian Slevin in 1978:

> Triad societies exist largely in name only, having degenerated from strictly
> controlled, politically motivated organizations into loose-knit gangs of
> criminals that merely usurp the names of triad societies of the past. Such
> gangs have their 'fellow travellers' but infrastructure has gone; such little
> leadership as there is revolves around individuals who have gained prestige
> or influence by virtue of their criminal background, and it is generally limited
> to the gang only.[5]

One concern was that disaffected youths on rundown housing estates had formed
triad-style gangs. This problem had been recognised several years earlier:

> In the slum areas of the city and densely populated new residential areas,
> there is a tendency for youths to group themselves into gangs, whose
> members profess triad affiliation to achieve recognition of their power and
> to intensify their illegal activities. However, they have no true allegiance to
> any triad society.[6]

The police in Hong Kong, generally, have played down the idea that triads
were a major factor when it came to organised crime.

However, it is a fact that in 1958 a special police unit, the Triad Society
Bureau, was set up. This unit was reformed in 1978 to carry out 'in-depth
investigations of important triad personalities and more serious types of triad
activities'. The following year, the Triad Society Bureau became a division
of the Organised Crime Bureau. Later the police admitted that several triad
groups were well structured and held boardroom-style meetings to review
policy and organise their activities.

Professor Harold Traver, a leading figure in the Hong Kong Society of
Criminology, pointed out:

> Apparently, triad societies had been only 'temporarily' disorganized and
> fragmented. Attention also turned to assessing the degree of triad involvement
> in organised crime. The result was a major revision of the strategy to counter

triad activity, which involved disbanding the Triad Society Division and establishing the Organised and Serious Crime Group which comprised two bureaux: the Organised and Serious Crimes Bureau and the Criminal Intelligence Bureau. The disbanding of the Triad Society Bureau generated considerable public controversy at the time but was defended on grounds that frontline police action against triads should be concentrated where it mattered most – on the streets at regional and district level.[7]

The Hong Kong police have records listing more than 300 triad groups. In the 1970s there were about fifty gangs, split into four main groups, the 14K, Chiu Chow/Hoklo, Wo and Luen.

Yiu Kong Chu, an academic who carried out a special study of triads, wrote in 1999: 'There is little doubt that triads are a menace in both Hong Kong and the international community. The word 'triad' conjures up many things to people: fear, intrigue, mystery, brutality and violence.'

He added:

Since Hong Kong triads are believed to be increasingly active in drug trafficking, human smuggling and economic organised crime such as credit card fraud, counterfeiting and money laundering, western police predict that these triads will replace the Italian Mafia as the most powerful criminal organisation in the world in the next century.[8]

A key activity of the triads has been control of labour markets and this can be traced back to 1857. Coolies who came to Hong Kong entered the Triad Society 'as a rule'. Some genuine labour associations ended up forming their own fighting sections to counter triad intimidation.

Violence is often a feature of triad activity. A member of the Sun Yee On gang was quoted as saying:

Many times I crippled people over a small monetary dispute. It was all to do with face and keeping order among members. A lot of times it was a show of power and your standing in the society. To show that we could do anything to anyone if they got out of order.[9]

Favoured weapons are choppers, iron bars and meat cleavers. Two cases from the 1970s, believed to have been drug-related, illustrate the brutality. 'We had one body floating in the Tai Tam reservoir,' said a murder squad detective.

It was decomposed, stab wounds all over him, his eyes had been cut out and acid poured on his face so that he couldn't be identified, and they'd cut off all his fingers as well so that we couldn't even get fingerprints.

Then I did another one found floating in Lai Chi Kok Bay to the west of Kowloon about a couple of years later. This one was in a sack and he had been sawn in half at the third vertebra with an electric saw. Not only that. They had disarticulated his ankles. So not only did he have no head, no finger or footprints but the thing was that in the first case, in the reservoir, the press had said – wrongly as it happens – that, even though the culprit had cut off the fingers, the clever police had identified him by his footprints. In actual fact, we never did – probably because his footprints weren't on record – but, because of this, in the second case they had taken steps to destroy his footprints.[10]

In another case, a businessman was sent the severed head of a dog as a warning. It probably involved extortion, and he ignored the warning. One week later the businessman was murdered by a suspected triad with a meat cleaver at a tennis club parking lot in front of women and children.

But triads are not averse to fighting each other. In the fifteen months up until 31 March 1973, police recorded 132 gang fights involving five groups, the 14K, Chiu Chow, Wo, Luen and Tung.

Chief Inspector Ben Munford of the Triad Society Bureau told a court that 'information indicates that triads are involved in a disturbing proportion of the colony's violent crimes'. He added:

> There is evidence that triads are attempting to expand their areas and influence, which must inevitably lead to clashes of interest and thus to violent crimes. Most of the triad activities came to police notice after gang fights occurred.

Facing the court were fifteen people who admitted being involved with the 14K gang. Two of the accused were a thirteen-year-old boy and a girl of eighteen who were arrested at a triad initiation ceremony in a hotel room, where police found an altar, triad flags, candles, an incense burner and gang papers.

'Five of the defendants were wearing the official triad red headband, denoting that they were office bearers,' said Munford.

> They also had gold flowers in their headbands showing that they were undergoing a promotion ceremony. Two of them were seen to have their lips stained red showing that they had just drunk from the cup of red flower wine mixed with their blood, and therefore had just been initiated into the triad as ordinary members.[11]

Another gang with a fearsome reputation is the Big Circle Boys, which was originally made up of former Red Guards and Chinese soldiers. Gang members arrived in Hong Kong as illegal immigrants between 1969 and 1975. Most of them had escaped after being detained in a purge in the Guangdong province of China. They are not strictly triads, but they embarked on similar activities, even shocking some gangs with the extent of their violence. Putting their military training to use and often armed with assault rifles and grenade launchers, they carried out brutal raids on banks, gold dealers and jewellery stores. Later, some members joined recognised triad gangs. The 14K took on so many that a special group was formed, the 14 Big Circle, or 14 Tai Huen.

Superintendent Norman Temple of the Triad Society Bureau had this to say of triads:

There are no redeeming features whatsoever to triads. They are not local Robin Hoods ... They are no more than common criminals and hoodlums. In the majority of cases triads are either professional criminals or the followers and supporters of professional criminals. In most cases they are thugs dedicated to nothing but their own immediate financial and material benefit. To a man they display total regard for the law and stand permanently prepared to exploit all means available to further their criminal ends regardless of consequences.

Remove the triad ritual, remove the triad titles, remove the hypocrisy of blood oaths and you are left with nothing more than common thugs and common criminals, professional 'frighteners' in no way different from the scum that prey upon civilised communities elsewhere.

The triads in Hong Kong function more or less in the Chinese community. They are not limited to any one Chinese ethnic group, although for obvious reasons triad thugs from the same ethnic group tend to stick together. In the matter of age there is no limitation. To describe triads as teddy boys or mere bully boys casually putting in leisure time in gang pursuits is to mislead. Equally, the description of triads as highly organised and efficient mobsters controlled by one or other mastermind, the Mr Big etc, is also misleading.

Too often one is asked to draw comparisons between the Hong Kong triads and the Mafia. When this question is put to me I have to remind myself that in most cases the image the questioner has in mind of the Mafia is the illusion, in most cases the celluloid illusion at the moment so frequently presented to us via our cinema and television screens, the ultra romanticised presentation of over imaginative fiction writers, in brief the Marlon Brando image, which is linked to the present unpalatable trend of idolising and publicising what are no more than cheap and nasty hoodlums.

If one can however reduce all such fantasy to a more realistic picture of the common American thug represented by the Mafia or syndicate hoodlum then there is little difference between such a 'frightener' and Hong Kong triad thugs, nor indeed to professional 'frighteners' elsewhere, be it London, Paris or what have you.

In respect of age, triad involvement covers a wide scale. There are on file cases involving 15 and 16 year olds taking part in triad gang activities, some taking part in gang attacks organised by triad gangs to establish or maintain criminal monopolies. There are 20 to 25 year olds on record as leaders of set triad gangs. There are 30 year olds identified as functioning as organisers of triad criminal monopolies, directing as it were the activities of their thug followers. There are men in their 40s and 50s, some even in their 60s still actively involved in the direction of day-to-day triad gang activities.

As in most businesses, mergers do occur even in the world of crime. Police naturally take a very dim view of any attempts in this direction and indeed one of the main tasks of the Triad Society Bureau is to vigorously discourage all and any such attempts, acting as an anti-monopoly board, as it were. From time to time in Hong Kong triad factions lay claim to holding set territories or areas. However, much of this is a figment of their over worked imaginations and reflects more what they would like to believe they have than what in fact exists. However, occasionally areas become temporarily over frequented by members of the same triad gangs who then concentrate their criminal activities in that area and so present to the uninformed a picture of total triad control in the area, which on the surface at least seems to be supported by fact.

The whole matter of where triads are requires to be carefully viewed and seen in perspective. All too often prominent local personalities tend to comment that this or that area is totally controlled by triad gangs. This tends to present an erroneous picture of a total breakdown of law and order in the area and of criminals freely operating there unhindered, and so holding entire areas of the colony to ransom.

Temple added:

No one, and particularly not the police, would ever wish to reduce the dangers posed to the community by triad gangs, nor indeed to lessen the need for vigilance on the part of the public against such thugs. But gossip and gross exaggeration help no one but the triad gangs. Circulating rumours or gossip about alleged triad activities is every bit as bad as complacency. Fear breeds fear, so let us at least try by example to reduce the opportunities for the same.[12]

CHAPTER 11

Colony of Corruption

Corruption was a way of life in Hong Kong in 1971. For many it was known euphemistically as 'tea money'. Few areas of public service were unaffected. Bribes could secure most things: an ambulance to get to hospital; firemen to extinguish a blazing home; a licence for a restaurant; planning permission; accommodation; a loan. Graft, certainly, had been around for a long time – the colony's first anti-corruption law had been passed in 1897 – but it was a growing problem in the 1960s and early 1970s. One area of particular concern was the police.

The issue of police corruption exploded with the case of Chief Superintendent Peter Godber. There are still question marks over how Godber came to be unmasked. One report suggested that it all began when the Royal Bank of Canada in Vancouver carried out a routine check on dormant accounts, one of which happened to be in the name of Peter Fitzroy Godber. He was listed as a British diplomat in Hong Kong – and he had acquired a lot of money. The bank got in touch with the Foreign Office in London to check if he was still alive.

A puzzled Foreign Office contacted Hong Kong and the routine enquiry ended up in the office of Commissioner of Police Charles Sutcliffe. It did not take long to work out that the only Peter Fitzroy Godber in the colony was the chief superintendent.[1] Another suggestion is that Sutcliffe was tipped off about Godber by a jealous colleague or an irate member of the public. Curiously, Sutcliffe retired to Salt Spring Island, near Vancouver. There is a story that he had an account with the same bank and on an earlier visit to Canada he was told by a clerk: 'We know your boss – Peter Godber.'

Until then, Godber had been a highly regarded officer. He distinguished himself during Communist-inspired rioting in 1967 and was subsequently honoured, Princess Alexandra presenting him with the Colonial Police Medal for meritorious service.

When police raided Godber's home in 1973, they found boxes of silver bars and a 'trail of fortune' leading to bank accounts in Canada, Australia,

Singapore and other countries. The investigation soon revealed that Godber's resources totalled more than 4.3 million Hong Kong dollars, nearly six times his total net salary from the time he joined the force in 1952 until May 1973, when the alert went out. That figure was a conservative estimate, and Godber is believed to have amassed a great deal more. Under Hong Kong law it was an offence for a police officer to have wealth that could not be explained.

Godber must have known that his time was running out because in January 1972 he asked to retire, citing his wife's poor health. This was agreed and he was given a leaving date of 20 July 1973. With the net closing in, he asked to go on 30 June, but on 3 June, in the office of Deputy Commissioner Christopher Dawson, he was charged – and fainted. He was not, however, arrested. He was allowed a week to 'make representations'. On 7 June his wife left Hong Kong. The next day, carrying a pass giving him unrestricted access to Kai Tak Airport, he evaded the security there, boarded a Singapore Airlines flight and fled to England. According to the travel agent who sold him the plane ticket, Godber's wallet was so bulging with $500 (Hong Kong) bills that he could not fold it. His escape caused outrage in the colony and led to serious repercussions in Britain. Godber was found living in a cottage near Rye, Sussex, where he attracted a lot of media attention.

In Hong Kong, a judge, Sir Alastair Blair-Kerr, was appointed to conduct an inquiry. It soon became apparent that Godber could not be extradited because the offence of unexplained wealth was not recognised under English law. However, the runaway policeman was eventually returned to Hong Kong on 7 January 1975 to face charges of having accepted a bribe – HK$25,000 – and conspiracy. He was jailed for four years.

The main prosecution witnesses were interesting choices – two other corrupt policemen, Superintendent Ernest Hunt and Superintendent Cheng Hon-kuen. Cheng had given Godber the HK$25,000 bribe in return for arranging the Chinese officer's appointment as head of the Wan Chai division on Hong Kong Island. At the time this area was noted for prostitution, drugs and illegal gambling, and provided a lot of scope for police corruption. Hunt, who had been serving a jail sentence for corruption, and Cheng were both granted an amnesty for testifying.

The judge, Yang Ti-liang, revealed that during the trial he received letters threatening violence if he did not impose a tough sentence. 'Nobody said I did a good job,' he said. 'Instead many people were dissatisfied with my judgment. They thought the penalty was not heavy enough.'

Godber, once a constable pounding the beat in Hastings, Sussex, was released on 3 October 1977 after serving thirty-one months. He returned to Britain and later settled in Spain – as did Hunt.[2] For years Spain had been a favourite destination for British criminals, safe in the knowledge that there was little chance of them being extradited.

The reserved Godber and the flamboyant Hunt were both from the 'Class of 52', a group of expatriate policemen who joined the force in 1952 and amassed many millions from rackets. In 1975, Hunt told the London *Daily Express* that the police were in charge of running crime in Hong Kong. 'Make no mistake about it, I was a villain,' he said.

> You name it and I've done it. And I was not the only one either, not by a long way. I have seen corruption extend to the deepest roots of government. There were lots of us at it and, from the knowledge at my disposal, there are many still at it.

Later, in an interview with the BBC, he said that corruption was 'as natural as going to bed at night and brushing your teeth in the morning'. He claimed that 95 per cent of the force was corrupt and said he was only 'a small fry compared with what my fellow officers were taking'. Hunt estimated he had made about HK$6 million in bribes.

He might well have been right in suggesting that he was only 'a small fry'. In 1971, a police staff sergeant named Hon Sum retired – and in 2006 it was revealed that he had a fortune of least HK$140 million. In his thirty-one-year police career he would have earned a total of less than HK$200,000. After retiring he moved to Canada, but since 1976 he had been a target of the Hong Kong authorities for having assets 'disproportionate' to his salary. According to court papers, he had amassed his fortune through bribes and running Hong Kong's heroin trade, along with four other officers. He owned property in Hong Kong, Bangkok, Vancouver and Florida, and had a weakness for women and flashy cars. Shortly before an extradition hearing in 1978 he fled to Taiwan. Hon died in 1999, and in an out-of-court settlement in 2006 his family agreed to pay the Hong Kong authorities HK$140 million from his estate, but that figure only covered assets in the former colony.

Another notorious sergeant was Lui Lok, who would often arrange 'show' police raids, which had the bonus of eliminating competition from triads. One drug gang leader, Ng Shek-ho, said he paid the detective sergeant HK$30,000 to HK$40,000 every one or two months to prevent police interference. Lui made an estimated HK$8.5 million in the fifteen months up until his retirement in 1969.[3] But he was known as the 'Five Hundred Million Dollar Detective Sergeant'. Lui initially went to Taiwan, but he also invested part of his fortune in Vancouver. The Hong Kong authorities pursued him and a settlement was reached with his family in 1986. It was estimated that nearly fifty corrupt former members of the Royal Hong Kong Police had settled in Canada.[4]

The staff and station sergeants were all-powerful when it came to policing in Hong Kong Island, Kowloon and the New Territories. They were said to be on good terms with some triad leaders, meeting them in restaurants and nightclubs – apart from those who clashed with their own interests.

The sergeants found their lower ranks easy to handle:

> It was not difficult for syndicate bosses to recruit members. New arrivals at a station had money put in their lockers; if the cash was pocketed, it was taken as a sign of assent. The majority did participate, almost routinely, and took their weekly or monthly cut, a useful supplement to low official salaries. The amount received varied according to rank and seniority; the average constable might receive, in the early 1970s, only about $20 to $50 a month; the big money went to the station sergeants and to senior officers. But they were all bound together, as it were, by a sense of collective guilt.[5]

The few who declined to accept tainted money were transferred.

Senior officers such as Godber and Hunt probably received most of their money from staff and station sergeants, who were known as 'caterers'. Lower ranks – corporals and constables – were used as 'collectors' and 'runners'. Corrupt officers formed their own syndicates, milking particular criminal activities, and in many cases those who had retired from the force were still active and on the payroll.

Commissioner Sutcliffe had tried to erode the power of the sergeants with reforms in 1972. Corporals were upgraded to sergeant and the rank of corporal was abolished. The number of station sergeants in a division was increased from two to eight in the hope that influence would be diminished. But the changes did little to reduce corruption.

The police service was roughly divided in two: the inspectorate and senior ranks were usually held by Britons, and the lower ranks were mostly recruited from the Chinese population. Police corruption had been an open secret for decades, and one Elsie Elliott, a teacher and former missionary, proved a thorn in the side of the authorities. She came to prominence during the so-called Star Ferry riots in April 1966, when thousands opposed an increase in fares for the link between Hong Kong Island and Kowloon. During the 1960s and 1970s she was a fierce critic of corruption in all areas of public life, and the influence of triads. Special Branch kept her under surveillance, and she claimed that police had tried to frame her.

Walter Easey, who had been a police officer in the 1960s, pointed out:

> When Elsie speaks of corruption, brutality, callousness and indifference on the part of government employees – believe her. The Hong Kong government has endlessly tried to discredit Elsie as some kind of paranoid, a nut case, a bleeding heart liberal or self-promoting publicist. Nothing could be farther than the truth. Elsie is telling the truth, as she has always done. To my shame,

I can corroborate what she says, having seen, practised or connived at it from the other side.[6]

In 1971 Elliott published a pamphlet entitled *The Avarice, Bureaucracy and Corruption of Hong Kong*. On 23 January 1973 the *China Mail*, an English language newspaper in Hong Kong, ran a story with the headline 'Triad grip on CID says Elsie'. She must have been doing something right. Four years later she was awarded the CBE.

Corruption was not, of course, confined to the police. It was well established in most government departments – housing, education, immigration, commerce and industry, and transport. Successive governors had turned a blind eye to the problem, deciding that corruption was endemic in a Chinese society. Sir Murray MacLehose, who became governor in 1971, was a reformer but he, too, was reluctant to tackle graft, initially at least. Godber, Hunt and the other high-profile cases forced his hand. The police had an anti-corruption unit and senior officers were keen to put their own house in order. One argument was that any major change would probably lead to a collapse in police morale. But with the 'shocking' escape of Godber, MacLehose decided it was time to set up an independent body to fight corruption. He told the colony's Legislative Council on 17 October 1973:

> I believe that it is quite wrong, in the special circumstances of Hong Kong, that the police, as a force, should carry the whole responsibility for action in this difficult and elusive field. I think the situation calls for an organisation, led by men of high rank and status, which can devote its whole time to the eradication of this evil. A further and conclusive argument is that public confidence is very much involved. Clearly the public would have more confidence in a unit that was entirely independent, and separate from any department of the government, including the police.

In February 1974 the Independent Commission Against Corruption was set up. There were jokes that ICAC stood for 'Investigating Chinese Ancient Customs' or 'I Can Accept Cash'. But the commission's first head, Jack Cater, was serious about rooting out corruption. He had served in the Royal Air Force during the war and he had a wealth of experience in the public service. *The Times* would say of him:

> Cater was paired with Sir John Prendergast, the former director of Special Branch in Hong Kong who had worldwide intelligence experience. While Prendergast was the iron fist of the operation, Cater was the public face; one which Hong Kong had already learnt to trust. His eloquence and amiability were priceless in command of a body which, answerable only to

the governor, held draconian powers. Because police officers were recruited fresh from Britain to train Chinese officers, some suspected that the ICAC was a colonial body with oppressive aims. With 29 years of experience with marginalised communities, Cater was the best counter to such anxieties, and when he thumped his desk and told reporters that 'We will break the back of organised corruption in two or three years', he was entirely credible.[7]

The commission began with a staff of 369, including 181 police officers and forty-four civilians who were on loan from the disbanded Anti-Corruption Office. There was criticism over the use of so many police, but in the early days it was difficult to recruit a large number of people capable of carrying out investigations. Needless to say, relations between the commission and the Royal Hong Kong Police were strained.

The first major task of the new organisation was to return Godber to Hong Kong from his sanctuary in Britain. Less than three months after the commission had been formed, the runaway police chief was charged in London with accepting a HK$25,000 bribe, an offence recognised under English law. Godber, held in custody, fought extradition but on 7 January 1975 he arrived back in the colony. The fact that he was convicted thanks to two other corrupt police officers – Hunt and Cheng Hon-kuen – was noted by the *Far Eastern Economic Review*:

> Hong Kong has witnessed a man found guilty on the evidence of two self-confessed crooks, evidence which was obtained by means of immunity deals. One witness, a Chinese police superintendent, got away scot-free, with even his pension rights intact. The other, a contemptible European police officer, had only spent eight months in jail, most of that time in air-conditioned comfort.

Cater commented that Godber's conviction was 'an important milestone in the advance of the commission'. In his annual report for 1975, he referred to the 'titanic struggle which lies ahead', and identified syndicated corruption as the main target. Syndicated corruption was not confined to the police. It was also found, for example, in government departments dealing with housing, immigration, fire services and licensing.

Victims or alleged victims of police corruption had been quick to take advantage of the commission's crackdown. In its first year of operation, the commission received 1,443 complaints against the police, which resulted in seventy convictions. The police had by far the highest number of complaints, followed by the private sector (410), housing (226), and urban services (188). By March 1977 Cater's team was investigating twenty-three syndicates – and eighteen of them involved police.

The activities of the commission took a toll on police morale. In July 1976 a depressed senior superintendent, Jack English, shot himself. English had been appointed head of Kowloon CID after being seconded to the ICAC for two years. It was a bewildering time for many officers:

Traditionally, the Hong Kong police had been top dogs; they had overawed the lumpen proletariat and dominated the workers; they were given deference by the lower middle classes; avoided by the middle classes; but sometimes treated with scant respect by very rich Chinese or by the educated. Generally speaking, the police were feared …[8]

October 1977 was an uncomfortable month for corrupt police. The ICAC arrested about 140 officers, ranging in rank from constable to superintendent, from three Kowloon divisions. Shortly afterwards a further thirty-four men were held, including three British superintendents. Discontent in the force was growing, with complaints of unfair treatment and harassment. One day, some 300 officers gathered in the canteen at the Kowloon headquarters and drafted a nine-point letter for the commissioner of police. One point they made was that all the witnesses in corruption cases were either convicted criminals or involved in criminal activity. Commissioner Brian Slevin failed to placate his men, and further meetings were held. On 28 October around 2,000 officers gathered near the Star Ferry terminal on Hong Kong Island, where a Chinese superintendent addressed them. They headed to police headquarters at Wan Chai, and a delegation went to see Slevin, who agreed in principle to a demand for a rank-and-file association. The news brought cheers from the men who were waiting outside in a car park. However, a small group who included sacked officers decided to carry on to the office block housing the headquarters of the ICAC, which was stormed. Five of the commission's employees were injured in fighting. Estimates for the number of protesters ranged from forty to 100, but a special police investigation led to only one man, a retired sergeant, being charged. The local press dubbed him 'the lone raider'.

Slevin's concession did not bring an end to police protest meetings, which largely involved junior ranks who were influenced by still-powerful sergeants. The governor, MacLehose, was getting increasingly worried about the prospect of police anarchy, and on 5 November he stunned the colony by announcing an amnesty for officers who had been involved in corruption before 1 January 1977, except for the most serious cases. It was a serious blow to Cater and the ICAC. The leaders of the demonstrations were jubilant but they wanted a complete amnesty and they gave the governor an ultimatum. MacLehose was aware of the danger:

Concessions to such demands under pressure would invite pressure on other issues; next it would be the suppression of the ICAC itself, possibly to have persons in prison released, and so on, until we had a situation in which the law was being administered in the interests of the corrupt.

The governor was on the verge of putting troops on the streets. With the support of community leaders, the commissioner of police was given powers of summary dismissal. Moderate police representatives pledged loyalty, and the rebels were outwitted. But a large number of police had escaped the possibility of corruption charges.

Eight months later, Cater stepped down as commissioner of the ICAC and was replaced by Sir Donald Luddington. The commissioner's report for 1978 admitted that the events of the previous November had shaken public confidence:

> Considerable effort had therefore to be devoted to reassuring both the commission's staff and the public that government had no intention of reducing its efforts to combat and steadily to eradicate corruption as a feature of life in Hong Kong and that there were no plans to reduce the efforts or the strength of the commission.

Sir John Prendergast, the commission's director of operations, revealed the immediate effect of MacLehose's amnesty – the scrapping of eighty-three investigations into offences alleged to have been committed before 1 January 1977. New complaints of police corruption showed a sharp drop in 1978, a reflection of public scepticism.

The strength of the Royal Hong Kong Police grew from 12,000 in 1970 to more than 18,000 at the end of 1977. Between 1970 and 1977, 497 police officers were sacked. There were 3,149 resignations.[9]

CHAPTER 12

Colony of Spies

China, Taiwan and the Soviet Union saw Hong Kong as an important base for spying in the early 1970s. Keeping an eye on their activities were hundreds of men employed by Special Branch of the Royal Hong Kong Police, along with members of MI6 and the CIA. Espionage, of course, was not a new problem.

In 1955, the colony had been the setting for a plot to kill the Chinese premier, Chou En-lai. On 11 April an Air India plane named *Kashmir Princess* took off from Kai Tak for Jakarta, Indonesia, carrying a Chinese delegation that planned to attend a conference at Bandung. Chou should have been on the plane, which was on a refuelling stop from Beijing, but at the last moment he changed his travel plans. He never boarded the airliner. Instead, three days later he flew to Rangoon for talks with the Burmese leader U Nu and the prime minister of India, Jawaharlal Nehru, before going on to Bandung.

On the evening of 11 April, at 18,000ft, a bomb exploded in the wheel bay of *Kashmir Princess*'s starboard wing, blowing a hole in a fuel tank. One hour away from Jakarta, the plane ditched into the sea. Three crewmen survived but the remaining sixteen people on board were killed. Chou almost certainly was tipped off about the plot. The day after the disaster China's foreign ministry described it as 'murder by the special service organisations of the United States and Chiang Kai-shek'.

Eleven years later, a US Senate committee investigating CIA operations was told of a 1955 plot to kill an 'east Asian leader', and in 1977 William Corson, a retired US Marine Corps intelligence officer, said the target had been Chou En-lai.

At the time the Taiwanese had a network of about ninety agents operating in Hong Kong under a major-general, Kong Hoi-ping. A cleaner at Kai Tak named Chow Tse-ming was recruited. When the Air India plane landed for refuelling he planted the bomb, which had an American-made detonator,

according to Indonesian experts. As police began questioning staff at Kai
Tak, Chow – also known as Chou Chu – fled to Taiwan on a plane operated
by Civil Air Transport, which was run by the CIA and would become better
known as Air America during the Vietnam War. Taiwan refused to allow the
extradition of Chow, who was believed to have pocketed HK$600,000 for
planting the bomb. In 1967 John Discoe Smith, a former CIA employee in
New Delhi, claimed that he had passed on the bomb that downed the Air
India plane to a Taiwanese agent.[1]

In July 1971 police in Hong Kong arrested twelve men who were smuggling
weapons to Taiwanese agents and 'anti-Mao revolutionaries' in China. The
swoop followed a seizure of arms and explosives. The twelve men were taken
to the Victoria Road detention centre – run by Special Branch – before being
deported to Taiwan. The authorities were particularly concerned because
bombs were found in buildings in densely populated areas. Earlier, 200 lb of
explosives had been discovered at the Tsz Wan Shan estate, home to 133,000
people. Two Taiwanese agents were arrested.[2]

Chinese Communist agents were already in place in Hong Kong before
the Nationalists fled from the mainland to Taiwan in 1949. China's key
intelligence service went through several reorganisations and name changes
over the years. In 1955 it was known as the Central Investigation Department.
Beijing's eyes and ears in the colony were to be found mostly at its unofficial
embassy, the Xinhua News Agency. Xinhua employed a large number of
people. Everything of significance that happened in Hong Kong filtered back
to Mao Tse-tung. During the 1950s, all Chinese embassies had a special section
devoted to gathering intelligence under the control of the Central Investigation
Department. The Cultural Revolution of 1966–67 saw the abolition of
the organisation – many of its leaders were sent to the countryside for 're-
education' – but it returned to prominence in the early 1970s, eventually
becoming the Ministry of State Security.

Hong Kong was facing a major problem in 1971 with a flood of Chinese
'refugees'. An estimated 4,000 people arrived in the colony illegally during
May and June. Only about 930 had been caught. Many more were expected.
According to security sources, nearly all the 'refugees' were young people
'well indoctrinated in Mao thought'. One source said: 'The big question is
whether they are disillusioned Communists, or are they infiltrators? If they
are infiltrators this way of getting into Hong Kong is fool-proof.' It was
government policy to allow refugees to stay unless China demanded their
return. One report said: 'The high rate of illegal entry from China coincides
with local Chinese reports that the Communist front in Hong Kong has
become very active in spreading its influence since the 1967 disturbances.'[3]

Mao's relations with the Soviet Union had been poor for about a decade.
Early on, there was a fawning relationship with Joseph Stalin, which resulted

in significant aid and military hardware, although the Soviet leader always made sure that he remained the puppet master. Mao was once reported to have leapt up in front of a Soviet envoy and raised his arms, shouting three times: 'May Stalin live 10,000 years.' Despite repeated requests, Stalin refused to give China the atom bomb. He died on 5 March 1953. His successor, Georgi Malenkov, made it clear that the Soviet Union wanted to lessen tensions with the west and to end the Korean War, which Mao had largely instigated.

Serious cracks in China's relationship with Moscow started to appear in 1960, when Mao argued that 'as long as capitalism exists, war cannot be avoided' and suggested that the Soviets, under the leadership of Nikita Khrushchev, were becoming servants of imperialism. Khrushchev complained that the Chinese were 'spitting in our face'. Addressing a conference of Communist leaders in Bucharest on 21 June, he said: 'No world war is needed for the triumph of socialist ideas throughout the world. Only madmen and maniacs can now call for another world war.' He told colleagues: 'When I look at Mao I see Stalin, a perfect copy.'[4] Mao and Stalin certainly had a lot in common – ruthless dictators who were responsible for many millions of deaths in war and peace.

That year saw the Soviet Union withdraw all its advisers from China because of divisions prompted by the Great Leap Forward. This was Mao's master plan, unveiled in 1958, to turn the country into an economic superpower but which instead sent China reeling backwards. His insistence on exporting huge quantities of food led to widespread famine, costing the lives of an estimated 38 million people through starvation and overwork.[5]

He remained desperate to acquire a nuclear bomb, but in July 1963 Khrushchev signed a test ban treaty with the United States and Britain, which prevented the Soviet Union from passing on secrets. Khrushchev was denounced as a 'revisionist', one of Mao's worst insults. The description was often fatal in China – literally. Khrushchev, who had pursued a policy of de-Stalinisation, much to Mao's annoyance, was ousted in October 1964 to be replaced by Leonid Brezhnev. Khrushchev died on 11 September 1971. But Brezhnev was no admirer of Mao, who wanted the new Soviet leader to end the policy of de-Stalinisation.

The 1960s was also marked by border disputes between the two countries. The Soviet Union increased the number of its divisions along the border with China from thirteen to twenty-one between 1965 and 1969, when there were deadly clashes. Chinese troops ambushed Soviet border guards on Zhenbao Island, killing thirty-one. The Soviets retaliated by bombarding Chinese positions along the Ussuri River and storming the island. The fighting led to speculation that the Soviet Union was planning a major strike against China. The number of Soviet border divisions increased to thirty in 1970 and to forty-four the following year.

In 1971 Britain was worried about the number of Soviet spies who were entering Hong Kong posing as merchant seamen or cruise ship passengers. Edward Heath's government was keen to improve relations with China. The Foreign Office in London carried out a special analysis of the espionage problem:

> Over the past year the Russians have succeeded in establishing a considerable, though fluctuating, presence in Hong Kong through visits of Soviet merchant vessels and through arrangements for the repair of Soviet merchant ships in the colony dockyards. The risk of Soviet subversive activities and of embarrassment in our relations with Peking has increased and seems likely to continue to grow unless we take steps to control the scale of Soviet access to the colony. For many years the Russians have sought to expand their official presence in the colony but both we and the Hong Kong government have always refused.

The Soviet 'official' presence was restricted to two engineers in the docks. The Foreign Office report continued:

> The Russians have now succeeded over a period of time in circumventing our ban on a further official presence by having large numbers of Soviet seamen in the colony at any one time, either on ships putting into the colony during a cruise visit, or on ships undergoing repair in the dockyards. The full extent of the Soviet presence ... is clearly considerable and is growing. For example, in any one month in 1970 there was an average of no less than 362 Soviet seamen in the colony. Thirteen Soviet merchant ships were repaired in the dockyards in 1970; many stayed for long periods. The crews include Mandarin speakers, who have established contacts. There is at present no restriction on their movements in the colony. It would not be difficult for the Russians to maintain some continuity in the personnel by sending back the same people on different ships under different names.
>
> The situation has recently become even more disturbing. On February 9 this year local Hong Kong newspapers reported that the crew of a Soviet ship had been distributing pamphlets criticising Chinese policy to local Chinese dockyard workers. We expressed surprise and regret about this incident to the Soviet Embassy [in London], and were subsequently told by a member of the embassy that this was a 'private initiative and that no doubt the necessary steps were being taken'. In mid-April the Soviet Embassy asked permission for two 'scientific research vessels' to put into Hong Kong for three days each in July and August to replenish supplies. The governor's advice is that we should refuse both requests.
>
> The Chinese have not yet protested about the numbers of Soviet seamen in the colony although there have been warning hints in the Communist

press in Hong Kong that they are aware of the situation. The Chinese are understandably sensitive about Soviet activities in Hong Kong. It is clear that the Russians are interested in Hong Kong as a source of intelligence on China and possibly also as a springboard for intelligence activities directed against China. We are concerned about the possibility of Soviet subversive activities within the colony itself. We must assume that if the Russians are allowed to maintain and increase their present access to Hong Kong, they will eventually mount operations there on a large scale. Hong Kong Special Branch are already fully stretched in dealing with other security problems such as surveillance of Chinese and Nationalist Chinese intelligence organisations. They do not have the facilities or manpower to deal with Soviet activities as well.

Ideally, we should have liked to tell the Russians that they must reduce the number of ships which put into the colony or have repairs carried out there. However, our shipping policy has always been to encourage free entry to merchant ships all over the world. The Hong Kong government would be reluctant to agree to banning Soviet ships being repaired in the colony since this would entail a major row with the dockyards. We should also have liked to tell the Russians to confine the crews of ships under repair, and the crews of cruise vessels, to their ships while in port.

The question of keeping crews confined to their ships had taxed the minds of lawyers, who came to the conclusion that such a move would probably contravene an international convention on seamen's rights. The report continued:

Legal advisers see no reason however why we should not establish a limit of six hours per day. They agree that even in the case of crew with valid identity documents we could also justify restricting parties of visiting seamen to 12 at, say, hourly intervals. In addition we could give the Russians warning that any breaches of these restrictions or other misconduct would result in the immediate confinement on board of the group concerned in the event of minor breaches or misconduct, and of the whole crew in the event of serious breaches or misconduct, in either case until the ship left port. As regards Soviet passengers on Soviet cruise vessels, the only sanction open to us is to insist that they should have valid visas for Hong Kong if they wish to go ashore.

The Foreign Office doubted that there would be Soviet retaliation. Interestingly, the British Embassy in Moscow made it clear that it would prefer not to be involved – and that 'any approach to the Russians should be made in Hong Kong through the chairman of Kowloon docks'.[6]

The battle of wits carried on during 1971. The Soviet Union ignored the ban on its 'scientific research vessels'. In September, the Soviet research ship *Poseydon* arrived in Hong Kong unannounced and stayed four days.

Hong Kong's defence secretary, Peter Lloyd, warned the Foreign Office:

We see such unannounced visits by state-owned research vessels and government vessels on non-commercial service as another ploy in the Soviet attempts to obtain access to Hong Kong. So we should like to stop them from coming here. But we realise there might be awkward complaints if we simply refused to allow non-naval vessels to enter port. Moreover there would in any case be certain practical difficulties about doing this, as the ships might reach the quarantine anchorage before we identified them.

The upshot is that we are obtaining from the Ministry of Defence a list of the ships which might come. When any do, we now intend to tell them to go, once they have cleared quarantine, to an isolated anchorage in the west of the harbour. Although we do not propose to give a reason the justification could be, on port operational grounds, that the more central buoys are needed for working ships. Only essential persons (e.g. the agents) will be allowed to board and the ships' stay will be limited to 48 hours, during which time they will be under surveillance, with police and immigration representatives aboard. And only their masters will be allowed ashore.

In short, we shall do all we can to make life difficult for them without denying them the opportunity to take on essential supplies. There is no intention of being drawn into argument or defending our position with the masters or the agents. The sole reason given for the restrictions will be that 'government has decided'. However much any master may argue, we think it unlikely that he will disobey the limitations imposed on his stay. We also hope that the more public his argument and any subsequent Soviet government protest, the more Peking will be aware that we are not encouraging or conniving at visits by this class of Soviet ships.[7]

In August 1972 it was reported that Special Branch officers had 'smashed' a Soviet spy ring operating in Hong Kong. Two Taiwanese businessmen were arrested, along with two of their Russian handlers, who had arrived on a Soviet cruise ship, the *Khabarovsk*, masquerading as seamen. The businessmen had been asked specifically to obtain information on relations between Britain and China and the activities of Taiwan. The Russians were expelled after questioning. They were named as Andrei Polikarov and Stepan Tsunaev [Tsuanaev], a former university lecturer who was listed on the crew manifest as a stoker. Another man, Ho Hung Yan, a stateless Chinese, was also deported to the Soviet Union. He was put on board a Soviet ship, the *Kavalerovo*, which was destined for Vladivostok, but the captain refused to sail. The Hong Kong authorities would not allow Ho to disembark, and the stalemate lasted ten days. The captain eventually agreed to take Ho, who had no papers, on 'humanitarian grounds'. One of the Taiwanese businessmen was sent back to Taiwan and the other was released because of insufficient evidence.[8]

It was a busy time for Special Branch. In December detectives rounded up a Taiwanese spy ring. It was claimed that agents had planned to send letter bombs to Chinese officials in Beijing, Shanghai and Canton. The London *Daily Express* reported:

Officials in Hong Kong believe they prevented any of the bombs reaching China but, just in case, a warning has been sent to the Communists. British Special Branch police of the Royal Hong Kong force have staged raids throughout the colony and arrested at least 16 men. Last night it was learned from reliable sources that 12 Taiwan spies were still being held without trial under Hong Kong law, which commits aliens to be detained while awaiting deportation.[9]

In a confidential telegram to the Foreign and Commonwealth Office, the colony's governor, Sir Murray MacLehose, said:

You will have seen in the Hong Kong press recently certain speculative reports about police operations against the Kuomintang intelligence service. I can confirm that a recent routine operation, which was one of a series, resulted in arrests, 14 people are still under detention. In the course of this operation several explosive sabotage devices were seized. These comprised one limpet mine, 16 minor incendiary devices, of which six were concealed in men's leather belts, and three detonators. These last were inserted inside rolled magazines and were apparently intended for despatch through the post inside China.

The telegram ended: 'We are maintaining a "no comment" line with the press.'[10]

There was a serious complication to the Special Branch swoop. One of the men arrested was not Taiwanese but South Korean – one Kang Beik-hung, an assistant manager of the Korean Trade Centre in Hong Kong. South Korea, of course, was a 'friendly' nation. MacLehose reported to London:

He [Kang] holds an official passport and, although not on the consular list, is regarded by the Korean consul-general as a member of the Korean government service. A number of intelligence documents were found in his possession and he has admitted using this KIS [Kuomintang intelligence

ON THE STOCKS: The *Queen Elizabeth* takes shape at Clydebank. Her construction began in December 1936. (*J. & C. McCutcheon*)

RIVETING WORK: The hull rises up and the liner's immense length can be seen.
(*J. & C. McCutcheon*)

LAUNCH DAY: The *Queen Elizabeth* gliding down the slipway on 27 September 1938.
(*J. & C. McCutcheon*)

MAIDEN VOYAGE: A scarce picture of the liner making her secret dash across the Atlantic from Scotland to New York in March 1940. (*J. & C. McCutcheon*)

THREE GIANTS: The *Queen Elizabeth* (nearest), *Queen Mary* and *Normandie* berthed alongside each other in New York in March 1940. (*J. & C. McCutcheon*)

THE GREY GHOST: A drab *Queen Elizabeth* in her wartime role as a troopship. The odd bulge on her hull is a degaussing device to foil magnetic mines.

IN COMMAND: Winston Churchill, in naval rig, on the bridge of the *Queen Mary* with Commodore Sir James Bisset, a future master of the *Queen Elizabeth*. The prime minister was returning home in the liner after the Quebec conference in September 1944. (*Imperial War Museum*)

SAFELY BACK: Winston Churchill with his wife Clementine after disembarking from the *Queen Mary*, which had brought them home from the Quebec conference in September 1944. (*Imperial War Museum*)

WE'RE OFF: The Churchills leaving their London home to join the *Queen Elizabeth* in Southampton on 9 January 1946 for an Atlantic crossing. Winston Churchill had lost power after a general election and he was taking a long holiday in Florida. (*Imperial War Museum*)

STANDING ROOM ONLY: The *Queen Elizabeth* packed with troops. Her record for a single voyage was 15,932, including the crew. (*J. & C. McCutcheon*)

HOME AGAIN: The troopship *Queen Mary* returning to Southampton after wartime service. Her record for the greatest number of people carried on a single voyage was 16,683, including the crew. (*J. & C. McCutcheon*)

DRAWING THE CROWDS: The troopship *Queen Mary* gets admiring glances as she nears her berth in Southampton. (*J. & C. McCutcheon*)

ON THE BRIDGE: The *Queen Elizabeth* arriving in Southampton from the Clyde before entering commercial service after wartime duties. In the distance is the *Queen Mary*. (*J. & C. McCutcheon*)

AT SPEED IN PEACETIME: The *Queen Elizabeth* scythes through the water.
(*J. & C. McCutcheon*)

REGAL: The *Queen Elizabeth* shows her graceful lines during the golden years of Atlantic travel. (*J. & C. McCutcheon*)

NUDGED AWAY: Tugs in Southampton help to send the liner on another voyage. (*J. & C. McCutcheon*)

OLD FRIEND: The *Queen Elizabeth* arriving in New York on one of her many transatlantic voyages during the 1950s and 1960s. (*J. & C. McCutcheon*)

CHECK-UP: The liner easing into dry dock in Southampton. (*J. & C. McCutcheon*)

TOWERING: An impressive bow shot of the *Queen Elizabeth* in dry dock. (*J. & C. McCutcheon*)

Cunard

SPACIOUS: The main restaurant of the *Queen Elizabeth*. (*J. & C. McCutcheon*)

FINE DINING: Cunard promised 'world-renowned' cuisine. (*J. & C. McCutcheon*)

COMFORT AND STYLE: A bedroom in a suite aboard the *Queen Elizabeth*. (*J. & C. McCutcheon*)

ARRIVING AND DEPARTING: The *Queen Elizabeth* berths in Southampton as the *Queen Mary* sets off for New York. (*J. & C. McCutcheon*)

PASSING: The *Queens* off England's south coast on their weekly Atlantic run. (*J. & C. McCutcheon*)

service] unit to obtain intelligence on China as a basis for reports to the Korean government. He claims that his controller is Dong Suk-cho, the number two in the Korean consulate-general. The Korean consul-general ... has volunteered that the best solution might be to get Kang out of Hong Kong as quickly as possible. I agree and propose to have Kang handed over to the consul-general tomorrow morning provided the latter is prepared to give an undertaking that Kang will be flown to Seoul forthwith.[11]

MacLehose was prepared to mislead when it came to answering questions about the important South Korean official:

The press are now on to this story, including the involvement of Kang Beik-hung ... we shall say as little as possible when asked to comment. We have already been obliged to confirm that a number of persons have been arrested. In answer to a direct question we have said that no Korean is at present under detention. The Korean consulate-general are believed to have confirmed to an enquirer that Kang had been detained for a time but that it was all due to a misunderstanding. The consul-general has again been asked to get him out of Hong Kong tomorrow.[12]

CHAPTER 13

Fire!

On the morning of Sunday, 9 January 1972, BBC correspondent Anthony Lawrence was on the phone to his London office discussing a planned story on the *Queen Elizabeth*'s new life as the *Seawise University*. Suddenly, the voice at the other end exclaimed: 'The bloody thing's on fire!' The man had just seen a news agency report. A surprised Lawrence went to a window of his apartment in the Mid-Levels district of Hong Kong Island, located half way up Victoria Peak, with a fine view of the harbour. London was right.

Photographer Bob Davis was enjoying a barbecue on a rooftop at a friend's home in Central on the island when he spotted smoke pouring from the liner. Davis had been on the ship a short time earlier. C. Y. Tung wanted a photographic record of the conversion, which was coming to an end, and Davis was approached about the possibility of a commission. 'I duly went out there on one of their boats with a whole bunch of labourers,' he recalled.

> I immediately realised this was going to be an enormous job. I looked around various places on the ship and thought maybe I should go back to them and ask how many days have you got and what do you want me to shoot. I could see it running into weeks.

The day after his visit he contacted a Tung company representative and said he would be able to start the following week. But Davis was told it would be 'an inconvenient time to go next week' and the job would have to be postponed. The commission went up in smoke, literally.[1]

Another man who would always remember 9 January 1972 was John Hudson, a chartered accountant working in Hong Kong. His fiancée's parents were visiting the colony from England, and it was decided they would all go out in a small boat to take in the harbour sights. Hudson gave this account of an unfolding drama:

What caught our attention from a distance across the water was smoke coming from the ship's portholes – not just one or two portholes but from almost all of them from stem to stern on one side. Considering the size of the vessel and no visible signs of any other problems, the sight of smoke was alarming but also rather fascinating. There was no sign of added human activity on board, no fireboats alongside and no sign of anything out of the ordinary other than smoke billowing out of the portholes.

Hudson had taken along a camera and began taking pictures.

We cruised slowly around the vessel for upwards of three hours getting no closer than 20 or 30 feet. For the duration of our stay on the water there were no fireboats or any other official rescue craft, which might suggest that either none was called or their arrival was delayed. The only sign of officialdom was a harbour police launch that arrived and looked to be giving instructions to crew members assembled at the stern. A small contingent of junks, sampans and work barges came and went. Some stayed alongside perhaps as they would have done on a more ordinary day. Few if any workers or crew appeared to be assembling on board in the expectation of being taken off. None of the lifeboats were being swung into action. It was clearly evident that whatever was burning on board was more than a grease fire stemming from a worker accident. What had started as puffs of smoke from portholes turned into a raging inferno in the upper superstructure generating huge volumes of smoke. As the volume and intensity of the smoke increased we decided to move away. The wind had picked up and we did not want to get caught close up down wind if the direction of the wind changed.[2]

Other than to say they spent 'upwards of three hours' in the vicinity of the ship, Hudson did not give any times. Official accounts state that the first police launch at the scene arrived half an hour after a fire alert on the ship, which came at about 11.20 a.m.

Three cabin boys had been sweeping up rubbish – paper, scraps of carpet and bits of electrical wiring – on Main Deck. They took the rubbish in a box to a disposal point next to an open shell door on A Deck, one deck below, where there was already a pile of rubbish. A chute had been set up at the shell door to send waste to a barge waiting below. The cabin boys started to make their way back to M Deck to collect more rubbish when they spotted smoke. It was coming from an alleyway towards the stern on A Deck. A closer look revealed small flames in a pile of rubbish. After an abortive attempt to use a fire extinguisher, the cabin boys ran about 100 yards along an alleyway in the opposite direction shouting, 'Fire!' They met a three-man fire patrol making a routine inspection. Two of the men headed for the scene of the fire and the third, deck cadet Kwong Ving-kuen, went to report to the duty officer, whose office was nearby. The cadet was ordered to phone the public address centre and tell the man in charge to make a general announcement about the fire. But the line was engaged. An officer then went to the public address centre, on M Deck, and sent out an urgent call saying that fire had broken out aft on A Deck. All the ship's firefighters were to go there. Cadet Kwong was then told to phone the fire services ashore. He dialled 999 but there was further confusion – the operator thought the *Seawise University* was a building. It took another call to explain that there was a fire on the ship. The cadet said he checked his watch and the time was 11.45 a.m.

However, records show that Hong Kong's fire services were first alerted by a police message at 11.52 a.m. Police launch No. 10 had seen smoke and at 11.45 a.m. it sent a report to the headquarters of the marine police, which in turn called the fire control centre. There were other calls, including one from the Marine Department's Green Island signal tower, which phoned the ship to ask for confirmation that there was a fire on board.

By 11.50 a.m. police launch No. 10, under the command of Inspector Ted Ho Sze-ming, was under the liner's stern to co-ordinate rescue efforts. 'Many people were trying to get down to nearby launches,' said Inspector Ho.

> Ropes were thrown from the stern and they slid down them into the police launch. There were women and a child aboard. With a police constable I tried to go aboard but was unsuccessful. I instructed people to tie the child with a rope and lower him over the side. He was picked up by a launch. About ten people jumped into the sea from the ship's windows or doors near the stern. At about 12.10pm I heard a loud explosion and saw smoke and flames over the superstructure.[3]

Police launch No. 5, under the command of Sergeant Peter Cheuk Man-kei, arrived at the scene. 'We got there about 1200 and saw PL10 directing people by loudhailer to slide down ropes from the stern,' said Sergeant Cheuk.

> We started doing the same from the stern door, and then a few moments later there was a big explosion – flames seemed to sweep along the decks from bow to stern. That made the people move all right. A lot of them were panicking and had to be calmed down. We didn't pull away until we had taken 150 on board – ten times more than we were supposed to carry. We transferred most of them to PL10 and harbour launch 8, which had also arrived, and then we cruised round the ship looking for more. Right in the bow we found another group of 11 or 12 who had been cut off, and we got them off via the hawse-pipe and anchor chain. One of them turned out to be the foreman in charge of the work on board. He was weeping saying, 'The ship was being reborn. Now it is gone, all gone.'[4]

Senior Inspector Colin Reigate, in command of police launch No. 2, said:

> When we arrived at the scene the ship was well ablaze at the stern and a
> strong east wind was blowing smoke and flames towards the bow. It was
> obvious from the start that the fire was going to be uncontrollable. As
> police we could do little but assist the fire services, the workers and visitors
> scrambling to leave the burning ship by the bow. There was a suggestion
> from the Royal Navy at the time to blast the stern mooring so as to get
> the ship to come about so that the wind would blow away from the stern,
> but this was considered too dangerous, not knowing how the burning ship
> would eventually lie.

Later, with the help of Sergeant Cheuk, Reigate retrieved the tattered and
blackened Red Ensign that had been flying at the stern. The flag was framed
and presented to the Mariner's Rest, the officers' mess of the marine police.[5]

The first fireboat did not arrive alongside the ship until 12.27 p.m., more
than an hour after the three cabin boys had raised the alarm. The fireboat was
soon playing its hoses on the superstructure on the port side. Other fireboats,
including a command vessel, the *Alexander Grantham*, arrived, and they also
directed jets of water.

Doong Hwa was in command of the *Alexander Grantham*. He said he had
been alerted at 11.55 a.m. and the fireboat left its berth five minutes later. Soon
he spotted smoke rising from the liner. As his men made ready fire pumps and
deck monitors, the alert was upgraded to 'disaster alarm'. Drawing close to the
ship, Doong saw smoke and flames coming from portholes on the port side,
and three decks – P, A and B – were affected. Fire was burning fiercely in the
superstructure. Eight jets from the *Alexander Grantham* quickly opened up.
'There were many people fleeing from the gangway on R Deck and boarding
waiting launches,' said Doong, who would remain on duty until 9.30 a.m. the
following day. 'Some were sliding down ropes into lifeboats.'[6]

The ship's captain, Commodore Chen Ching-yien, went to the *Alexander
Grantham* and urged a full-scale operation to save the liner. It was not until
12.55 p.m. that a team from the fireboats boarded the ship, along with the
commodore. By that time the liner was probably beyond saving. Thick smoke
and flames were spreading throughout the vessel. The first alert had been
followed by reports of other fires.

At about 12.10 p.m., Assistant Chief Fire Officer Leonard Worrallo circled
in a helicopter and saw smoke pouring from the superstructure for half the
length of the ship. He sent out the highest fire alert, 'disaster alarm'. Some
250 crew and nearly 300 workmen were aboard when the emergency began.
There were also sixty guests who had been invited to a reception to celebrate
the ship's transformation. Before noon, Commodore Chen had ordered the

evacuation of everyone who was not involved in the emergency. C. Y. Tung's thirty-four-year-old son Chee-hwa [C. H. Tung] and other senior officials of the Island Navigation Corporation were among those rescued. Pleasure craft and other boats joined in the operation, taking survivors to the shore. 'I saw people jumping from the side of the ship into the sea to escape,' said a cook. 'Some people took off their trousers to protect their hands while they were sliding down ropes to boats waiting below. After escaping I heard explosions.'

By 1 p.m., about a dozen police launches were at the scene and they formed a cordon around the ship. At one point Director of Marine Kenneth Milburn, Director of Fire Services Alfred Wood, Herbert Hutchins, Chief Fire Officer of Hong Kong Island, and Assistant Commissioner Mike Illingworth, commander of the marine police, were on board the liner assessing the crisis. When Wood and Hutchins were told by a fireman that the sill of a starboard shell door on C deck was under water, they went to try to close it. Other shell doors on the same deck were also open but they could not reach them. A fire door that had been closed by the fireman blew open after an explosion, sending out a cloud of black smoke.

The ship was finally evacuated at 3.27 p.m. One minute later, with the liner listing 12 to 15 degrees to starboard, it was decided to stop the hoses. At about 5.30 p.m. the list had slightly decreased and the hoses were used sporadically, mainly to cool down the hull and superstructure. Surprisingly, there had been no deaths. Several people received minor injuries, including rope burns. One man ended up with leg and rib fractures after escaping through a porthole and falling onto a launch below.[7]

C. H. Tung and the other executives who had been rescued went to the headquarters of the Island Navigation Corporation in the Central district. A meeting saw 'emotional outbursts and loud bangs on tables ... the Tungs and aides were broken-hearted as the tremendous efforts and planning and work in reviving the old *Queen* had all vanished'. That night the company put out a statement saying the blaze had 'delayed' plans for the liner's sailing. C. Y. Tung was in Paris and he learned the news in a phone call. He had been in France for the launch of another ship for his expanding fleet. The next day he travelled to Britain, indicating that he would fly to Hong Kong to inspect the wreck. Before boarding a plane at Heathrow he made a brief comment: 'I feel so bad. It is the only historical ship left. We restored it to her former glory. It makes me cry. But I must be strong in my nerve.'[8]

Sea trials had been scheduled for 15 January and the liner was due to sail to Japan on 28 January to enter a dry dock for work on her hull and propellers.

The death of the *Queen Elizabeth* made world headlines on 10 January 1972. The banner headline on the front page of the *Hongkong Standard* was 'END OF THE QUEEN'. Part of the newspaper's report said:

Last night the inside of the ship was blazing furiously and the illustrious career of the world's largest liner was obviously at an end. Flames could be seen in the darkness through the portholes and the ship was listing 17 degrees to starboard. Early this morning the ship started to break up. The aft promenade deck on the port side collapsed to the main deck. And firemen shortly after midnight reported that the whole of the portside was becoming red hot – and added there appeared to be oil on fire below the main deck. About 200 workers were rescued from the ship. Nine were hurt. A series of thundering explosions, which rocked the entire ship, was heard throughout the day.

The *Hongkong Standard* had phoned the ship at 1.30 p.m. and managed to speak to one of the workers, who told of 'great confusion', with many men reporting fresh outbreaks of fire. 'I don't know where the fire first started, but it has now spread to almost every part of the ship,' he said. 'The police and firemen have just arrived. It is serious, very serious.'

Lloyd's List reported:

As the former Cunard liner *Queen Elizabeth* blazed from bow to stern in Hong Kong yesterday a senior harbour official declared: 'She will never sail again.' Several decks of the 82,998-ton gross ship, now named *Seawise University*, had collapsed, the official added. 'She is still burning and we cannot get close. Our policy is to let her burn herself out.'

The Times of London lamented:

For nearly everybody associated with the 83,000-ton liner *Queen Elizabeth*, builders, owners, passengers and crew alike, she was the most beautiful ship in the world. The liner, for so long the pride of Britain's passenger fleet, provided a unique service and atmosphere during the 30 years of her life before she was settled in retirement as a floating hotel at Port Everglades, Florida, in 1968.[9]

At noon on 10 January, with water still pouring in from open shell doors, the ship capsized on her starboard side, resting half submerged on the seabed. The next day the *Hongkong Standard* had another banner headline: 'SABOTAGE?' It was not the only newspaper to take that line. The *Hongkong Standard*'s front-page story began:

Suspicion mounted yesterday that the *Seawise University*, now a capsized wreck, may have been sabotaged. Local authorities refused to be drawn into it, but overseas there was speculation that the fire – which started on Sunday and has left the former *Queen Elizabeth* a charred, twisted hulk – could not have spread so quickly from natural causes.

In Britain, Commodore Geoffrey Marr, Cunard's last master of the *Queen Elizabeth*, was quick to suggest it must have been arson. 'I do not believe this fire could have started accidentally – the flames spread too quickly for that,' he said. 'It must have been sabotage.' He pointed out that the ship's fire-fighting precautions had been updated during her refit and were more than adequate. There were at least seven fireproof bulkheads with fire doors designed to close automatically. And there was an extensive sprinkler system. The fire could not have spread naturally from bow to stern in such a short time.

In 1973 Marr revealed that he had been kept informed of the 'excellent progress' of the refit in letters from C. Y. Tung.

> I had also read with great interest the announcements in the American press and travel magazines of her first 75-day luxury Pacific cruise, due to start from Long Beach, California, on 24 April 1972. It was therefore with shock and horror that I first heard the news in an early morning telephone call from the BBC that she was on fire fore and aft, blazing furiously, and expected to become a total loss. I just could not bring myself to believe that a ship with such a good fire safety record (and as a result of her reconversion should have been more fireproof than she had ever been before) could burn so quickly and so completely, unless fires had been deliberately started in several parts of the ship at the same time. My expression of these opinions in press and TV interviews caused a certain amount of consternation, and I even received a telephone call from a leading Hong Kong newspaper asking me to clarify what I based these opinions on. All I could say was that I felt I knew the ship very well, and as I had already suffered at the hands of an arsonist on board the *Carinthia* in Montreal, one does not forget the significant details.

Tellingly, Marr stated: 'Fire destroys all evidence so completely. I very much doubt – no matter how many "official inquiries" are held – whether anyone will ever know for certain just who, or what, caused the tragic end of this gracious lady.'[10]

Lord Mancroft, Cunard's former deputy chairman, was also immediately suspicious about the liner's destruction: 'She shouldn't burn like that from stem to stern. Something seems very funny there, very odd.' The comments of Marr and Mancroft riled Herbert Hutchins, Chief Fire Officer of Hong Kong Island, who said it was 'waffle' to suggest that the blaze had been anything other than an accident. Four days after the first alert, with one fire still burning inside the ship, Hutchins complained: 'They are living in the past. They are commenting from when they owned and worked the ship.' He seemed to be under the impression that there had been only one fire: 'We have not yet pinpointed the position at which the fire broke out. We just don't know.'

A group of five fire officers had boarded the ship the previous day. 'All the upper decks have collapsed into the centre of the ship and we found it almost impossible to find even a corridor to walk along,' said Assistant Chief Fire Officer Leonard Worrallo. 'Fifty per cent of the ship is flooded by dirty water with oil floating on the surface. The remaining part, which is above water, is just a mass of tangled and distorted metal.'[11]

The *South China Morning Post* commented:

> The loss of the *Seawise University* is far more than a local disaster of the first magnitude. It is an international tragedy and hundreds of thousands of people will share the grief of the C Y Tung group, which endeavoured to restore this magnificent vessel to seaworthy condition. The tragedy is all the more apparent today when one sees the deadly finality of it. The brave words put out by the C Y Tung group on Sunday about sailing plans being 'delayed' even then concealed the fact that the phoenix had perished and would never rise again from the ashes. There is no doubt that Mr Tung's lavish concern for this vessel was a labour of love. The amount of money he spent testifies to that, for the most optimistic shipping man would have doubted its chances of making money as a combined floating campus and luxury cruise ship.

The newspaper added:

> Certainly she was incomparable as a luxury liner and all who sailed on her or who served her will today join in the mourning for a great ship. It is indeed a tragedy to see the blackened hulk overturned in the harbour, and her disposal is the next problem her owners will have to face ... In many ways it is a pity that this great ship could not have met her end with greater dignity by slipping beneath the sea to disappear forever.[12]

Curiously, C. Y. Tung did not arrive in Hong Kong after his flight from London on 10 January. He was not seen for two weeks. On 23 January he flew to the colony from the United States. After an emergency meeting at the offices of the Island Navigation Corporation, he 'vanished ... all efforts to trace him proved fruitless. Both company officials and Mr Tung's family declined to disclose where the shipping magnate was'.

He had been met at the airport by a small number of relatives, friends and aides, and avoided reporters by leaving the terminal building through a side door. On 28 January he flew to Singapore, saying he was unable to meet the press as he had promised because of 'pressing business commitments elsewhere'. However, in a statement he pledged to continue his floating educational programme, admitting that the tragedy had 'broken my heart. To me the *Seawise* was a labour of love and not merely a commercial enterprise'. He thanked the people of Hong Kong for their 'goodwill and kindness' and officials of various government departments for their 'co-operation and assistance'.

Director of Marine Kenneth Milburn prepared a special background report for the governor, Sir Murray MacLehose. It outlined Tung's success as a shipping tycoon and how the *Queen Elizabeth* came to end up in the colony – 'it is presumed Hong Kong was selected as a base for the conversion because it would be cheaper'. Of the loss of the ship, he said:

> Government services were prompt and efficient in their reaction. There was the customary splendid co-operation, which we take as a matter of course, between fire services, police and marine departments. The rapid spread of the fire was on the knowledge available at the present time beyond comprehension ... By the grace of God and swift human response there was no loss of life.[13]

The *Queen Elizabeth* was not the only casualty that month. Sir Basil Smallpeice left Cunard following a takeover by Trafalgar House, a property and construction group run by Nigel Broackes and Victor Matthews. All the members of the group board lost their jobs, with the exception of managing director Norman Thompson. Smallpeice recorded:

> We held the last meeting of the board of Cunard as an independent company of 93 years standing on August 25 1971. I stayed on as a member of the Trafalgar House board for another five months, but there was little or nothing I could do there to help the Cunard ship; and then, with sadness in my heart, I let myself quietly over the side and went ashore.[14]

Smallpeice had little to say about the loss of the *Queen Elizabeth*. It was, he noted, 'a sad end'.

CHAPTER 14

Ghost of the *Normandie*

Saving the liner was probably an impossible task from the outset. She was too big. There were too many fires. But did she have to capsize? Director of Marine Kenneth Milburn admitted: 'The capsize resulted from the vain attempt to control the fire.' He added:

> Passenger ships are by design initially tender. Beaching was not a feasible proposition for practical reasons. It can theoretically prevent capsize if carried out at an early stage and if precise control is possible. The French liner *Normandie* in New York and the British liner *Empress of Canada* in Liverpool also capsized as a result of fire-fighting operations with the ships lying alongside in relatively shallow water.[1]

It was shortly after 3 p.m. on 9 January 1972 that Herbert Hutchins, Chief Fire Officer of Hong Kong Island, noticed the ship 'give a big heave' and develop a serious list. His men on board were told to withdraw and an order was also given to stop pumping water to their hoses. Some firefighters were forced to leave their equipment behind as they rushed to safety. The fireboats were also told to stop. An estimated 9,300 tons of water had been pumped into the ship and 5,000 tons remained, flooding many of the decks. It was feared that the ship would capsize, rupturing her fuel tanks and sending 3,200 tons of oil into the sea. Open shell doors letting in water were another factor. 'We feared that the *Seawise University* might go over at any moment,' said Hutchins. Fireboats, police launches and other vessels were told to move up to 1,000 yards away from the blazing ship. The order to stop the hoses was given by Director of Fire Services Alfred Wood. But C. H. Tung, the rescued son of the shipping tycoon, urged him to continue fighting the fire for as long as possible. Wood replied that as a fireman he would be happy to carry on, but he had been advised by Milburn to stop.[2]

The actions of the firefighters drew criticism from one of Hong Kong's leading salvage experts, Captain William Worrall: 'About the worst thing you can do to a burning ship is to continually pour water into her blazing hull.'

Worrall gave as an example his experience with the Norwegian freighter *Ala*, which was abandoned by her crew about fifty miles from Hong Kong in October 1956 after a flash fire in the engine room threatened the superstructure. The salvage tug *Tai Koo*, under Worrall's command, found the ship, still burning, and managed to attach a towline. As the *Tai Koo* headed to Hong Kong with her charge, the big fireboat *Alexander Grantham* arrived to help. 'As far as I was concerned this was a mixed blessing,' Worrall recalled.

> With a fire burning in an empty ship, there is a fair chance that the blaze will burn everything that can be burned, then die out leaving the gutted remains still afloat. But once you start pouring water into a steel hull, the water will find its own free level. The ship will start to list, and the more water that goes into her the worse the list will get. But now she was on the spot, the *Alexander Grantham* could play a role in helping to stop the fire from spreading from the engine room. I asked the fireman in charge of the boat to direct his powerful jets of water on to the hatches fore and aft. This water would damp down the wooden hatches and prevent them from catching fire and would flow overboard.
>
> The *Alexander Grantham* steamed alongside the *Ala* as I took her under tow towards the harbour, with her hoses pouring water on the ship at the rate of thousands of gallons a minute. Then, for reasons known only to those aboard, the fireboat started to pour its load of water on to the blazing engine room area, and this was absolutely the last thing I wanted. 'What the hell are you up to?' I demanded over the radio. 'Turn the damn hoses off.' I feared the water trapped in the hold would cause a list, which would get worse until the *Ala* rolled over and sank. This is what caused the *Queen Elizabeth* to capsize when she went down in Hong Kong harbour after saboteurs set her on fire. But I couldn't reason with the fireman. He kept on directing his hoses at the engine room until I finally ordered him away.

The Marine Department told Worrall that he could not bring a burning ship into the harbour, but he carried on and the *Ala* was anchored safely in Junk Bay – still on fire. Eventually the flames died out, and insurance assessors discovered that she was not a total write-off. The ship was towed to Japan and rebuilt. A few years later, renamed *Moon*, she sank after a collision.[3]

It was, of course, the *Alexander Grantham* – spraying columns of water into the air – that led the armada of boats welcoming the *Queen Elizabeth* to Hong Kong in July 1971. And the fireboat had helped to sink the liner. In July 1979 one of the firemen who fought the blaze revealed that the loss of the ship would always be a painful memory. Standing on the bridge of the *Alexander*

Grantham, Jo Tai-chang, a divisional officer, said: 'It was terrible. It was the worst fire we experienced and the only ship we lost. We tried to fight it for four hours but it was a losing battle. Every other time we've managed to save the ship.'[4] The *Alexander Grantham* was decommissioned in 2002 after forty-nine years' service and is now a tourist attraction at Quarry Bay Park, Hong Kong Island.

For two weeks in March 1940 New Yorkers were treated to a spectacular sight – the world's three greatest liners, *Queen Elizabeth*, *Queen Mary* and the French Line's *Normandie*, berthed at adjoining piers. When the *Normandie* entered service in May 1935 she was the largest and fastest passenger ship. Her lavish interiors were marvels of Art Deco design. She epitomised French style. Her life, sadly, was comparatively short, though she became a transatlantic legend. The *Normandie* arrived in New York on 28 August 1939 after a crossing from Le Havre and, with war only days away, there she stayed. It would turn out to be her last voyage. The French Line did not want to risk a possible U-boat attack on the return journey despite the fact that the ship was capable of 32 knots, a speed that could render submarines impotent. By October only a skeleton crew was on board. Outwardly, she still looked splendid in her traditional colours – black hull, white superstructure and red and black funnels – unlike her neighbour, the *Queen Mary*, painted from stem to stern in wartime grey. Within, she was eerily quiet.

After France's surrender in June 1940, the Vichy government demanded the return of the *Normandie*. The American response was to put her in 'protective custody' with an armed guard. When the United States entered the war in December 1941 after the attack on Pearl Harbor she was formally seized and renamed USS *Lafayette*. The *Queens* had already proved their worth as large troopships, and the US military wanted a similar role for the *Normandie*. Shipyards were under pressure because of the war effort, and a decision was taken to carry out the conversion at her berth, Pier 88. Some 2,000 workers were soon swarming aboard. Paintings, Art Deco fittings and a huge quantity of furniture were taken away for storage. Chaos reigned as workers faced changing plans and an unrealistic completion date. The contract had been awarded to the Robins Dry Dock & Repair Company, but the US Navy was in overall charge, supported by the Coast Guard.

At about 2.35 p.m. on 9 February 1942 fire broke out in the main lounge, the grand salon, on Promenade Deck. There are remarkable similarities in the fate of the *Normandie* and the *Queen Elizabeth* almost thirty years later. There was a delay of between ten and fifteen minutes in alerting Manhattan's fire department. The first alert came from a call box on Pier 88, not the ship. By 3 p.m. flames were sweeping across the upper decks. Lower decks were filled with choking smoke. But the ship was without power to pump hoses. Communications to firemen and navy personnel on shore were difficult, and sailors on board were reduced to waving flags in semaphore signals.

Fire engines descended on Pier 88 and three fireboats directed jets of water. Strong winds blowing across the Hudson River fanned the blaze. There were nearly 3,000 people on board – civilian workers and navy and coast guard personnel – and they evacuated the ship. About 200 were injured, and one man died after an explosion.

The officer in overall command was Rear Admiral Adolphus Andrews, whose Third Naval District headquarters was in Manhattan. Shortly before 3 p.m. he had picked up his phone to be told by one of his officers that the *Normandie* was on fire. According to one account, this was the conversation:

'How bad is it?'

'I'd say it's out of control.'

'What happened? What started it? Was it sabotage?'

'No one knows for sure, sir. It may have been sabotage. It may have been a welding accident'

'I'll be there in a few minutes.'

That was the first time that Admiral Andrews visited the ship.

It soon became apparent that the liner was listing, and fire chiefs were asked to stop the hoses, but they insisted in carrying on because they thought the adjacent piers were in danger. Fate took another turn – among the people who gathered at the scene was Vladimir Yourkevitch, a Russian naval architect who played a key role in designing the *Normandie*'s revolutionary hull. He had moved to Manhattan and set up a ship design company. Yourkevitch pointed out to fire and navy chiefs that the ship was likely to capsize but this could be prevented by opening the sea cocks, with the inrush of water allowing her to settle on the river bed. He knew the location of all the sea cocks. His plea was ignored, though whether the flames and smoke would have allowed access to them remains open to question.

At 12.22 a.m. on 10 February the *Normandie*'s list was 15 degrees – about the same as the *Queen Elizabeth*'s on 9 January 1972. At 2.25 a.m. the *Normandie* capsized on her port side. One estimate suggested that four million gallons of water had been directed at the ship.

Sabotage was the immediate suspicion – German agents were to blame for the blaze. The true explanation, however, was less elaborate – it was a simple case of carelessness. Unlike the *Queen Elizabeth*, only one fire was responsible for the tragedy and it was not sabotage, but like the former Cunarder there were major questions about fire precautions and the ability to fight a blaze. That afternoon on 9 February in the main lounge on Promenade Deck, several workmen had been trying to cut away a tall metal light stanchion using an oxyacetylene torch. The main lounge was being used as a storage area for more than 1,400 bales of life jackets containing kapok, a highly inflammable

material. The torch sent out sparks which ignited one of the bales. According
to America's National Fire Prevention Association, the events that followed
resembled a 'Hollywood slapstick comedy'. Fire extinguishers failed to work
and a man hurrying to the blazing bale with a bucket of water tripped, spilling
the contents. Burning bales were thrown around by the panicking workmen,
only to spread the blaze. Because of the conversion work decks were full of
combustible material, including rolls of linoleum and mattresses.

Rumours of sabotage continued until the FBI carried out an investigation
and confirmed the original source of the fire. Agents even recreated the main
lounge scene in a warehouse, with a metal light stanchion, a bale of life jackets
and the same group of workmen equipped with an oxyacetylene torch. Sparks
quickly set the life jackets on fire.

Several high-level inquiries were held. Although the US Navy had accepted
responsibility for the liner, it emerged that little was done to protect her. 'Fire
watchers' lacked training, fire-fighting equipment was not checked, navy
personnel were unfamiliar with the ship's machinery, switches on the bridge
to sound a general alarm had been disconnected, gas masks were faulty and
American hoses would not connect to French valves.

The 83,423-ton *Normandie*, lying on her port side between two piers like a
giant beached whale, was a remarkable sight, a magnet for sightseers. The US
Navy was so embarrassed that it erected a high plywood fence to screen the
wreck from the road running past the piers.

The job of carrying out what was then the world's biggest wreck removal
went to the New York salvage company Merritt-Chapman & Scott. The
superstructure was completely removed and the hull was refloated. Eighteen
months after the fire, a dozen tugs towed the remains of the ship to the
Brooklyn Navy Yard. Later she was transferred to another berth and after
the war she was sold for scrap. Once again she was taken in tow, this time
to Port Newark to be broken up. By 6 October 1947 all that was left of the
magnificent *Normandie* was a 75-ton section of plating.[5] It had been a long,
lingering death.

It would be the same for the *Queen Elizabeth*.

CHAPTER 15

Court of Inquiry

A decision to set up a Marine Court of Inquiry into the loss of the *Queen Elizabeth* was taken quickly. Despite the liner's chequered history since her Cunard days, she had become a British ship once again, flying under the flag of the Bahamas. The Governor of Hong Kong, Sir Murray MacLehose, and his advisers decided during a meeting at Government House on 14 January 1972 that an inquiry should be held 'as soon as possible' in view of the public interest. The task was given to Judge Art McMullin and two assessors, John Robson and Captain John d'Oyly Green, a retired member of the Royal Naval Reserve. Hearings were set for various days in February and March, plus 4 April. The court's report was completed in late June and released in July. There were ninety-two witnesses, who included crewmen, workers, executives of the Island Navigation Corporation, fire and marine department chiefs, police personnel and shipping experts. C. H. Tung, son of C. Y. Tung, was not among the witnesses.

Before hearing any evidence Judge McMullin and his assistants needed to familiarise themselves with the layout of the ship and the fire precautions.

From the top there were these decks: Sports Deck, Sun Deck, Boat Deck, Promenade Deck or P Deck, Main Deck or M Deck, A Deck, B Deck, Restaurant Deck or R Deck, C Deck, D Deck, E Deck, F Deck and G Deck. A Deck extended the length of the ship. There were public rooms and cabins on all decks from the Sun Deck down to D Deck. Holds, baggage rooms and storerooms were below the accommodation. There were fifteen main watertight bulkheads below R Deck. These were fitted with watertight doors. In addition, there were twenty-one watertight doors in bulkheads dividing the passenger accommodation on C Deck. When fire broke out on the morning of 9 January, every one of these doors was open.[1]

Above R Deck the ship was divided into eight main zones by fireproof bulkheads, which were generally in line with the watertight bulkheads below. In the bulkheads above R Deck and in stairway enclosures, workmen were in the process of fitting fireproof doors. Out of total of 251 doors, 175 had been completed – but on 9 January very few of them were closed.[2]

There were four main stairways, as well as minor ones, three large restaurants, lounges, smoking rooms, drawing rooms, bars, libraries, shops, offices, a theatre and a cinema. P Deck had an open-air swimming pool and on C Deck there were thermal baths. The ship's layout was 'vast and intricate'.

The liner was well equipped to fight a fire. Throughout the vessel there were 367 hydrants with hoses and nozzles, 184 soda acid extinguishers, ninety CO_2 extinguishers, fifty-nine foam extinguishers, thirty-seven dry-powder extinguishers and 480 buckets with sand. Breathing apparatus and protective clothing were also available. An alarm system covered all the accommodation areas and could alert the chartroom, the officers' quarters on the bridge and the engine room. A smoke detector and alarm system covered holds and baggage spaces. A sprinkler system was fitted in the accommodation areas, public rooms and galleys. The ship had two fire stations, one on R Deck and the other on C Deck. The R Deck station had panels with warning lights that could indicate the location of a fire. On 9 January it was discovered that nozzles for some of the hoses were missing. The ship had a temporary public address system, which ceased working after the first announcement of a fire.

How many firemen were on duty at any one time in case of an emergency on the world's largest liner? The answer was four. Twelve professional firemen were employed, and they were divided into three groups. Each group of four men was on duty for 24 hours and then had 48 hours off. While on duty one man would occupy the fire station on R Deck and the other three would either go on patrol, check fire equipment or rest in their quarters. Three firemen would usually go for lunch in the main restaurant at 11.30 a.m., leaving the fourth man in the fire station.[3]

This was the procedure in the event of a fire:

Warning would be given in the fire station [R Deck] by an alarm bell and by the lighting of the panel showing the approximate location of the fire. The fireman on duty in the fire station would immediately phone the public address office and tell them to announce the outbreak of the fire and its location. He would then send fire-fighting appliances and gear to the scene of the fire. The duty officer of the day would hear the announcement and would set up a fire control centre in the deck officer's office on A Deck square. He would be kept advised of the progress of the fire by telephone or by messengers, and would take appropriate action. Should a more senior officer than the duty officer be on board, he would take command, and whichever officer was in command would decide if and when shore assistance should be called for. The officer in charge at the scene of the fire would decide whether shell doors, watertight doors or fireproof doors in the vicinity should be closed, bearing in mind the need to maintain escape routes for workmen on board and for those dealing with the fire.[4]

But the inquiry report noted:

> From the evidence it seems probable that the fire station was not manned at the time the first alarm was raised, and the evidence shows that it was not manned for about 20 minutes after the public address announcement of the fire, apart from those members of the crew and others who went to the fire station for extinguishers and breathing apparatus during that time.

Twelve crewmen also had been given training to carry out fire patrols. They worked in three shifts of four men. The first shift was from 8 a.m. to 4 p.m., and there were four routes, one man for each one, and the patrols usually took forty minutes to complete. The patrols were done every hour on the hour, starting and finishing at the R Deck fire station. The men were young and did not have any sea-going experience, but they had either attended a two-day course at a fire school ashore or received training from the chief fire officer on the ship. About 100 crewmen had attended the two-day course.[5]

There were twenty-four security guards on the ship who were provided by a sub-contractor. They worked in two shifts of twelve hours each. Their main duties were to check crew, workmen and visitors who were arriving or leaving the ship, and to watch over valuable material and places where there was a special fire risk. They were also expected to carry out patrols, but the inquiry report noted:

> Although it was a specific provision in their standing orders that no part of the ship should remain unvisited for more than two hours, it is clear that patrolling was a minor consideration throughout their employment on the *Seawise* and was done only to the extent that men were available when they had covered their other duties. They had no training in fire prevention or fire fighting and in an emergency their main duty would be to assist in the evacuation of workers etc from the ship.[6]

Some 2,000 workmen were used in the ship's conversion. Their hours were usually 8 a.m. to 11 a.m. and from 1.30 p.m. to 4.30 p.m., seven days a week. Surprisingly, in view of the lengthy process, most of the men employed by the Island Navigation Corporation went ashore in launches for their lunch, leaving at about 11.15 a.m. and returning at 1.15 p.m. The crew ate on board, the ratings at 11 a.m. and the officers at 11.30 a.m., and so did most of the workmen employed by sub-contractors, between 11 a.m. and noon. These meals were taken in the first-class restaurant on R Deck.[7]

About sixty welders were working on the ship on 9 January. They had jobs on several decks and involving the funnels, but a total of nineteen firewatchers were at the locations as a precaution. The welders would usually stop work at 10.55 a.m., report to an office on Main Deck and then go ashore for lunch, returning at about 12.45 p.m. They were hired on a daily basis, although their foremen were employees of the Island Navigation Corporation. The possibility that welding work started any of the fires was ruled out. But not a single welder gave a witness statement. Judge McMullin and his assessors reported: 'We were told that it was impossible to trace any of the welders who had actually been working upon the ship on Sunday, 9 January …'[8]

In the early days of the ship's conversion many decks were scenes of chaos. With the work nearing completion, the amount of rubbish reduced significantly and so did the potential for fire. Rubbish was loaded on barges and taken away twice a day. Gas for burning and oxyacetylene welding was kept in bottles in two storerooms, one on C Deck and the other on Sun Deck. Bottles were distributed to work sites when they were needed, and empty bottles were sent ashore. On 9 January there were seven full bottles of gas and twenty full bottles of oxygen in the C Deck store. A few bottles were distributed around the ship. Paint was brought on board in relatively small quantities and kept in a storeroom on B Deck.[9]

But could the crew, generally, cope with a major fire? It appeared not. The marine court noted:

> Duties were not nominated and there were obvious difficulties in the way of such nominations including the fact that recruiting was going on and of those members already recruited there would be a turnover as a result of leave of absence. The only way, therefore, for each man to discover his precise duties at a time of fire would be to muster with the others at the appointed fire control centre so that the senior officer on duty could tell them of it and explain their duties to them. There is no evidence that this was done. A high proportion of the newly recruited crew were hotel staff most of whom had never been to sea and who knew little about the fire-fighting equipment on board and topography of this very large and complicated ship.

CHAPTER 16

Fire? It's Lunchtime

The fate of the *Queen Elizabeth*, from the time that the three Philadelphia businessmen became involved until the day she went up in flames, is nothing less than bizarre. But it did not end there. The court of inquiry would throw up many puzzling questions. And then there was the behaviour of some of the witnesses … In the event of fire, head straight for the restaurant and have lunch. That was the thinking of several of the men working on the ship.

Two carpenters told the inquiry that they saw smoke but did not report it. They took their meal break as usual. The men had been fitting beds in cabins on A Deck. Man Kwok-shui said he saw the smoke at about 11.35 a.m. as he left a cabin.

'It appeared to be coming from the small alleyway in the direction of the stern,' the carpenter recalled.

> After seeing the smoke we went down the aft main staircase to B Deck. On the way down I looked back into the cross alleyway leading to the shell door and saw the ceiling of the alleyway was in flames. It wasn't clear to me where the flames were coming from.

There were no signs of a fire on B Deck and he went to a storage room to change his clothes.

> Then I went towards the stern and down to the R Deck restaurant where I had a meal. I didn't see any excitement among the people in the restaurant although some were talking about a fire on board. After the meal we sat in the restaurant for a short time and some of the lights went out.

He heard a public address announcement but the words were not clear. He did not see any sprinklers working. Of his first sighting of smoke and flames, the carpenter admitted:

It didn't strike me as extraordinary. I didn't report it to anyone in authority. I had not been given instructions as to what to do in such a case. I had been working on the ship for only 11 days.[1]

An eighteen-year-old colleague, Poon Yat-lai, told a similar story. He saw the smoke and flames on A Deck at about the same time, went to the storage room to change his clothes and then headed for the restaurant.

When I had finished eating I went into the kitchen to get a cup of tea but the kitchen was full of light smoke. I returned to the restaurant and saw a few workers in white boiler suits running aft with fire extinguishers. After a few minutes I saw smoke slowly coming from the lighting fixtures in the false ceiling. There were many people in the restaurant and there appeared to be some excitement in their conversation. They did mention the fire but I didn't pay any attention to it. Neither myself nor my friends said anything to anyone about the fire. I had been working for eight or nine days and did not pay any attention to any instructions posted in the ship.

Eventually he became 'frightened' and along with about a dozen workers he was told to leave the ship. They were lowered over the port side to a waiting barge. It was about 12.15 p.m. and by that time 'the aft portion of the ship from A Deck upwards was well alight'.[2]

Two of the cabin boys involved in the original fire alert also revealed that they went the restaurant for lunch.

Lin Hung-sun had been working as a cabin boy on the ship for nine days. 'On January 9th I started work at 9 a.m. cleaning the cabins on A Deck with a group of six other people,' he said.

Later we went to M Deck where we worked for two hours sweeping the port side clear of dust and rubbish. We took the rubbish to A Deck where we dumped it in a wooden box and emptied the box twice, at 10.30 a.m. and 11.40 a.m. The second time we put down the box of rubbish I saw a little smoke which appeared to be coming from the stern along the side alleyway. After putting down the box, three of us hurried along the alleyway to take a look. In that stretch of alleyway other workmen had also smelled the smoke and gone to take a look. I saw some smoke and small flames among the rubbish in the alleyway leading to the shell door.

He and two other cabin boys ran back towards a staircase, shouting 'Fire!' They found a fire extinguisher and returned to the scene. 'By that time the smoke had become very dense and the place had become very dark,' said Lin.

I got dizzy from the smoke, dropped the extinguisher and went back to the main staircase where we met some firemen, who chased us away. I went back up to Main Deck where I saw my other workmates and went with them to R Deck and there was no fire there. I wished to have lunch so I went to the restaurant. I got as far as the kitchen but saw some smoke. I didn't pay much attention to where the smoke was coming from – it wasn't very dense – but after noticing it I decided not to have lunch.

He went to a port side gangway and waited 'quite some time' until marine police told him to leave the ship. It was between 12.30 p.m. and 12.45 p.m. He did not hear a public address announcement or any alarms.[3]

Tsim Fook-shing said that after spotting smoke coming from rubbish on A Deck he and the two other cabin boys 'immediately went back to the main staircase to raise the alarm and met someone who wore a white engineer's suit and a helmet and carried a torch'. He went on:

When we shouted Fire! he asked where it was and we pointed to the stern. Then the three of us picked up a fire extinguisher, intending to put out the fire. We weren't quite half way there when we found ourselves almost choked by the smoke. We dropped the fire extinguisher and went back to the main entrance. There I saw firemen wearing breathing apparatus and at the request of some people we left to go to R Deck for lunch. I didn't notice any smoke on the way down to R Deck but I went through to the kitchen where I saw a large number of people having a meal there. I could see there was smoke in the kitchen so two of us decided to leave that place and go back to the alleyway. After we dropped the fire extinguisher we received no instructions from anyone.[4]

The cabin boy told the court that he first saw smoke at about 11.35 a.m., but the inquiry report revised this time, suggesting that it was in the region of 11.20 a.m. to 11.25 a.m. The report pointed out:

Few witnesses looked at their watches at any time during the emergency, and very few observed times. The times logged by the fire services, marine department and the police, and the times of some of the photographs, have been used as anchor points. Witnesses' estimates of times given in their evidence have been checked against actions taken, distances covered etc, and corrected as necessary to give a reasonable correspondence with each other. In some cases witnesses' recollections were, or appeared to be, out of sequence, and this has also been taken into account.[5]

A service manager, Jim Poon, told the court that he searched the ship for almost two hours to alert and evacuate cabin boys. He was in charge of 153, most of whom had been hired a week earlier. Their main duties were to clear rubbish and clean cabins. During his search the manager did not see any sprinklers working or hear any alarms. There was a public address announcement but he did not understand what was being said. He found fireproof bulkhead doors open.

Poon, who had been working on the ship since 1 October 1971, became aware of the first fire at about 11.35 a.m. 'I was waiting impatiently on P [Promenade] Deck for nine cleaners to come back from lunch to start work,' he said.

> Finally I went down to M [Main] Deck to hurry them up. We were going to have a luncheon party on board that day and I wanted them to clean the veranda grill on the Sun Deck. As I was stepping down from P to M Deck at about 11.35 a.m. or 11.40 a.m. I became aware of the fire. It was near the front of the vessel. After stepping on the Main Deck I saw smoke coming from both alleyways. The smoke was very light. It looked just like fog. At the same time I heard people shouting. I walked towards the stern to see whether it was the source of the fire on the Main Deck. But I saw no sign of fire. I then went down the main stairway to A Deck and saw a few people standing there who told me there was a fire. At that point I could see smoke on A Deck and it appeared to be coming from the aft, along the port alleyways.

Poon began walking towards the source but met two colleagues rushing towards him with fire extinguishers, and they advised him to retreat. 'The smoke was getting denser and I realised I should inform my staff to evacuate or stand by,' said the manager, who was then joined by one of his assistants.

> At the main square of P Deck we couldn't get into the main lounge because the smoke was too dense. We retreated to B Deck, intending to go up another main staircase to search for people. The forward part of B Deck was quite normal – there was no smoke at all. But when we got up to the Sports Deck we saw smoke and the higher we got the heavier the smoke became. Between the Promenade Deck and the Sun Deck we were shrouded in heavy smoke and began to feel uneasy. But we continued to the Sports Deck. It was hard to find our way.
>
> Only the emergency lights were on. Apart from the stern end, the Sports Deck was free from smoke. But underneath the bridge wing, very black smoke was shooting up both sides. We saw no flames, only black smoke.

They did not find any of their staff. Poon went alone to A Deck 'where smoke was very black and I heard crackling sounds'. He continued:

I went down again to R Deck and heard what sounded like something crackling and burning. A few minutes later – I'd estimate the time at 12.35 p.m. or 12.40 p.m. – two firemen came equipped with breathing apparatus and carbon dioxide fire extinguishers. I told them the fire was upstairs and followed them up to A Deck. The firemen had come from the forward part of the ship on R Deck. Half way up the stairs between A and B Deck I saw flames burning through the bulkhead and spreading out. The ceiling of the stairway was aflame. I went back down to R Deck and met my assistant and a number of people who were standing by. We saw flames coming from down below R Deck on the port side.

Poon and an engineer grabbed a fire extinguisher and tried to deal with a fire in a lift shaft. 'At that point I heard an explosion in the lift shaft,' said the manager. Soon afterwards he left the ship and was taken to safety in a police boat.

He told the court: 'We had no particular assigned duties in the event of fire but, according to the ship's schedule, we would be trained in fire-fighting techniques.'[6]

CHAPTER 17

My Impossible Task

The fire chief on board the liner told the court of inquiry that he had no time to co-ordinate operations to deal with the emergency on 9 January. Wong Pao-lung was leading the special three-man patrol that the cabin boys encountered after they spotted the initial blaze on A Deck. Wong and a fireman went to the scene of the fire after the third member of the patrol, deck cadet Kwong Ving-kuen, was told to alert the duty officer. For a time the fire chief and the fireman were the only ones battling the blaze on A Deck. Wong assumed that other crewmen were co-ordinating fire-fighting efforts, and that help would soon arrive. At that stage he believed there was only one fire.

'I was mainly concerned with fighting the fire on A Deck and we didn't have time to convey any messages,' said Wong. 'I rushed to the scene of the fire immediately after it broke out, broke the alarm glass and activated the alarm.' Several firemen did arrive with equipment. Later the fire was brought under control.

Wong continued:

But I could not determine the seat of the fire because it was pitch black – the electricity supply had been cut and there was a lot of smoke. By the time we had brought the first fire under control, other fires had broken out. An engineer told me there was a fire on B Deck. Immediately he took me to B Deck via the port side staircase. We went through the bulkhead door and came to the fire door on the left hand side of an alleyway. The door was closed and he told me there was a fire inside. I noticed that a fire hose was already laid out on B Deck and water was passing through the main bulkhead door. To my mind the fire had come from the lower decks, mainly via the wooden staircase. The floor at the bottom of the staircase was not ablaze because it wasn't made of wood but the walls around the staircase floor were burning, as well as the wooden panelling. I feel quite sure the fire was not a pile of garbage burning but something that looked like a stack of cartons. Other people were there and I got hold of a hose and aimed a jet at the stack of burning material. Next I directed it at the burning panels and the wall, when I noticed that water from the hose on the other side had stopped. I had almost put out the fire on the wall in the mid-bulkhead when I left the spot. I met a fireman with whom I had patrolled the vessel earlier. I took his breathing apparatus and went back to the hot spot and tried to put out what was left of the fire in the bulkhead wall. I then went to the portside alley and found the main staircase well ablaze.

Wong said the fireproof bulkhead door on A Deck had been open when he was fighting the first blaze.

The fire came from the staircase and the flames came out of the staircase and the wind blew it through the bulkhead door. The same staircase was ablaze on A and B Deck. When I put out the fire on A Deck I went down to the same stairway on B Deck and found it blazing. What arouses great suspicion is that all of the four staircases were ablaze.

He went to the main restaurant on R Deck where several senior members of the crew had gathered. 'There was no fire on R Deck but there was a fire on the upper deck. I was so tired at that time I took off my breathing apparatus.' After resting he went back to B Deck and found the fire out of control. He returned to R Deck.

Wong suddenly found he was surplus to requirements:

On R Deck I met a fireman who had brought about 20 firemen aboard the vessel. A European fire officer was leading the crew and he indicated we were to stand to one side while they did their work. We weren't allowed to take part in the fire-fighting operations.

With others, he spent the rest of his time on board searching for people who needed to be evacuated, although the task was difficult because of the darkness. At one point he went to the engine room. 'From the time until I left the vessel we looked for people and also closed all the fire doors on R Deck. I left the ship at about 3.30pm.'[1]

The court had this to say about the fire on A Deck:

It is clear from the mass movement of men and equipment to that scene that, at the outset, it was regarded as the only serious threat to the ship. At one time or another in the first half-hour after the alarm was raised, that site was visited by the majority of the witnesses who have spoken of fighting the fire prior to the arrival of the fireboats – some 26 witnesses in all. From the start this locality swarmed with helpers fetching fire extinguishers, breathing apparatus etc and making them available to the trained firefighters and also assisting with the hoses. But it was Mr Wong Pao-lung and his assistants, Mr Ko Ngan-wan and deck cadet Kwong, who played the major part in dealing with this fire.

The fire extinguishers had proved ineffective, and the fire, fanned by draughts, spread rapidly, setting alleyway panelling alight.[2]

The court believed that it took 75 minutes to bring the A Deck fire under control. It noted:

Yet at that very moment of seeming victory nearly 80 yards aft and more than 200 yards forward of this hard-won battle, and quite unconnected with it, there were raging fires of such size and intensity, and so inadequately confronted, that it is clear that the ship was already beyond saving.[3]

The inquiry report also noted:

Throughout the whole period of emergency the fire forward in the decks above A Deck had gone unchecked because of the scarcity of men to locate and fight it and because of the paramount need to ensure that workers, visitors and others who might be in that area and elsewhere in the ship should be found and conducted to safety.[4]

When the fireboats began to arrive, the ship was pouring smoke from most of her superstructure, from the bridge to the swimming pool aft on P Deck. 'The fireboats began at once to train their jets on the blazing superstructure from the port side of the vessel,' said the report. 'The starboard side was thickly covered by a pall of smoke which by now was clearly visible for miles down the eastern reaches of the harbour.'[5]

Fireman Ko Ngan-wan, who played a significant role in dealing with the A Deck blaze, revealed that at least one of the fire doors had failed to operate. The doors were designed to close automatically when the temperature reached a certain level. But a fire door near a burning staircase on B Deck remained wide open. Firemen on board the ship had not been given any instructions about fire doors. 'There was another group of officers aboard the ship whose sole responsibility was to look after the fire doors,' he pointed out. 'Instructions about fire doors weren't the concern of our section. I don't know who it concerned.' Questioned by the court, he said fire instructions were on prominent display throughout the ship. The firemen had a special set of instructions. Ko had served with the colony's fire service for eight years, joining the ship soon after she arrived in Hong Kong.

Of the A Deck blaze, he said:

> Many people, including Mr Wong, helped fight the fire and because I had
> breathing apparatus I moved ahead with the fire hose. Mr Wong was behind me
> and because of the dense smoke had to retreat a little. The smoke was so thick it
> was like having a black bag over my head and my vision was also limited by my
> firefighter's helmet. I couldn't see but I sensed the place in front of me was red
> hot and about all I could do was direct the hose upwards. I heard sizzling noises
> when the water was discharged. I exhausted the oxygen supply in my breathing
> apparatus – it lasts about 30 minutes – and when it was finished I handed the
> hose to Mr Wong and went for a replacement. I intended to return to the scene
> of the fire but when I went out I heard someone call there was a fire on B Deck.

With another fireman he headed down to B Deck to investigate and saw smoke
coming from between two cabins and the 'light of a flame' behind a staircase
door. He played a hose on the staircase. 'I attempted to open the door but
found it was very hot and shouldn't be opened wide if there was a fire behind
it.' Fireman Ko checked another fireproof door and found it was wide open.
'Looking into the stairway, I could see the fire quite clearly. It spread from the
ground level onto the wall and ceiling, but I didn't notice what was burning.'
He continued fighting the fire and then a warning signal on his breathing
apparatus flashed on to signal that the air supply was nearly exhausted. By
that time he thought he had the fire under control.

He went to R Deck to change his breathing apparatus but ended up boarding
a marine police launch, which took him to one of the fireboats. He asked the
officer in charge to put a put a crew on board the liner. Ko told the court:

> He ordered a group of firemen to go with me and we went by marine police
> launch to the *Seawise*. When we boarded, the firemen of the Fire Services
> Department told us to stand aside. I assisted them in extending fire hoses,
> which they'd brought over the side, and stood by. I was very cold and tired
> and took off my breathing apparatus to have a rest. I rested until firemen
> said they had to give up, and we left the ship.[6]

His statement that the ship's firemen had not been given any instructions
regarding fire doors was later contradicted by one of the liner's chief officers,
Liu hen. Liu told the court that instructions on fire doors were part of the fire
crew's standing orders. 'In the vicinity of the fire zone any fireman present
should close the fire door if it is possible,' he said.

> They knew about the instruction because I told them. Every professional
> fireman, including the fire patrolmen, knew that fire cannot continue

without combustion, therefore they must shut the fire off from the oxygen supply. Since the ship was being renovated all fire doors were not in a working condition and firemen knew that the fire doors must be closed in such circumstances.

He explained: 'Each of the chief officers had a specific duty and mine was supervision of fire-fighting and life-saving services.'

Kwong Ving-kuen, the deck cadet who was a member of the special patrol alerted by the cabin boys, told how he ran to the deck officer's office on the starboard side of A Deck to report the first fire.

> He (the duty officer) asked me to go to the broadcast office at the aft of the Main Deck and have a public announcement made. I tried to make a telephone call to that office from A Deck but failed. The telephone line was busy. I reported to Chief Officer Liu, who asked me to report to Chief Officer Zee Su-tang on A Deck. Mr Zee already knew about the fire and told me to phone the fire brigade on shore. According to my watch it was 11.45 a.m. I went to an office on A Deck, found the Fire Services Department number and tried to call them on the harbour telephone. I failed to get through because somebody else was talking on the line. I dialled 999 and reported a fire aboard the *Seawise University*. But the person who answered the telephone misunderstood me. He thought that I was reporting a fire somewhere on land. It is possible he confused the word 'university' with something on land. Eventually he understood me and I left the office and met Commodore Chen outside, and I told him I'd made the phone call. He told me to go to the engine room and tell the crew to supply steam to the ship's whistle. I ran down the main stairs on A Deck to R Deck where I used another stairway to C Deck. There was smoke coming from the port alleyway on A Deck. Later I saw fireman Ko and helped him to take a fire hose into a doorway at the aft of B Deck in a staircase. Inside the stairway enclosure I saw the wall was burning. The smoke was thick and my vision was limited so I couldn't see what object was burning.

The cadet remained at the scene until the fireman said his breathing apparatus was exhausted. Later he went to help fire chief Wong Pao-lung. When men from a fireboat came on board, he assisted them.

> I then returned to C Deck because there were people trapped there. I located two workers. They seemed to be scared. I took them upstairs to the gangway on R Deck. I stayed there until we left the ship at about 3.15pm. The firemen had given up on the ship, and everyone was leaving.[7]

Chief Officer Liu told the court that he helped to evacuate crewmen and workers before escaping. He threw two ropes over the side after he found a group of workmen trapped near the bridge. He helped men over the side of the ship but several wanted to go down to R Deck because they had 'company affairs to attend to'. Liu said:

> After escorting these people to the first-class entrance on R Deck I returned to the Main Deck and saw that fireboats had come around. By that time most of the vessel was clouded in smoke and it was impossible for me to return to R Deck or go down the ropes because no one was there to drop me down. Finally I went down the anchor chain over the side.

He recalled the moment that deck cadet Kwong alerted him about the first fire.

> He was shouting 'chief officer, chief officer' and rushed into my office and told me fire had broken out on the aft of A Deck and there was much smoke. I looked down the port alleyway and saw smoke and told cadet Kwong to phone M Deck. He told me he could not contact the fire officer on M Deck and I went myself to the Main Deck office via the main alleyway. There was no smoke on M Deck, where I met Commodore Chen, who instructed me to rush to the bridge to sound the emergency whistle and the general alarm in the wheelhouse. I immediately went to the navigation bridge and saw smoke coming from the starboard side of the Sun Deck. I saw smoke in the wheelhouse and it was hard to decide where it came from. On the captain's bridge there was a telephone and after reaching it I came up the main stairway to P Deck. The wind was coming from the port side and the smoke was grey and brownish. I didn't have any breathing apparatus with me so I rushed back to the A Deck office.

Liu said he did not have a chance to visit the A Deck fire, and he did not know if any other senior officer had visited the scene.[8]

The man in charge of the main fire station on R Deck admitted that he was away from his post for 20 minutes after the first alert. The fire station had a board with warning lights that could indicate emergencies in different areas of the ship. Red lights were activated by manual alarms, yellow lights by sprinkler alarms and green lights by thermal alarms. At about 11.30 a.m. a red light flashed, indicating a fire at the aft of A Deck. Lui fai, a foreman fireman, told the court:

> I was in the fire station on R Deck when the fire signal light flashed and an alarm bell rang. I heard a public address announcement that fire had broken

out at the aft of A Deck. The announcement was first made in Cantonese and again in Mandarin. My first thought was to telephone the broadcast office but after hearing the public address announcement I realised it was unnecessary. After hearing the announcement I took a bag of tools to the fire. I stayed at the scene for 20 minutes then returned to the fire station on R Deck. There I prepared equipment for firemen who were rushing to the fire station. Mostly I put together spare oxygen tanks for breathing apparatus and fire extinguishers. More alarms flashed on while I was in the office. At 11.30 a.m. when I left for the scene of the fire only one red light was showing on the board. When I returned to the fire station additional yellow lights were on indicating fire in the aft staircase of A and B decks. A yellow light came on showing fire on B Deck near the forward staircase. Another came on near the front staircase of R Deck at about 1pm. I turned off the main lights of the ship when I went to the A Deck fire. The staircase of R Deck was not burning because it was metal but the wall panelling was on fire.

He was told to leave the fire station when men from the fireboats came on board. He went to help pull up hoses from the fireboats.[9]

The liner's staff captain, Hsu Pang-tsuey, joined in the efforts to fight the fire on R Deck, but faced an immediate problem. He connected a firehose to a hydrant – and then discovered there was no nozzle. Also, the water pressure was too low. 'The fire became worse and I fought it without result because the of the low water pressure,' he said. But a deck engineer, Cheng huan, insisted that the water pressure remained good during fire-fighting on R Deck. He did admit, however, that there was a problem with missing firehose nozzles. 'When two of the hoses were rigged there were no nozzles for them,' said the engineer. Two nozzles were eventually found. In later testimony to the court it was suggested that nozzles had been pilfered. Engineer Cheng said he first became aware of a fire when he opened his cabin door on the Sun Deck and saw dense smoke drifting towards the forward part of the ship. He also saw fires on B Deck and R Deck.[10]

A public relations officer, Tuan Nu-ming, spoke of flames nearly five feet high on A Deck. He had just returned from an inspection of the ship when he heard that fire had broken out. 'I picked up a fire extinguisher and walked aft to the port side of the main staircase and saw dense smoke,' he said.

The shell door in the cross alleyway was open and wind was blowing the smoke inside. I directed my fire extinguisher at the source of the smoke near the shell door and flames suddenly flared nearly as high as my forehead. I ducked into a cabin to get a breath of air and came back to help fight the fire with a hose. Then I saw fire on the main staircase but the two fires were not connected. The second fire was coming from inside the staircase enclosure. I heard shouts that there was another fire on R Deck aft.

On R Deck he saw people waiting to be rescued. Three firemen with hoses were trying to put out flames but 'it was so hot the water immediately evaporated as steam'. He left and found the handrail of the B Deck staircase burning. Panelling was also on fire. 'In my opinion the fire couldn't have spread so fast from R Deck – it must have started from a different source. On R Deck I heard an explosion.' Tuan said he left the ship at 2.45 p.m. on the orders of Commodore Chen, who sent him to a fireboat with a special message. 'The commodore asked them not to give up their fire-fighting efforts and to try to save the ship,' he said.[11]

Dense smoke was also reported in the boiler room. It was 'so thick that those who worked there could hardly open their eyes', said Yung Pak-lam, the staff chief engineer. He rushed up decks to report the emergency to Commodore Chen, who ordered the boiler room staff to 'stick to their posts'. When Yung returned to the boiler room, the smoke had become worse. It was about 1 p.m. Earlier, he had gone to the scene of the A Deck fire after hearing the alert on the public address system. Then he hurried down to the engine room to check that the fire pump was working to supply water for the hydrants and hoses. Returning to the choking boiler room, he talked to the chief engineer, Wong Chung-wing, about seeking fresh orders from the commodore. They went to C Deck where they found some empty oil drums, which they thought could be dropped into the sea and used as floats. Looking out from a shell door on the deck, they spotted a boat, which signalled to them to escape. The oil drums were left behind as they climbed down a rope ladder to safety. It was about 2 p.m. About twenty other crewmen also used the ladder.[12]

Engineer Chow lin-chang saved himself by jumping into the sea. He was on C Deck heading for the restaurant when he heard the fire warning on the public address system. He rushed down to the aft engine room on the lowest deck, G Deck. 'There was only one person in the engine room and I told him to attend to the fire pumps,' he said.

The time was about 11.35 a.m. I remained in the engine room until 1.30 p.m. or shortly afterwards. One fire pump was running all the time and the other two pumps were not operating but were in working order. While we were in the engine room we were ignored by everybody until the chief engineer [Wong Chung-wing] telephoned to tell me to turn off all machinery in the aft engine room and also the generator in the turbo generator room. I left the engine room ... all lights went off at the same time. The generators to power the lights had been turned off by other people elsewhere in the ship. I left the ship by jumping into the sea.[13]

On 17 March 1972 the court of inquiry asked Commodore Chen to explain why so many fire doors and shell doors were open on the day that fire swept through the liner. The commodore pointed out that about 2,000 workers were renovating the ship and said: 'These doors were left open to provide sufficient ventilation and light to facilitate their work. And more important it was necessary to maintain free access for so many people in the event of fire.' The question of fire doors had been discussed at a meeting of the ship's officers after a fire on the liner in November 1971.

> We discussed the possible cause and result of the fire and concluded no blanket order could be made about closing shell and fire doors in the event of fire. We felt it should be left to the discretion of various ship's officers. The policy formed at that meeting was that some fire and shell doors should remain open and others should be closed.

The commodore admitted that after taking command there had not been any formal fire drills on the ship. He explained that the ship's general alarm was activated manually in the wheelhouse on the bridge.

> In accordance with our rules, fire-fighting operations would be controlled by the fire station but there was no general alarm switch there. If fire broke out during the period of renovation, we would use the public address system to sound the warning. There were some 50 loudspeakers on the ship and if broadcasts were made they would be heard.

Judge McMullin commented that previous evidence suggested that not all the people aboard had heard the announcement. The commodore replied: 'If the announcement had been repeated it would have been more effective but there was no chance to do so.' As for sounding the general alarm, it had not been possible to reach the wheelhouse.

Commodore Chen had boarded the ship at about 10 a.m. and carried out a general inspection. One hour later he went to a meeting of ship's officers and those in charge of the work. 'At about 11.30 a.m. Staff Captain Hsu Pang-tsuey reported a fire on A Deck,' he said.

> I returned to my office on A Deck and made enquiries. Then I met a number of people on the main staircase who said there were fires on A Deck, on B Deck and on the Sun Deck. I felt the situation was extraordinary, especially since the reports came from officers experienced in working on the ship.

The commodore gave various orders, which included evacuation of the ship by those not involved in fire fighting. 'I didn't instruct anyone to close the fire doors or the shell doors,' he said. 'I left that to the discretion of responsible people on the spot.' He tried to telephone the main broadcast office but the telephone was out of order. 'The telephone was absolutely silent,' he said. 'Since it was temporary it could have been damaged by fire.' On his failure to get to the wheelhouse, he said: 'I wanted to reach the bridge to assess the position from there. I was thinking about lifeboats and other routes of escape for people.' The commodore went to his office on A Deck and made a 999 call.

> I was rather excited and told the operator we were in a very serious situation and I wanted them to send fireboats immediately and notify the Marine Department. The Fire Services Department operator told me fireboats were on the way.

It was about noon. He added: 'Chief Officer Liu [Liu hen] told me he had been to the bridge and found a great deal of smoke there. Mr Liu said he had failed in an attempt to sound the general alarm.'[14]

At 3.15 p.m. on 9 January Alfred Wood, Director of Hong Kong's Fire Services, gave the order to stop all fire-fighting operations. Herbert Hutchins, Chief Fire Officer, Hong Kong Island, who was on board the liner, told the court: 'At this time we feared the *Seawise University* might go over at any moment.'

CHAPTER 18

The Court's Findings

There were at least nine separate fires – probably eleven – on the liner, the court of inquiry concluded. A, B and R decks were mainly affected, particularly the stairways. In addition, smoke was reported on the Promenade Deck and the Sun Deck. But no fire-fighting was done on these decks. Only one fire was precisely located – the first one on A Deck. 'A matter of minutes after it was detected there were reports which proved reliable of a fire 40 yards aft of it on B Deck and a fire 150 yards forward of it in the area of the Sun Deck close to the captain's bridge and wheelhouse,' said the inquiry's report.

> The precise sources of these fires have not been identified. The possibility of the spread from this one precisely known source, by conduction of hot gases or flame with explosive suddenness, to the other areas through connecting alleyways and ventilation trunking even with fire doors and dampers open is too remote to be reasonably entertained.

The court acknowledged that Commodore Chen did not have enough men to tackle the Promenade Deck and Sun Deck emergencies. The fire that cut off the wheelhouse probably started below in the officers' quarters, and it spread rapidly, unchecked. 'It is of interest that the burnt-out hulk of the *Seawise* shows two major areas of collapse,' said the report. 'One is forward in the region of the bridge and one aft and slightly forward of the swimming pool where several decks appear to have buckled and fallen in upon each other through the intolerable stress of heat.'[1]

Many witnesses spoke of hearing explosions, but the court was unable to discover what caused them or where they occurred, apart from one case, when the blast came from a lift shaft. Gas cylinders in areas where welding had been carried out may have exploded, and a build-up of gases could have been responsible.[2] But had explosives been used?

One significant difficulty for the court was deciding where and when fires had started. It was 'unfortunate' that the ship's main fire station was unmanned at a crucial time.

> Had it been vigilantly observed, the control panel would have been able to provide, by its arrangement of coloured lights, information as to when and where any fire had started and which alarm had notified its existence ... On his own evidence Mr Lui fai, foreman of the party of four firemen on duty that day, cannot have been at his post in the fire station when the first alarm was raised at about 11.30 a.m. as he only heard the bell and saw the red indicator light just before he heard the public address announcement at about 11.37 a.m. Moreover, he left the fire station almost immediately with equipment and went to the scene of the fire where he stayed to help for about 20 minutes before returning to the fire station, where he saw more lights on the panel. The court has thus been deprived of evidence which might have been of inestimable value in pin-pointing the times and places of the various outbreaks.[3]

A handicap for the crew was the failure of the public address system after the first alert. Confusion grew as reports were made of further fires. The commodore and his officers tried to maintain an emergency fire centre on A Deck 'but it crumbled under the pressure of events and the action became increasingly incoherent and uncoordinated'. The crew had not taken part in regular fire drills and that was a factor. However, the court believed the commodore and his officers had shown energy and initiative in dealing with the crisis. The commodore's handling of the emergency was impressive: 'It reflects much credit on him that no lives were lost.' There was also praise for those involved in fighting the fires:

> Within the limitations of their training and their understanding of their duties the motley force which rallied immediately after the alarm endeavoured to deal with an appalling situation with great courage and tenacity. It would be invidious to single out individuals in this matter. All who dealt with the fires, the carrying of equipment and relaying of messages etc acquitted themselves well.[4]

Months earlier the Director of Marine, Kenneth Milburn, had made recommendations about nominating individuals and their duties in case of an emergency but 'no instruction of this sort appears to have been given'. The fire patrolmen knew virtually nothing about ships and had received little training. In the court's view there should have been at least double the number of patrolmen. There was also a question mark over the number of firefighters. The engineers came closest to following standing orders:

Almost without exception they moved to their posts at the pumps and other machinery and waited in conditions of considerable suspense, and eventually of great discomfort from smoke, for orders and for news of the progress of the fire.

Many fire doors were open when the emergency began, and no general order to close them was given. Some doors were shut when the fire-fighting operation was almost over. In his evidence, Commodore Chen explained that it was important to have free access because so many people were on board the ship. But previous courts of inquiry into similar disasters had stressed the importance of closing fire doors and fire dampers (no fire dampers were shut on 9 January). 'It is understood that the difficulty of deciding when to shut fire doors may be considerable when the operation covers a very large area under conditions of confusion such as prevailed upon the *Seawise* on the day in question,' said the report.

> But the real criticism here is that no general instruction appears to have been given as to the importance of carrying out this manoeuvre and this once again reflects a weakness in the nature of the instructions given and the failure to hold muster drills.[5]

And why were so many shell doors open? It was necessary to have some open, but they should have been kept to a minimum, especially those at the lower levels such as C Deck. Again, the commodore gave safety of life as the main reason. The court's view:

> Nothing in the evidence, however, has persuaded us that this paramount necessity would not have been equally well served, even as events fell out, by keeping open a sufficient number of doors on the higher R and B decks and providing them with rope ladders permanently at the ready for lowering to the water. The sealing of C Deck by closing the shell doors in time might have saved the vessel from capsizing.

It will be recalled that Hong Kong fire chiefs Herbert Hutchins and Alfred Wood, along with one of the ship's firemen, tried to close a C Deck shell door as water came in. Photographs of the ship on 9 January showed a large number of portholes open. All portholes in cabins where work had been completed were supposed to be closed. 'It is a reflection on those charged with inspection or patrolling that there were so many open,' the report noted. 'During the emergency no order was given to close the portholes and there is no evidence that any were closed.' According to Chief Officer Liu hen, there was a general order to the effect that all fire doors, fire dampers, port lights and port shell doors must be closed in the event of fire. The report said:

This instruction, with others aboard the ship, was lost by fire and one can only say that if such a general instruction was in existence and had been made known to the responsible officers, no attempt to implement it appears to have been made in the course of the emergency on 9 January.[6]

Alfred Wood, Director of Hong Kong's Fire Services, had stressed to the court that the opening minutes of any fire were crucial as to whether it would turn out to be a minor or a serious outbreak. He believed that if trained firemen in significant numbers had gone to the fires on the ship quickly it might have made a significant difference. The court observed:

A half-hour's delay in this matter is very often decisive. This makes it all the more strange that the earliest arrivals from the fire services waited about half an hour after arriving at the *Seawise* before putting a party on board. The court takes the view that it would have been advisable for the fire services officers to have put some of their men on board the entrance on the R Deck at the earliest opportunity, where their training and skills could have been better used in that way than by simply directing water on the superstructure. Their failure to do so has not been explained.

It may have been the result of poor liaison between the fire and marine departments, the Island Navigation Corporation and the ship's company. But the court did acknowledge that by 12.30 p.m., when the first fireboat arrived, it was probably too late anyway.

When they did go board, the firemen, including some of their senior officers, at considerable risk to themselves, worked in conditions of extreme discomfort and danger in a clearly deteriorating situation, for some two to three hours before eventually abandoning the ship.[7]

Commodore Chen was commended for ordering an early evacuation of the ship. The security guards were effective in directing people to the main exits on R Deck. There were many confused and frightened people, who were shown how to escape using ropes or rope ladders or lifeboats, 'for which the expectations of the day and their normal occupations had ill prepared them'. As the liner began to list, senior officers, some crewmen and fire services personnel carried out searches

in the nether regions of the ship in areas grown unfamiliar with the darkness and the list, down companionways slippery with streaming water from the hoses … Considering the size of the ship, the disastrously rapid advance of the fires, the general lack of coordination, the lack of light at all levels and the steady encroachment of smoke, it is an astonishing fact that not a single soul was lost.

The police were also praised for the way they used their launches and other craft to pick up survivors.[8]

Should the liner have been beached? The Marine Department had put forward the possibility in a contingency plan in the event of a serious fire. Such an operation would take time and require the use of at least four tugs, whether or not the ship could use her engines. Director of Marine Kenneth Milburn decided it would be too dangerous to move the ship, already burning fore and aft, because of the proximity of an oil installation on Tsing Yi Island, a power station, a container ship berth at Kwai Chung and an explosives depot at Green Island. The liner might also have become a grave danger to other ships in the harbour. The court said: 'With all these observations we are in full agreement.'[9]

One irony is that the liner had been at greatest risk during the early stages of the conversion work. As the court pointed out:

> The earlier phases of the work were necessarily those of the greatest danger. The fire-fighting equipment and installations were below par; the organisation was untested and the project team was still feeling its way; extensive welding operations were in progress; all kinds of materials were distributed over many areas; a large work force was everywhere in the ship, yet she survived all this with a few minor fires which those on board had coped with without difficulty. As the time of completion approached, the risk of fire from these sources diminished ...

After the ship's arrival in Hong Kong the fire and marine departments had made a number of recommendations regarding the safety of the ship, and many of them had been followed. But the departments could have done more:

> The Marine Department and the Fire Services Department, from their greater experience, could have emphasised to the inexperienced master and owners the additional dangers inherent in this great ship being two and a half miles from the company's workshops and 20 minutes sailing time from the nearest help from the Fire Services Department, and the consequent need for adequate patrolling and fire-fighting forces backed up by a trained crew having regular musters and fire drills. The fire services personnel should have sought opportunities of familiarising themselves with the ship and her officers whereby their value in an emergency would be greatly enhanced. Valuable time was wasted on 9 January because there was no immediate contact between the ship's senior officers and the fire services personnel.[10]

Eleven fires were reported, and the court came to the conclusion that there were at least three major sites and that these blazes started within minutes of each other. 'While there is no direct and conclusive evidence on the matter, the court is also satisfied that by far the most likely cause of the fires was a series of deliberate acts by a person or persons unknown,' said the inquiry's report. The factors supporting the view that it was arson:

> The number and size of the independent outbreaks. The speed with which each gained ground and became uncontrollable denotes an initial outbreak of considerable size and of great immediate spread indicating the possibility of the use of some highly inflammable reagent; once firmly alight in several places, of course, the immensely rapid spread was due principally to the readily inflammable miles of seasoned timber, panelling and furniture, with the plentiful supply of air through the long open corridors and with the huge open squares acting as chimneys. The outbreak occurred when virtually all the workmen had withdrawn for lunch either in the restaurant or ashore when most of the areas initially affected could reasonably be expected to be, and to a large extent were, free of human traffic. The mere timing of the outbreaks is, therefore, in itself, significant.[11]

The court ruled out welding, cigarette smoking and faulty electrical wiring as possible causes. By 9 January most of the welding work on the ship had been carried out. Those welders still employed went off duty at 10.55 a.m. – about half an hour before the first fire alert.

The report said:

> The court has been impelled to what may seem a somewhat dramatic and disturbing conclusion. It has made no attempt to assign blame for any criminal act nor has it sought to determine the identity of the person or persons who, if we are right, must be responsible for the casualty.

Interestingly, Judge McMullin and his assessors revealed that during the inquiry they had received an anonymous letter, which named a person who was said to have been behind the plot to destroy the ship. The allegation was investigated by the police 'and we wish only to say that the form and tenor of it were such that we felt obliged to disregard it wholly and that it has played no part whatsoever in the conclusion to which we have come'.[12]

CHAPTER 19

A Reluctant Kojak

On 13 January 1972, four days after fire destroyed the ship, it was revealed that the police had been called in to carry out an investigation. The suspicions of the Hong Kong Marine Department were sufficiently aroused. It was unfortunate timing for Herbert Hutchins, Chief Fire Officer, Hong Kong Island. That same day, 13 January, he was reported to have dismissed claims of sabotage as 'waffle'. It will be recalled that Commodore Geoffrey Marr, Cunard's last master of the *Queen Elizabeth*, and Lord Mancroft, the company's former deputy chairman, were quick to question whether the blaze was an accident. Hutchins told a press conference that the two men were 'living in the past'. But on 10 January Director of Marine Kenneth Milburn had appointed one of his officials, Neville Matthew, to carry out a preliminary inquiry. Matthew did not take long to decide he needed the assistance of the police. Accordingly, a 'top detective' was assigned to work with him. The police declined to comment. Matthew was asked to write a report for the governor, Sir Murray MacLehose.[1] Soon afterwards the governor was advised to set up a major inquiry because 'worldwide interest had made it inevitable'.[2]

The verdict of the subsequent Marine Court of Inquiry was arson. But when the inquiry's report was released in July, Judge McMullin and his assessors pointed out that they did not know who had been responsible. Indeed, it had not been one of the court's tasks.

> There is nothing in the evidence which could fairly be said to support even speculation in the matter, nor do we believe that the pursuit of any line of inquiry in the present form, beyond those actually pursued before us, could have resulted in more than the promotion of speculation

said the report.[3]

It was a matter for the police. After the release of the report it was announced that a special squad of detectives had been set up to carry out a full investigation. The officer in charge was Superintendent Charles Mayger of the marine police CID.[4] The squad was based at the headquarters of the marine police, a splendid colonial building on the Kowloon waterfront, which underwent a transformation in 2009 to become a luxury hotel.

Iain Ward, an inspector, was assigned to the team for several weeks because of his Merchant Navy experience. He had been in the navy for several years before joining the police force in 1966, and it was thought that his knowledge of big ships would be helpful. 'The investigation was initially under Charlie Mayger but he passed the file on to another officer when he was transferred,' said Ward.

> They were the officers in command of marine CID at the time, but the real work was done by Chief Inspector "Taffy" Bere. It was a very long drawn-out and inconclusive investigation and quite a few people passed through the investigation team, including me.

Derek Bere, who was bald, would acquire another nickname – 'Kojak' after Telly Savalas, the follically challenged actor who played a New York City detective in a popular 1970s television series. 'Bere was a very loud Welshman, a no-nonsense character,' said Ward.

> Some senior officers didn't like him because he was his own man. He upset people, and he was posted to the marine police as a kind of punishment. But he was a very good detective, especially when it came to murder cases. He solved a lot of murders, some of them quite complex. He was known as Hong Kong's Kojak because he was a good detective – and bald. Many Chinese held him in awe. He was a man who would kick down doors and then ask questions. Murder was his thing and he saw the *Queen Elizabeth* investigation as a lost cause. The ship had gone. He didn't put his heart into it. There were never any arrests. He was going through a pissed-off period because he had been sent to marine. He went on to make a big name for himself. But he continued to upset people and was never promoted above chief inspector.

Remarkably, Bere did not rule out the possibility that the loss of the *Queen Elizabeth* could have been down to an accident. So many fire doors, shell doors and portholes had been open, and flames would have spread quickly along the alleyways, fuelled by all that wood and waste material. Safety precautions and fire prevention measures were 'close to non-existent'. Such reasoning, of course, made it easier to dispose of the case.

Ward, who rose to the rank of superintendent, spoke of police corruption. 'There was a lot of it in the 1960s and early 1970s,' he said.

It was like a bus. You could get on, you could run alongside, or you could try to stop it – and get run over. I'm glad I was not a more senior rank when that was going on. The higher you climbed, the more difficult it became. I guess I was running alongside the bus. But corruption was much worse in other services. The police service now is clean, one of the finest in the world.

Of Mayger, Ward recalled: 'Mayger was not a hands-on man. He was an administrative man rather than a top-star detective. He was not a terribly inspiring guy. Mayger moved on to police headquarters, where he stayed in administration.'[5]

David Hodson, a former assistant commissioner, who served in the force from 1962 until 1997, said of the *Queen Elizabeth* investigation: 'There was a feeling that it had not been thorough enough. Some people expected a better result. No clear motive emerged. Perhaps this was down to C. Y. Tung.'[6]

Trevor Hollingsbee, an intelligence specialist and a former senior superintendent, joined the Royal Hong Kong Police a couple of years after the ship's loss. 'I heard a lot about the fire over the years,' he said. 'There was indeed an inconclusive investigation. Reputedly the file remained 'open' and was retained at Central police station because of its sensitivity.'[7]

Indeed, the file has not been closed, as Commissioner of Police Tang King Shing confirmed in 2009. But the Hong Kong Police insisted that the contents would have to remain secret in case any disclosure prejudiced the investigation.[8] It seems highly unlikely, however, that anyone will ever be convicted over the destruction of the *Queen Elizabeth*.

Derek Bere certainly made a name for himself as a murder squad detective. In 1975 he led an investigation that produced a forensic first in Hong Kong. A teenage girl was found murdered in Happy Valley, and Bere was convinced that the body – in a cardboard box – would yield a vital clue. Forensic experts analysed fibres under the girl's fingernails and they matched those from a suit worn by the main suspect. The man denied murder but he was convicted on the forensic evidence, the first time it had happened in the colony. Thirteen years later the killer admitted his guilt.[9]

Peter Halliday, a former assistant commissioner, who was involved in the initial stages of the *Queen Elizabeth* investigation, said of Bere: 'He was a long-serving CID officer and investigated a considerable number of serious crimes. He was known for his tenacity and thoroughness.'[10]

Journalist Kevin Sinclair noted in the *South China Morning Post*: 'No other person in Hong Kong history has been pitured so frequently kneeling beside the hacked bodies of murder victims.' When Bere arrived at a crime scene, Chinese onlookers would chant 'Kojak! Kojak!' The detective would grumble: 'That Telly Savalas has a lot to answer for.' According to Sinclair, Bere's boundless energy was matched only by a 'limitless capacity' for San Miguel beer. The burly officer, who wore a shirt 'large enough to pitch as a tent', usually made a grand entrance when he descended on bars. 'Bere's the name, murder's the game', he would shout. On other occasions customers heard the cry 'Yabba dabba doo', catchphrase of Fred Flintstone of the American cartoon series *The Flintstones*.[11]

Bere had joined the police in 1952, an entry year infamous for officers who would end up being accused of corruption. Five years later he found the time to serve in the force – and run a pub. In 1997, aged 78, he told colleagues:[12]

> I'm still surviving. More than surviving. I used to have a well-known pub called Ye Olde Buffalo Bar in Wan Chai in 1957. Many people have had many a drink there and admired the buffalo head – which I shot after it killed two people – on the pub's wall.[12]

Despite his run-ins with authority he was awarded the Colonial Police Medal for meritorious service. He retired from the force in 1980 and ended up in Spain. Bere died in Malaga on the Costa del Sol in 2002.

Charles Mayger was promoted chief superintendent in 1978 and retired in 1985 after 36 years in the force. He had been awarded the Queen's Police Medal for distinguished service and the Colonial Police Medal for meritorious service. The father of five died in Goring-by-Sea, West Sussex, in 1998, aged 69.

John Turner, a former chief superintendent, revealed that there was a serious drug problem among workers on board the *Queen Elizabeth*. Men converting the liner were high on heroin. Turner was among a group of marine police who were invited to tour the ship during the work.

He recalled:

> The impression we got on our tour was that health and safety measures were virtually non-existent on board. Workmen smoked everywhere. Tobacco and heroin were evident in all parts of the ship. Cheap Chinese cigarettes were most popular but there were also tell-tale signs of foil used by drug addicts. We thought afterwards that it was not surprising the ship caught fire!

At the time he was a superintendent and Divisional Commander for Islands Division. On 8 January 1972 he was returning to harbour from Lantau Island and saw the liner bathed in 'a gorgeous sunset' and took several photographs. The *Queen Elizabeth* would have less than a day to live. The next day he returned to the scene in police launch No. 3 as part of the rescue. He still had his camera – and this time took pictures of a blazing *Queen Elizabeth*.[13]

CHAPTER 20

Rioting in the Streets

The police investigation was inconclusive, so who was probably responsible for destroying the *Queen Elizabeth* in 1972? It is necessary to visit the year 1967 and an artificial flower factory in Kowloon, and to examine the influence of Communists in Hong Kong and the power of Beijing.

On 6 May 1967 there were disturbances outside the artificial flower factory after bosses tried to impose tougher working conditions. Police were called and twenty-one people were arrested. The next day the colony's pro-Communist Federation of Trade Unions (FTU) became involved, making five demands – the release of those arrested, the punishment of those responsible, the payment of compensation, a guarantee of workers' safety and a pledge that police would not interfere in labour disputes. It would signal the start of months of civil disorder, with riots and killings, and fears that China would invade Hong Kong.

The swift intervention of the FTU was more a reflection of what was happening on the political front in China than on any concerns about sweatshop labour in Hong Kong. At this time Mao Tse-tung's China was in turmoil, with Red Guards on the rampage. As one commentator put it:

Mao Tse-tung's Great Proletarian Cultural Revolution had unleashed thousands of Red Guards to purge those opposed to his leadership. Looking and listening over the border through the eyes and ears of Radio Peking, Hong Kong's nine Communist newspapers, and the tales of returning comrades, Hong Kong's Communist leaders grew increasingly fearful. They realised that had they been living in China they would have been quickly branded as 'revisionists', publicly humiliated and purged. All rubbed hands with the capitalists each day; for all, profit was the key concern ... As the reverberations from the Cultural Revolution grew ever louder, the colony's Communists frantically searched for a way to proclaim themselves true Maoists, to prove their revolutionary purity, and to forestall their own purge and possible recall to China.[1]

The Hong Kong Communists had been encouraged by two recent events. On 15 November 1966 there was a scuffle between police and demonstrators at the site of an illegal Communist school in the Portuguese colony of Macau, west of Hong Kong. The dispute escalated, and eight Chinese were shot dead and more than 100 injured before order was restored. Local Communist leaders demanded public apologies by Macau's governor, the sacking of officials and compensation for the deaths and injuries. The Chinese government backed the demands and also requested the handing over of seven Taiwanese agents who had been arrested in 1963. The Portuguese government capitulated and effectively lost control of Macau. The second event involved the Hong Kong Seamen's Union. In early 1967 it forced Royal Interocean Lines to apologise publicly and sack the captain of one of its ships who had shot and wounded four Chinese crewmen in Australia. Hong Kong Governor Sir David Trench, MacLehose's predecessor, observed:

> Pro-Communist workers in a number of other companies began to put pressure on their managements and a new spirit of militancy amongst the rank and file became obvious. At the same time it became clear that pro-Communist leaders had released the tight control which they had hitherto exercised over their union members and were, in accordance with the precepts of the Cultural Revolution, allowing the 'masses' greater freedom to 'struggle'. The pro-Communist press was also becoming increasingly abusive, attacking the government on a variety of grounds ...[2]

After the showdown at the artificial flower factory it did not take long for the dispute to escalate. On 11 May there were further clashes, which saw the arrest of 143 people. Demonstrations involving 'paid hooligans' were staged outside courts when those who had been held appeared to face charges. Soon the number of arrests totalled 556, and sixty-seven people were injured, twenty-eight of them police. A bystander was killed by a stone.

It seemed that China might be trying to do another Macau. On 15 May Beijing condemned Britain and the Hong Kong authorities for 'acts of brutal suppression and fascist atrocities in collusion with the United States'. It supported the demands of the Communist-led unions in the colony but, despite all the chaos in China, Mao's regime knew that it needed to tread carefully – a lot of money was at stake. Hong Kong was an important source of foreign exchange. For years the Communist regime had been building a network of businesses and banks in the colony, and in 1967 more than US$500 million a year was flowing into the Bank of China in Hong Kong, plus around $85 million from Chinese living abroad.[3]

The troubles had been confined to north and east Kowloon, but on 16 May they shifted to Hong Kong Island. Pro-Communist delegations, including the so-called All Circles Anti-Persecution Committee, appeared at the gates of Government House, demanding 'in an offensive and peremptory way' to see the governor. 'When this was refused, the temper of the demonstrators became hotter,' Trench reported.

> The numbers of delegations quickly grew and their members became increasingly arrogant, demanding and noisy. Quantities of posters were affixed to the gate at the entrance of Government House grounds. By 20 May crowds of over 3,000 were involved and, being denied immediate access to Government House, spread out into the city creating trouble wherever they went, egged on by inflammatory and anti-European broadcasts over loudspeakers from Communist-owned concerns, particularly the Bank of China. The climax came on 22 May when a major trial of strength took place. Twice the crowds tried to break through the police cordons round Government House and a well planned but poorly executed attempt was made to dramatise police brutality by the manufacture of false victims and the maximum exploitation of real casualties. Elsewhere in the city dangerous crowds built up and traffic was brought to a standstill when bus drivers abandoned their vehicles blocking all the major roads, while there was renewed trouble in Kowloon.

Many demonstrators carried Mao's Little Red Book and shouted quotations from it. Order was restored after a night curfew in the north of Hong Kong Island and the banning of marches and meetings without police permission. The total number of arrests rose to 816, with 106 people injured, 35 of them police. Trench noted that the police had behaved with 'exemplary restraint'.

Special Branch of the Hong Kong Police produced a report on the threats and how they could be countered. It identified the Federation of Trade Unions and the Hong Kong Office of the Xinhua News Agency as the key organisations behind unrest, but pointed out that they would almost certainly be acting under the control of Beijing. Labour, propaganda and political action were the three main targets. Of the first, the report said:

> The Communists have a wide choice of action in the field of labour and, by agitation, could spread disaffection in many sectors of essential services. However, they would probably choose to avoid, initially at least, any action where the weight of its effect would fall on the Chinese population, since they would be reluctant to be charged with causing hardship to the local population whose interests they claim to champion.[4]

Special Branch identified a particularly sensitive threat:

Communists in Hong Kong have the capacity to organise public demonstrations and the manpower to present a considerable problem to the police. One of their most effective weapons is the use of schoolchildren, indoctrinated in left-wing schools, full of the enthusiasm of youth and armed with the invincible Thoughts of Mao Tse-tung. An organised march by children from left-wing schools, on Government House for example, would pose an extremely difficult problem for the police, on tactical as well as humanitarian grounds. This particular manoeuvre was used to great effect in Macau and the efficacy of this means of 'persuasion' cannot have been lost on the leaders of the left-wing here who, during the past few months, have made a close and detailed study of the 'Macau campaign'. The participation of schoolchildren in any demonstration of protest is a severe handicap to police action, and one which the left-wing can use to make more effective their harassing tactics designed to reduce morale in police and government.[5]

Special Branch stressed the need for the 'utmost restraint' in dealing with demonstrations, particularly those involving children, but pointed out that the authorities could not hold back, as this would be seen as a sign of weakness and 'matters might easily get out of hand'. The report said:

When it is known that children are to be used for such purposes, it is essential that the full force of government's information media be brought into play and parents be cautioned against allowing their children to be used for political purposes, making it clear at the same time that all who break the law, children as well as adults, will be treated with due process.[6]

On 23 May, shortly after the Special Branch report was circulated to senior government officials, the Communists switched tactics to the labour field, which had been identified as the first main target. A series of strikes began in all public transport and utility companies 'as well as in other concerns where Communist influence predominated'.

Trench acknowledged that he was now battling to preserve public confidence. And he was well aware that he could not give Beijing an excuse to invade Hong Kong. The turmoil in China itself was also an important factor:

Accounts of disorder approaching anarchy continue to come in. It may become increasingly difficult for Peking to exercise firm control over local Communist hotheads, both here and in Kwangtung [Guangdong, a province on the southern coast of China]. There is always the possibility that extremists in Canton might try to come to the aid of their fellow countrymen here, in defiance of Peking. However, the Chinese army is the authoritative body in Kwangtung and it exercises firm control over the border area.

GARDEN WITH A VIEW: The *Queen Elizabeth* sails past the grounds of a hotel at East Cowes on the Isle of Wight. (*J. & C. McCutcheon*)

TAKING ON FUEL: An Esso tanker alongside the liner in Southampton. (*J. & C. McCutcheon*)

TIGHT SPOT: The *Queen Mary* manoeuvring at Clydebank.
(*J. & C. McCutcheon*)

UNDER WATCHFUL EYES: The *Queen Mary* passing the cruiser HMS *Sheffield* during
a 1955 voyage. On board was the Shah of Persia. (*J. & C. McCutcheon*)

IN DRY DOCK: The *Queen Mary*'s bow does not have the same rake as the *Queen Elizabeth*'s. (*J. & C. McCutcheon*)

THE DODGY BUYERS: Robert Miller and Charles Williard, two of the Americans whose original purchase of the *Queen Elizabeth* ended in fiasco.

Above left: CUNARD'S BOSS: Sir Basil Smallpeice trained as an accountant and he was unsentimental when it came to selling his ships. (*Cunard Archives, University of Liverpool*)

Above right: GANGSTER: Angelo Bruno, head of the Philadelphia Mafia, was friendly with the American businessmen who bought the *Queen Elizabeth*. He would end up being murdered.

OPPOSITION: Commodore Geoffrey Marr was critical of Cunard's decision to sell the *Queen Elizabeth*, believing she could have remained in service for several years. (*Cunard Archives, University of Liverpool*)

FAREWELL: The Queen Mother leaving the *Queen Elizabeth* accompanied by Sir Basil Smallpeice in Southampton on 6 November 1968. She had launched the ship in 1938 and this would be her last visit. (*Cunard Archives, University of Liverpool*)

THE ROCK'S SALUTE: Royal Air Force jets pay tribute as the liner sails away from Gibraltar on her final cruise in November 1968. (*Luis Photos, Gibraltar*)

SAD GOODBYE: Only a few people gather on the shore as the liner leaves Southampton for the last time on 29 November 1968, heading for her new home in Florida. She goes without ceremony and Commodore Marr's wife describes it as a 'shameful departure'. (*Southern Daily Echo, Southampton*)

NEW HOME: The liner at Port Everglades, Florida. She arrived on 8 December 1968 to a warm welcome but her stay would not be a happy one. (*J. & C. McCutcheon*)

Above and below: CHALLENGE: Television documentary maker Alan Whicker interviewing C. Y. Tung in Hong Kong in November 1971 about his plans to restore the *Queen Elizabeth* as the world's greatest liner. The tycoon, a supporter of Taiwan, admitted he was having problems with his Communist-led workers. (*ITV Yorkshire Picture Archive*)

HOURS TO LIVE: John Turner, a superintendent in the marine police, took this picture of the *Queen Elizabeth* in her new colours on 8 January 1972 as she was bathed in 'a gorgeous sunset' in Hong Kong harbour. The next day he returned to the scene as part of the emergency, taking more photographs – of the ship in her death throes. These pictures are published for the first time. (*John Turner*)

DESPERATE FIGHT: The fireboat *Alexander Grantham* spraying jets of water on the port side of the blazing ship on 9 January 1972. (*John Turner*)

DOOMED: Bow shot of the *Queen Elizabeth* taken from marine police launch No. 3. (*John Turner*)

ENGULFED: The liner can barely be seen on the right as huge clouds of smoke pour from the ship, fanned by the wind. (*John Turner*)

BURNING FROM STEM TO STERN: The *Queen Elizabeth* before she capsized. Inset, the two warning light panels from the liner's main fire station. They were recovered from the wreck and are on display at the Aberdeen Boat Club, Hong Kong. On the day of the

emergency, the duty fireman was not at his post when many of the warning lights started flashing. (*Main image, J. & C. McCutcheon*)

Above and below: LYING FORLORN: The rusting wreck of the *Queen Elizabeth* in Hong Kong harbour was a sad sight for several years. Work to remove the ship with cutting gear and explosives did not start until December 1973 and the operation was abandoned in March 1979 as too dangerous. Some 23,000 tons of the liner remain buried in the harbour. (*J. & C. McCutcheon*)

Above left: POLICE CHIEF: Superintendent Charles Mayger was put in charge of the criminal investigation in July 1972 after the court of inquiry ruled that the *Queen Elizabeth* had been the target of an arson attack.

Above right: 'KOJAK': Detective Chief Inspector Derek Bere, who played a key role in the investigation but made no arrests, receiving the Colonial Police Medal for meritorious service from Hong Kong Governor Sir Murray MacLehose in a 1977 ceremony.

COLONIAL SPLENDOUR: The headquarters of the marine police in Kowloon, where the investigation was based.

SHAKE ON IT: President Nixon's historic meeting with Chairman Mao in Beijing on 21 February 1972, six weeks after the *Queen Elizabeth*'s destruction.

Above left: GO-BETWEEN: Nixon's special envoy, Henry Kissinger, who had secret talks with the Chinese Communists on the future of Taiwan.

Above right: CONTROVERSIAL: C. H. Tung took over his father's shipping empire and was picked by Communist China to be Hong Kong's first chief executive in 1997 after the British handover.

NEW STAR: The *Queen Elizabeth 2* in Southampton in 1969, months after the *Queen Elizabeth* left the port for the last time on her way to Florida. (*J. & C. McCutcheon*)

REBORN: Cunard's new *Queen Elizabeth*. The ship was named by Her Majesty Queen Elizabeth II in a ceremony in Southampton on 11 October 2010. (*Cunard*)

He warned:

> The crisis is by no means over. We have weathered the initial storm pretty well; and, at the time of writing, appear to have forced the Communists to think again. This, however, the local hard core are doing with a malevolence probably enhanced by their initial failures. The keys to the future lie in maintaining Hong Kong's confidence in itself; in maintaining the confidence of the world outside in us – for if our economy fails, all fails with it – and in our ability to continue to do business; and, finally, in the attitudes towards us of a China in convulsions.[7]

In London, Prime Minister Harold Wilson was pleased with Trench's handling of the crisis. A message to the governor said: 'He has been particularly pleased to note from your telegrams how common sense, grace and good humour have been uppermost, despite the gravity of the situation …'[8]

The message was sent one day after a meeting of the Cabinet's defence and overseas policy committee at which the Secretary of State for Commonwealth Affairs, Herbert Bowden, presented a report on Hong Kong. The first point:

> We have always known that Hong Kong was vulnerable. But it is valuable to China and we had assumed that it was in her interests to maintain the status quo. Indeed there has been evidence in the past that the central government have controlled and restrained the Communists in the territory.

The picture had changed dramatically, but how far would China go? There were three possibilities: Beijing was simply trying to score a propaganda victory; it wanted to impose a 'Macao solution'; or it had decided to forsake the economic benefits of the colony and wanted the British to leave. Bowden noted:

> We cannot resist a determined attempt to force us out altogether and we could not tolerate the humiliation of remaining in Hong Kong without effective control. I am convinced that a Macao solution would be unacceptable.

It was important not to escalate the crisis, but certain measures needed to be taken. The commando carrier HMS *Bulwark* would soon arrive in Hong Kong. The governor wanted to 'neutralise' buildings being used by the Communist organisers, detain several of the leaders and to close the printing press of the main left-wing newspaper. Interestingly, Bowden pointed out that there was a complete split between the Communist unions and the unions that supported Taiwan. 'The Communist unions are basically disinterested in genuine industrial issues,' he said. But there was an urgent need for labour reforms in the colony.[9]

The arrival of the commando carrier *Bulwark* riled Beijing, which accused Britain of indulging in nineteenth-century gunboat diplomacy. The *People's Daily*, the official newspaper of the Communist Party of China, carried a commentary saying the Chinese people and their Hong Kong compatriots did not 'give a jot for a few broken-down warships', and suggested that Britain had not learnt any lessons from the *Amethyst* incident [the attack on the frigate HMS *Amethyst* on the Yangtze River in 1949] or the Suez affair. The article concluded: 'We once again warn British imperialism, Hong Kong compatriots directed by Mao's thoughts, will certainly fully settle accounts for your terrible crimes in Hong Kong.' Communist newspapers in Hong Kong also joined in the condemnation. The newspaper *Ta Kung Pao* predicted: 'With the strong motherland in the rear and the thoughts of Mao Tse-tung pointing the way, the struggle will definitely be victorious.' Describing *Bulwark* as a paper tiger with one tooth and half a claw, the newspaper *Wen Wei Pao* said the Chinese had never been intimidated, and cited the Opium Wars and the Boxer Rebellion, as well as the *Amethyst* incident, seemingly unaware that all three events had ended in defeat of some kind for China.[10]

June was marred by further protests, strikes, hundreds of arrests and several deaths. It was apparently in revenge for these killings that the most serious attack so far was carried out. On 8 July a police station at Sha Tau Kok on the border was targeted and five policemen were shot dead. The identity of the attackers remains unclear. They may have been militia or soldiers who were not wearing the uniforms of the People's Liberation Army. Chou En-lai is said to have sanctioned the attack.[11] Days later police went on the offensive, raiding buildings and arresting Communists – and seizing weapons. Workers announced a boycott of the port.

The Foreign Office decided it was necessary to carry out another assessment in light of the violence, particularly the attack at Sha Tau Kok. A report noted that the *People's Daily* had described the police and security forces as assassins, warning that 'those who kill people must pay with their lives'. The report said: 'To this extent Peking must be held responsible for the recent wave of violence against the police.' But there was still no evidence that China wanted to take over Hong Kong. Its aim seemed to remain limited to humiliating Britain as it did the Portuguese in Macao. 'Clearly we must still avoid creating a situation which will encourage Peking to decide positively to take over Hong Kong since they would almost certainly succeed,' said the report. 'What we must do is to demonstrate conclusively that the present violent tactics are not going to succeed.'[12]

Also keeping a close watch on events was the CIA. The agency questioned the economic wisdom of China's challenge, particularly as its foreign exchange earnings were increasing rapidly:

Almost all of this would be lost if Peking took over the colony, and a significant proportion would go by the board if the Chinese Communists took action short of seizure, which in effect would put Hong Kong out of business.[13]

The firm but measured response of the Hong Kong authorities, which included the closing of three leading Communist newspapers after inflammatory articles, saw a new phase of violence from August – bomb attacks, mainly aimed at shopping centres, police stations, army buildings and public transport.

On 22 August the focus switched to Beijing itself. A crowd of around 10,000, stirred by the crackdown in Hong Kong and a general hatred of foreigners, gathered outside the British Embassy. Diplomats and their wives were prevented from leaving the building by soldiers who said they could not guarantee their safety. Men with petrol cans were seen approaching the embassy, and the crowd rushed forward when a flare was fired, lighting up the night sky. The eighteen men and five women inside the building went to a strong room. Red Guards with battering rams smashed down a wall of the embassy, and soon the building was on fire. Diplomats and their support staff were forced to leave, only to face a mob shouting, 'Kill! Kill!' Punches were thrown, and female Red Guards grabbed at the testes of the men as male comrades ripped clothes from some of the women. After nearly an hour of this treatment the soldiers were persuaded to intervene.

Two days later in Hong Kong a double murder shocked and angered many people. A popular radio presenter, Lam Bun, who had publicly criticised the Communists, was stopped by a group of men posing as road maintenance gang as he drove to work. He and a cousin were doused with petrol and set on fire. They died in hospital. No one was ever arrested.

The CIA returned to the subject of Hong Kong and forecast that the local Communists would step up their efforts to create disorder, encouraged by the sacking of the embassy in Beijing. There was also a warning that the authorities might eventually lose control of the colony:

Renewed Chinese Communist pressure on the British over the situation in Hong Kong raises new questions concerning the immediate future of the colony and the prospects over the longer term. The increasingly fluid situation in Peking and the continuing 'revolutionary' disorder throughout China make confident predictions of Chinese behaviour more difficult than ever. Nevertheless, China's demeanour in the past three months has led us to conclude that the Chinese authorities intended from the outset to keep the Hong Kong issue hot and to continue their support for dissident elements in the colony. We have also concluded that Peking undertook a campaign aimed at gradually eroding the position of the Hong Kong authorities and thus preparing the ground for a new attempt by the local Communists to seize de facto control in a year or so.

The confidence of the colony's business community had been seriously shaken, and capital was beginning to flow out. The CIA warned: 'If a pessimistic trend should develop, the consequences over time would mean stagnation or even ruin for the colony.'[14]

Bomb disposal experts were kept busy and one of them, an army sergeant, lost his life. Some 8,000 suspect bombs were found and more than 1,000 were real. In one bomb attack a seven-year-old girl and her brother, two, were killed playing outside their home in North Point. But by the end of the year the Communist campaign had lost momentum, largely because of the response of the authorities and a public backlash against the violence. The confrontation cost the lives of fifty-one people, including the five policemen who were killed at Sha Tau Kok. More than 800 people were injured, 200 of whom were involved in law enforcement. There were 5,000 arrests and about 2,000 convictions. The police were honoured for the way that they had handled the troubles. They became the Royal Hong Kong Police.

Even by November 1967 it seemed that a degree of calm had returned:

A new generation of Suzie Wongs, more alluring than ever in their mini-cheongsams, still pester fuzzy-cheeked sailors to buy them 'one more' tea (masquerading as whisky). Suits can still be made in 24 hours, and shops with showcases bulging with gold, jade, cameras and watches still offer the luxuries of the world at a fraction of the cost paid elsewhere. The Hong Kong of myth, legend and travel poster lives on.[15]

To a degree. There were still many Maoist slogans urging the inhabitants to 'paint Hong Kong red from the earth to the sky'. But this was a 'people's war' largely without the people.

Little was heard of Communists in Hong Kong in the five years that followed the disturbances. But it would be wrong to assume that their influence had declined. In 1972 it was revealed that the reverse was true, particularly with trade union membership. In early 1968 left-wing unions claimed to have 126,000 members. By July 1972 the number was 150,000, a rise of 24,000. Most of the unions involved were affiliated to the pro-Beijing Federation of Trade Unions. Left-wing newspapers had increased their circulations significantly, and banking and commerce also saw Communist inroads. Three new Communist banks had opened in the past year, and some 20 per cent of banking facilities in Hong Kong were controlled by the left. Of the 3,550 fishing vessels in the Hong Kong fishing fleet, all but 400 had dual registration with China, which meant they were fully under Communist control. Education was another key target. Seventy new schools had been opened by the left since 1968, and 40,000 students were declared Communists.[16]

One Hong Kong newspaper, the *Kung Sheung Daily News*, gave this warning:

There is no sign that the ambitions of Maoists in Hong Kong are being abandoned following the recent diplomatic thaw between Peking and London. They will change their tactics but never their ultimate objectives, which will be pursued according to the exigency of the situation. Like other western countries, Hong Kong has been the target of Peking's recent 'smiling offensive' in an effort to court favour from the people. This mood of friendliness is diametrically opposite to that displayed in the 1967 episode ... Peking interprets 'friendship' in terms of a total and unconditional submission to it; otherwise it is 'animosity'. A recent survey shows that local Communists have succeeded in stepping up their infiltration into banking, trade and trade unions since the 1967 disturbances ... These findings point to the fact that the Communists are pursuing a double-faced strategy with the ultimate aim of controlling our economy, finance, education and industries. The colony's security will be jeopardised if only half of this malicious plot comes into fruition. Compared with their tactics in 1967, this is far more wicked. Instead of advocating open rebellion, they are trying to subjugate Hong Kong by strangling its throat.[17]

CHAPTER 21

Tricky Dicky

In 1967 the leader of the People's Republic of China, Mao Tse-tung, viewed the United States of America as a long-standing enemy. Korea, Vietnam and especially Taiwan were major obstacles, on ideological and military grounds. But four years later the manipulative Mao was ready for one of his spectacular somersaults. His long and expensive campaign to make Maoism a force in world politics had flopped, and he was fearful of the might of the Soviet Union and the growing economic power of Japan. Someone else was also in somersault mood – Tricky Dicky, President Richard Nixon, whose early political life had been notable for its attacks on Communism. The game of table tennis is popularly thought to have been the catalyst for one of the most significant changes of the twentieth century, but the so-called ping-pong diplomacy was simply a convenient way of explaining a process that had been gathering pace for some time.

Nixon, who took office as president in January 1969, had outlined a strategy to embrace China nearly two years earlier. He saw Mao as key to ending the war in Vietnam, peace with honour, as he would promise the voters. He also believed that China, with its huge population, deserved a place on the world stage. And he was keen to woo the Soviet Union to secure a strategic arms limitation agreement. Nixon believed that better relations with China would increase his leverage with Moscow. Mao was receptive to American overtures, though Beijing would continue to direct its rhetorical hostility at Uncle Sam for a long time. It was important not to show too much outward enthusiasm, especially as it might baffle the Chinese people, who had been brought up on a diet of propaganda denouncing 'American aggressors and their running dogs'. Nixon was not above baffling his own nation. In early 1969 he had a meeting with Charles de Gaulle and asked the French president to inform the Chinese leadership that the US was going to withdraw from Vietnam 'come what may'. Shortly afterwards he declared that China was the 'greatest threat' to world peace. His efforts to end the Vietnam War saw the US invade Cambodia in the spring of 1970, an attack that was supposed to secure a settlement from a position of strength. The Chinese were not impressed.

The picture began to change in October 1970. Nixon's national security adviser, Henry Kissinger, had been trying to establish channels with Beijing using the Romanian and Pakistani governments, which were friendly with the US and China. On 25 October Pakistan's President Yahya Khan was invited to the White House for talks. Yahya was described as 'tough, direct and with a good sense of humour. He talks in a very clipped way, is a splendid product of Sandhurst and affects a sort of social naivete but is probably much more complicated than this'. Yahya was on good terms with the Chinese premier, Chou En-lai, and he was asked to establish secret links between the US and China 'to enable the parties to say what was really on their minds and yet have absolute discretion'.[1] Two months later there was an encouraging response from Chou. He indicated that Mao would be interested in discussions that would bring about a high-level meeting in Beijing. Surprisingly, the US was making promises before any talks had taken place:

The meeting in Peking would not be limited only to the Taiwan question but would encompass other steps designed to improve relations and reduce tensions between our two countries. With respect to the US military presence on Taiwan, however, you should know that the policy of the United States Government is to reduce progressively its military presence in the region of East Asia and the Pacific as tensions in this region diminish.[2]

In January 1971 Nixon and Kissinger heard via the Romanians that the president would be welcome in Beijing. But Chou made one thing clear:

There is only one outstanding issue between us – the US occupation of Taiwan. The PRC [People's Republic of China] has attempted to negotiate on this issue in good faith for 15 years. If the US has a desire to settle the issue and a proposal for its solution, the PRC will be prepared to receive a US special envoy in Peking. This message has been reviewed by Chairman Mao and Lin Piao. [Mao's named successor, who died in a mysterious plane crash in September 1971 amid reports of a failed coup attempt][3]

Like Mao, Nixon was reluctant to appear enthusiastic. 'I believe we may appear too eager,' he told Kissinger. 'Let's cool it.' Then came the ping-pong diplomacy. In March 1971 the Chinese sent a table tennis team to the world championships in Japan. It was unusual because the Cultural Revolution had stopped such visits. The Chinese team had been instructed not to shake hands with the Americans. However, newspaper photographs showed an American player shaking hands with the Chinese men's champion. It led to Mao inviting the US team to China, although initially he turned down the idea. The Chinese player was not punished and ended up being described as a 'diplomat'. Of such minor happenings are momentous events born. The invitation generated worldwide publicity. Mao was delighted and so was Nixon, who now saw a presidential visit to Beijing as a smart move in the run-up to 1972's White House election. According to Kissinger, the president was 'excited to the point of euphoria'. And Mao, the revolutionary, after all the turmoil at home and abroad, the millions of deaths, was about to find himself on the world stage in the most peaceful way possible.

Chou told the US table tennis team that its visit to Beijing had opened a new page in Sino-American relations. China, of course, had an agenda, as a State Department intelligence briefing pointed out:

> Peking's most immediate consideration in adopting 'people's diplomacy' toward the US is presumably a belief that a show of reasonableness will fuel its current drive for international recognition and improve prospects for allocation of the China seat in the United Nations to the PRC this fall. But the more flexible approach will also enhance Peking's ability to affect the emerging four-power inter-relationship in East Asia … In addition, Peking presumably hopes that Taipei's predictably anguished reaction will contribute to the PRC's long-standing – and strikingly unsuccessful – effort to undermine morale on Taiwan and cause the Nationalist Government to collapse.[4]

In April 1971 Nixon told the American Society of Newspaper Editors that there were two long-term goals – a normalisation of relations between the US and China, and the ending of Beijing's isolation from the world community. Later that month Kissinger received a message from Chou – via Pakistan's President Yahya – that

> the Chinese Government reaffirms its willingness to receive publicly in Peking a special envoy of the President of the US (for instance, Mr Kissinger) or the US Secretary of State or even the President of the US himself for direct meeting and discussions. Of course, if the US President considers that the time is not yet right the matter may be deferred to a later date.[5]

That evening Nixon and Kissinger had an animated phone conversation about the person they might send as a special envoy.

Nixon: How about Bush? [George H. W. Bush, ambassador to the United Nations and US president from 1989 until 1993]

Kissinger: Absolutely not, he is too soft and not sophisticated enough.

Nixon: I thought that myself.

After dismissing other candidates Nixon suggested Nelson Rockefeller, the governor of New York:

> Nelson – the Chinese would consider him important and he would be – could do a lot for us in terms of the domestic situation. No, Nelson is a wild hare running around.

> Kissinger: I think for one operation I could keep him under control. To them a Rockefeller is a tremendous thing.

> Nixon: Sure. Well, keep it in the back of your head.

> Kissinger: Bush would be too weak.

> Nixon: I thought so too but I was trying to think of somebody with a title.

> Kissinger: Nelson has possibilities.

> Nixon: A possibility, yeah. Of course, that would drive State [the State Department] up the wall.

> Kissinger: He would take someone from State along but he despises them so much he will take our direction and I would send someone from our staff to go along.

> Nixon: Send Haig [Brigadier General Alexander Haig, deputy assistant to the president for national security affairs]. Really, he's tough.

> Kissinger: And he knows Haig.

> Nixon: Henry, it wouldn't have happened if you hadn't stuck to your guns. We played a game and we got a little break. It was done skilfully and now we will wait a couple of weeks.[6]

Nixon responded to Chou's invitation on 10 May. Yes, he was willing to come to Beijing. It was a historic decision. Nixon suggested sending Kissinger for talks with the Chinese premier to pave the way. Nixon's national security adviser could fly to a location in China that was a convenient distance from Pakistan. But everything must be conducted in secret:

> Dr Kissinger would be authorised to discuss the circumstances which would make a visit by President Nixon most useful, the agenda of such a meeting,

the time of such a visit and to begin a preliminary exchange of views on all subjects of mutual interest.

It was stressed:

> It is proposed that the precise details of Dr Kissinger's trip, including location, duration of stay, communication and similar matters be discussed through the good offices of President Yahya Khan. For secrecy, it is essential that no other channel be used. It is also understood that this first meeting between Dr Kissinger and high officials of the People's Republic of China be strictly secret.

It was agreed that Kissinger would fly from Pakistan to Beijing in July. President Yahya had promised that 'absolute foolproof arrangements will be made by us and he need have no anxiety on this count'. On 1 July Nixon, Kissinger and Haig held a meeting at the White House to discuss how the Beijing talks should be conducted. Nixon said Kissinger should build on three fears – fear of what the president might do in the event of a continued stalemate in the Vietnam War, fear of a resurgent and militaristic Japan, and fear of the Soviet threat on China's flank. Taiwan, of course, remained a big issue. Nixon

> emphasised that the discussions with the Chinese cannot look like a sellout of Taiwan. He instructed Dr Kissinger not to open up with a discussion of what we've done and the fact that we will not need troops there forever, but rather to restructure that point by emphasising that the Nixon doctrine provides for help to those nations who help themselves and thus it will not be essential for our military presence to remain in some areas forever ... In sum, the president asked him to review the entire discussion of the Taiwan issue so that we would not appear to be dumping on our friends and so that we would be somewhat more mysterious about our overall willingness to make concessions in this area.[7]

On 9 July Kissinger met Chou in Beijing. On Taiwan, the premier was tough but 'clearly understood the need for time on the political side'. He pointed out that Nixon was 'not responsible for the mistakes of the past which he inherited'. The next day Chou returned to the subject, insisting that the US had to recognise that only the government of the People's Republic of China represented the Chinese people, that Taiwan belonged to China, and that the Americans could not support a policy of 'two Chinas' or 'one China, one Taiwan'. He was pressing for normal relations between China and the US.

Kissinger said:

A visit by President Nixon to Chairman Mao has, of course, a considerable substantive significance, but it also has a tremendous symbolic significance because it would make clear that normal relations were inevitable …

He also conceded:

I am sure the president would be prepared to repeat to Chairman Mao, as I have told you, that we will not support the Taiwan independence movement. I am sure he will repeat that we will not support one China, one Taiwan.

Chou: Nor a policy of two Chinas.

Kissinger: I am sure that the president will repeat he will not support a two Chinas solution.

It followed that 'Taiwan belongs to China'. Kissinger added: 'Therefore, the only issue that we will have to leave until after the [US presidential] elections is the formal acceptance of the People's Republic of China as the sole legitimate government of China.' He also indicated that the US would not object if China took Taiwan's seat at the United Nations, providing there was a two-thirds majority vote.

There was another point:

The only president who could conceivably do what I am discussing with you is President Nixon. Other political leaders might use more honeyed words, but would be destroyed by what is called the China lobby in the US if they ever tried to move even partially in the direction which I have described to you. President Nixon, precisely because his political support comes from the centre and right of centre, cannot be attacked from that direction, and won't be attacked by the left in a policy of moving toward friendship with the People's Republic of China. You can see that I am speaking to you with great frankness.[8]

The talks continued on 11 July, and in a message to Haig at the White House Kissinger revealed: 'They were the most intense, important and far reaching of my White House experience.' The details were too sensitive to put in a cable, and he stressed:

Other side made special point about need to keep word meticulously. They will not understand even a minor leak and will consider it deliberate affront and proof of unreliability. Please keep PR types ignorant. A leak or even a hint is almost certain to blow everything. I cannot be too strong on this.

Soon afterwards Kissinger sent a lengthy assessment of the talks to Nixon. His discussions with Chou and senior Chinese officials had lasted a total of 21 hours. He stressed:

> Simply giving you a straightforward account of the highlights of our talks, potentially momentous as they were, would do violence to an event so shaped by the atmosphere and the ebb and flow of our encounter, or to the Chinese behaviour, so dependent on nuance and style.

Although the talks covered a number of subjects – Nixon's proposed visit, Indochina, relations with the Soviet Union and Japan, arms control, future American-Chinese communications – China's 'fundamental concern' was Taiwan.

Kissinger was clearly taken with Chou:

> He spoke with an almost matter of fact clarity and eloquence. He was equally at home in philosophic sweeps, historical analysis, tactical probing, light repartee. His command of facts, and in particular his knowledge of American events, was remarkable. He insisted in admitting faults in their society, and protesting that their lavish hospitality was only 'what they should do'. There was little wasted motion, either in his words of a man concerned both with the revolutionary fire of the next generation and the massive daily problem of caring for 750 million people, one who endured the tribulations of the Long March and was now inviting the President of the United States to visit his capital. Chou was also genial and urbane, with a refreshing sense of humour ... In short, Chou En-lai ranks with Charles de Gaulle as the most impressive foreign statesman I have met.

It was Chou, of course, who orchestrated the violence in Hong Kong in 1967, which included the killing of police officers. Kissinger, however, did show some realism about his hosts:

> These people were on their best behaviour ... Almost all of the positive qualities we saw are Chinese, not Communist, and can be found in Taiwan or Singapore or San Francisco. Much of their ideology is distasteful, and living in China today would be a numbing, depressing experience.

Kissinger outlined in detail China's demands over Taiwan. The Chinese wanted the withdrawal of all American forces from Taiwan and the Taiwan Strait. It was explained that the US had forces in Taiwan for two reasons – the defence of Southeast Asia, especially Vietnam, and to protect the island. When the Vietnam War ended, the relevant forces could be withdrawn, but any decision on those for the protection of Taiwan 'would depend on the general state of our relations with the PRC'. Two-thirds of the forces in Taiwan were linked to the Vietnam War.

Kissinger told Nixon:

> As a final point on Taiwan, Chou noted that the agreement on your meeting with Chairman Mao would 'shake the world'. Afterwards Chiang Kai-shek might collude with the USSR or Japan, and would demonstrate against you. Chiang would try to operate independently of the US. Chou knew this from his previous associations with Chiang, and the US 'should beware'.

Kissinger had obviously enjoyed the hospitality and he got a bit carried away in his summary of the trip:

> Those 48 hours, and my extensive discussions with Chou in particular, had all the flavour, texture, variety and delicacy of a Chinese banquet. Prepared from the long sweep of tradition and culture, meticulously cooked by hands of experience, and served in splendidly simple surroundings, our feast consisted of many courses, some sweet and some sour, all interrelated and forming a coherent whole. It was a total experience, and one went away, as after all good Chinese meals, very satisfied and not at all satisfied.

He predicted that the process the US had embarked on would send shock waves around the world. It might panic the Soviet Union into 'sharp hostility'. It might shake Japan 'loose from its heavily American moorings'. And it would cause a violent upheaval in Taiwan. There would be a major impact on other Asian allies such as Korea and Thailand. But it would be wrong to continue the isolation of one quarter of the world's 'most talented people and a country rich in past achievements and future potential'.

On Taiwan, Kissinger conceded that a damage limitation exercise would be necessary 'by reaffirming our diplomatic relations and mutual defence treaty even while it becomes evident that we foresee a political evolution over the coming years'.[9] Reaffirming diplomatic relations and the mutual defence treaty? Is that what Mao and Chou were expecting when Kissinger said the US would reject a 'two Chinas' policy? The question of Taiwan was not about to be solved quickly …

On 15 July 1971 Kissinger was back in Washington for a special meeting with Nixon and senior members of the White House staff. Nixon opened the meeting and explained why it was important to continue to keep the China mission secret – even from 'our good friends the British'. The Chinese had been happy to make developments public, but the president was convinced that secrecy remained the key to success. On the question of leaks, Nixon, who was never comfortable with media coverage, advised: 'The press has the least respect for the babblers. They have the most contempt for the people with diarrhoea of the mouth.' It had been a remarkable turn of events in a short time. The 'chief militant aggressive revolutionary power' was sitting down with the 'chief capitalist power'. Nixon acknowledged that Taiwan would be a problem.

Kissinger also emphasised the need for secrecy: 'Let me make one point, though it may seem ungracious. The most impressive thing we can do as far as the Chinese are concerned is to shut up.' He referred to the part played by Pakistan's President Yahya: 'The cloak and dagger exercise in Pakistan arranging the trip was fascinating. Yahya hasn't had so much fun since the last Hindu massacre!'

Newspaper speculation that the US had given China assurances on Taiwan was 'total nonsense'. Total nonsense? Chou had made specific points about what China wanted from the US over Taiwan, and Kissinger certainly gave assurances. Later, in his memoirs, Kissinger suggested that the subject of Taiwan had been 'mentioned only briefly'. He was corrected when the official records were released in 2002 and said: 'The way I expressed it was very unfortunate and I regret it.' It was also made clear to the Chinese that the US would give full diplomatic recognition by January 1975 if Nixon won re-election.

At the White House meeting Kissinger was asked if the British and French had much influence with the Chinese and he was dismissive:

> I talked with Chou for 20 hours. This is more than all the western ambassadors put together have talked with Chou En-lai in all the years they have had diplomatic relations. Ambassadors don't get to see Chou En-lai. The Soviets have a deputy foreign minister in China negotiating on the border issue but he has never seen Chou. The Chinese talk when they have something to say. Frankly, I sensed that the other western nations are of no account to them. They use the western Europeans. They're not interested in abstract friendship. The fact that the British recognised them in 1951 has no impact that I can see.[10]

The announcement that Nixon would visit China was made on 15 July 1971 at news conferences held simultaneously in Washington and Beijing. The trip would be made at an 'appropriate date' before May 1972. It shocked Taiwan, and the next day it lodged a strong protest and recalled its ambassador to Washington. Politicians in Taipei accused Nixon – seen as staunchly anti-Communist – of double-crossing their country.[11] Nixon sent California's governor, Ronald Reagan, to Taiwan as a special presidential envoy to explain the new policy to Chiang Kai-shek. Reagan was a long-time supporter of Taiwan, and he met an angry Chiang.

In April 1970 Chiang's son, Chiang Ching-kuo, who held the post of vice premier, had made an official visit to Washington. There was a meeting with Nixon, and the president reaffirmed his support for Taiwan, pointing out that he had been a friend for 23 years. 'The United States will never sell you down the river,' he said.

Nixon's planned visit to Beijing also took the Soviet Union by surprise – with an unexpected result. Four days after the announcement Moscow sent an invitation to Nixon, and stalled arms talks were reopened.

It is worth repeating that the announcement of President Nixon's visit to Beijing to meet Mao Tse-tung was made on 15 July 1971. The *Queen Elizabeth* arrived in Hong Kong harbour … on 15 July.

CHAPTER 22

Crisis at the UN

Something else of significance happened on 15 July 1971. That day saw seventeen countries begin a move aimed at expelling Taiwan – the Republic of China – from the United Nations and recognising the 'lawful rights' of Mao's People's Republic of China. It was not a new issue. The question of China's representation had become an annual event at the UN. From the early 1960s Albania, led by the Marxist-Leninist Enver Hoxha, had been at the forefront of a campaign to win the vote for Mao, without success because of the opposition of the US and its allies.

Chiang Kai-shek's Republic of China was one of the founding members of the United Nations in 1945, with a seat on the Security Council. Four years later the Communists seized power in the mainland and Chiang and his supporters fled to Taiwan, which had been under Japanese control until the end of the Second World War. The Japanese ceded Taiwan and other islands to the Republic of China as part of the price for peace. Chiang, from his island fortress, continued to insist that his government, not the Communists, represented all Chinese people.

Henry Kissinger had told Chou En-lai in Beijing that the US would not object to UN recognition of the People's Republic of China, providing there was a two-thirds majority. Chou did not embrace the concession with great enthusiasm, pointing out that China had lived without the UN for many years. Nevertheless it was an important step, and it would give the US a major headache. By September 1971 the campaign in support of Mao's China was gathering momentum. Kissinger had indicated in his talks with Chou that the US would not support a 'two Chinas' or 'one China, one Taiwan' policy, but its position at the UN was not so clear cut. It wanted China to be admitted – and it wanted Taiwan to remain. George H. W. Bush, the US ambassador to the UN, argued the point when he appeared before delegates on 18 October 1971. Once again, Albania had tabled a resolution in support of Mao's China.

'For 22 years the question of representation of the great nation of China in the United Nations has been a major international issue – a troublesome and intractable one,' said Bush. 'In the history of this issue the year 1971 can be, and ought to be, a year of change and decision.' But a dilemma remained:

> For 21 years the assembly faced, on this question, only two stark alternatives. We could either leave things as they were, with no representation here for the enormous population of the Chinese mainland, or we could agree to a formula which, in a single stroke, would make room for the People's Republic of China by expelling the Republic of China, a member and we all agree in good standing. As to this latter step, the assembly has always been aware of its drastic nature and its fateful implications for the UN itself – and year after year this assembly refused to take this step, even though it meant prolonging the absence of the People's Republic of China from this organisation. So the situation remained frozen.

There was a third possibility, however. It was 'perfectly possible' for the UN to accommodate both governments. Bush said the US had consulted most of the member countries, and he put forward a draft resolution that 'affirms the right of representation of the People's Republic of China' and 'affirms the continued right of representation of the Republic of China'. The 'most realistic, pragmatic and equitable solution' would allow Taiwan to remain in the General Assembly and give China a seat on the Security Council. All the people of China would be represented. Bush insisted that such a solution would not divide China into two separate states.

> It does not take either a 'two Chinas' position, or a 'one China, one Taiwan' position, or in any other way seek to dismember China. It is simply founded on the reality of the present situation as we all know it to be, but it does not seek to freeze this situation for the future. On the contrary, it expressly states in the preamble that a solution should be sought without prejudice to a future settlement.

Bush pointed out that in the 26-year history of the UN no member had been expelled. In fact, the membership had grown during that time from fifty-one to 131 nations.[1]

Two days later, on 20 October, US Secretary of State William Rogers weighed in with an analysis arguing the case for Mao's China and Taiwan. He warned the UN:

> It could become the first assembly in United Nations history to take action to expel a member – an action which would have the effect of expelling 14

million people from its councils. The path of expulsion is perilous. To open it for one would be to open it for many.[2]

On 25 October Albania's resolution finally prevailed. The US proposal was rejected. The UN admitted Mao's China and threw out Taiwan. Rogers said the US deeply regretted the decision to 'expel 14 million people'. He insisted: 'The Republic of China, of course, continues to be a respected and valued member of the international community and the ties between us remain unaffected by the action of the United Nations.'

Right-wing politicians in the US were angered, and there were claims that Resolution 2758 violated the UN charter. On 14 October 336 members of the House of Representatives had sent a petition to Nixon opposing the expulsion of Taiwan, and there were similar expressions of feeling in the Senate.[3] Chiang Kai-shek's government could still claim many friends in the US.

Taiwan's supporters would have appreciated one irony. Albania's resolution at last had been accepted, but the 15 July announcement of Nixon's planned visit to China shocked Enver Hoxha. He sent a message to Beijing saying the invitation to the 'frenzied anti-Communist' was 'incorrect and undesirable'. Relations between two countries quickly deteriorated, with China warning Albania that it could no longer count on aid. By 1973 Hoxha acknowledged that Albania was no longer regarded as the 'faithful special friend'.[4]

On 10 December 1971 Kissinger had a secret meeting with China's newly appointed ambassador to the UN, Huang Hua, at an apartment in New York City. Also there were Bush and Haig and several Chinese officials. The meeting showed how close the Americans and Chinese had become, on the surface at least. Kissinger told Huang:

Just so everyone knows exactly what we do, we tell you about our conversations with the Soviets – we do not tell the Soviets about our conversations with you. In fact, we don't tell our own colleagues that I see you. George Bush is the only person outside the White House who knows I come here.

The main topic of conversation was war between India and Pakistan, which had broken out on 3 December over tensions in East Pakistan, which would soon become Bangladesh. The US and China both supported Pakistan. Nixon feared that the conflict would lead to Soviet expansion in the region. The Soviets were backing India. As a further example of the new friendship between the Americans and Chinese, Kissinger said to Huang:

We are moving a number of naval ships in the west Pacific toward the Indian Ocean – an aircraft carrier accompanied by four destroyers and a tanker, and a helicopter carrier and two destroyers. I have maps here showing the location of the Soviet fleet in the Indian Ocean if you are interested. These are much smaller ships. They are no match for the US ships.[5]

The war ended quickly with a humiliating defeat for Pakistan, and Yahya Khan, the man who had played an important role in bringing about Nixon's visit to China, stepped down as president.

It appeared that Nixon and Kissinger were working well together as president and national security adviser, but they had been harbouring doubts about each other for some time. In December 1971 Nixon was thinking of the possibility of sacking Kissinger. The president was envious of his adviser's growing reputation, the clever charmer who was striding across the world's political stage. But away from the spotlight Kissinger could be gloomy. He was upset by press criticism over the Vietnam War and by his discovery that spies for the Joint Chiefs of Staff were sending back reports on the National Security Council. Two of Nixon's aides, John Ehrlichman and H. R. Haldeman, were concerned about Kissinger's 'mood swings' and the president himself is said to have wondered whether 'psychiatric care' might be necessary.[6]

According to Kissinger, Nixon was a loner who

would hole up in his hideaway office, slump in a chair and write notes on a yellow legal pad. For hours or even days he would shield himself from outsiders, allowing only a small circle of aides to join him in his rambling ruminations.

Nixon would sometimes refer to Kissinger as 'my Jew boy'. Privately, Kissinger referred to the president as 'that madman', 'our drunken friend' and 'the meatball mind'. And he was not impressed with some of the president's aides. He told British ambassador John Freeman in 1970: 'I have never met such a gang of self-seeking bastards in my life. I used to find the Kennedy group unattractively narcissistic, but they were idealists. These people are real heels.'[7]

However, as the clocked ticked down to the momentous visit to China, Nixon and Kissinger found themselves back on speaking terms.

CHAPTER 23

Nixon's Triumph

It was the week that changed the world, President Nixon declared. On 21 February 1972 Nixon arrived in Beijing. He made sure that he was the centre of attention, emerging alone from *Air Force One*. On the journey he had stressed to Kissinger and Secretary of State William Rogers that they were to remain on the plane until he had descended the steps and shaken Chou En-lai's hand. Just to make sure that his instructions were followed, a Secret Service agent blocked the exit. Nixon did not want Kissinger, his celebrity adviser, sharing the limelight. He also took revenge on those despised newspapermen by making sure that the travelling American press corps was weighted in favour of television journalists. His historic visit, the first by a US president to the People's Republic of China, would make good TV back home.

Nixon and his team received a surprise soon after arriving. They were taken to an unscheduled meeting with Mao Tse-tung. To Nixon's dismay there were no cheering crowds on the way to the Chinese leader's residence. As one report put it:

> The cool reception at the airport was duplicated on the drive into the city. Few Chinese were in evidence, and those that were about hardly bothered to glance at the motorcade as it sped along the streets of Peking.[1]

Unknown to the Americans, 78-year-old Mao had been seriously ill with heart problems and a lung infection. But he was still keen to meet Nixon and take his place on the world stage, even though he could barely walk or speak. Officially, Mao had been suffering from bronchitis.[2] Kissinger and Chou attended the meeting but William Rogers, embarrassingly, was excluded. After initial greetings, such a momentous occasion continued with a rather banal exchange in which there was a reference to Chiang Kai-shek.

Nixon: You read a great deal. The prime minister said that you read more than he does.

Mao: Yesterday in the airplane you put forward a very difficult problem for us. You said that what is required to talk about are philosophic problems.

Nixon: I said that because I have read the chairman's poems and speeches, and I knew he was a professional philosopher.

Mao: (Looking at Kissinger) He is a doctor of philosophy?

Nixon: He is a doctor of brains.

Mao: What about asking him to be the main speaker today?

Nixon: He is an expert in philosophy.

Kissinger: I used to assign the chairman's collective writings to my classes at Harvard.

Mao: Those writings of mine aren't anything. There is nothing instructive in what I wrote.

Nixon: The chairman's writings moved a nation and have changed the world.

Mao: I haven't been able to change it. I've only been able to change a few places in the vicinity of Beijing. Our common old friend, Generalissimo Chiang Kai-shek, doesn't approve of this. He calls us Communist bandits. He recently issued a speech. Have you seen it?

Nixon: Chiang Kai-shek calls the chairman a bandit. What does the chairman call Chiang Kai-shek?

Chou: Generally speaking we call them Chiang Kai-shek's clique. In the newspapers sometimes we call him a bandit. We are also called bandits in turn. Anyway, we abuse each other.[3]

From such comments is history shaped. Little of substance was discussed at that meeting, which lasted about an hour. Despite attempts by Nixon to touch on major issues, Mao refused to be pinned down. Afterwards White House press secretary Ronald Ziegler said the two leaders had been involved in a 'serious and frank' discussion.

That evening the president was the guest of honour at a state banquet, which Mao did not attend. Nixon made a flattering reference to the Long March, the episode that came to symbolise the Communists' determination to secure victory over the Nationalists. Nixon said:

> Let us, in these next five days, start a long march together, not in one step but on different roads leading to the same goal – the goal of building a world structure of peace and justice in which all may stand together with equal dignity and in which each nation, large or small, has a right to determine its own form of government, free of outside interference or domination.

Chou was less effusive. The visit 'provides the leaders of the two countries with an opportunity to seek the normalisation of relations between the two countries, and also to exchange views on questions of concern to the two sides'.[4]

The next day the issue of Taiwan did come up in talks between Nixon and Chou. 'We will support any peaceful resolution of the Taiwan issue that can be worked out,' said Nixon. 'And the reduction of the remaining third of our military presence on Taiwan will go forward as progress is made on the peaceful resolution of the problem.' Chou replied that China had waited more than 20 years 'and we can wait a few more years'.

On 24 February Kissinger and Chou tackled the subject once more. The Chinese premier appeared less keen to wait a long time for a solution and said it would be good if the 'liberation' of Taiwan could be achieved during Nixon's next term of office.

At the end of the US president's week-long visit the two countries issued what has become known as the Shanghai communiqué. The statement covered a number of points, including the Vietnam War, Korea and Japan. But Taiwan, of course, remained a key issue, and China said it was the crucial question obstructing the normalisation of relations with the US. It insisted:

> The Government of the People's Republic of China is the sole legal government of China; Taiwan is a province of China which has long been returned to the motherland; the liberation of Taiwan is China's internal affair in which no other country has the right to interfere; and all US forces and military installations must be withdrawn from Taiwan. The Chinese government firmly opposes any activities which aim at the creation of 'one China, one Taiwan', 'one China, two governments', 'two Chinas', an 'independent Taiwan' or advocate that 'the status of Taiwan remains to be determined'.

The communiqué declared that the US

> acknowledges that all Chinese on either side of the Taiwan Strait maintain
> there is but one China and that Taiwan is a part of China. The United States
> government does not challenge that position. It reaffirms its interest in a
> peaceful settlement of the Taiwan question by the Chinese themselves. With
> this prospect in mind, it affirms the ultimate objective of the withdrawal of
> all US forces and military installations from Taiwan. In the meantime, it will
> progressively reduce its forces and military installations on Taiwan as the
> tension in the area diminishes.

Observers have pointed out that the US gave way on Taiwan much more in
talks than the communiqué indicated. Curiously, at a meeting in the Oval
Office of the White House on 26 January, Nixon had reiterated that 'we still
recognize Taiwan and will continue to honour our treaty commitments'. The
US had signed a mutual defence treaty with Taiwan in 1954.

According to US columnist Jack Anderson, Nixon's wooing of Mao's China
left Chiang Kai-shek feeling isolated and embittered. The Nationalist leader
believed he had been double-crossed by an old friend. Anderson pointed out
that over the years Chiang wined, dined and financed Nixon. In 1950 the
generalissimo sent his nephew Louis Kung to California 'with a bankroll of
$100 bills' to boost Nixon's campaign for the Senate. The Chiang regime's
financial house, the National Bank of China, retained a public relations outfit
called Allied Syndicates to help elect Nixon. The Chiangs showered Nixon
with valuable gifts, including several Chinese paintings that used to hang in
the hallway of his fashionable Fifth Avenue apartment in New York City.
Anderson wrote: 'Old Chiang had every reason to believe that Nixon, in the
White House, would continue to be a close friend and dependable ally.'[5]

Tricky Dicky was taken to task by nearly 4,000 university professors in
Taiwan shortly after his arrival in Beijing. In a statement they complained that
'the hands Nixon is shaking in Peiping [one of the Chinese capital's names]
are covered with the blood of the Chinese people and Nixon's American
brothers'. They added:

> The Maoist regime is practically the initiator of the Korean and Vietnamese
> wars, the major source of trouble in the world and the murderer of more
> than several hundred thousands of Americans in the Korean and Vietnamese
> wars.

They expressed deep concern over Nixon's visit 'because of traditional Sino-
American friendship and our common interests in the anti-Communist
cause'.[6]

But Taiwan's unhappiness was outweighed by praise for Nixon's diplomatic triumph. Back home, the president and Kissinger enjoyed the plaudits. Howard Smith of the television network ABC said: 'Mr Nixon deserves credit for a master stroke both opportune and statesmanlike.' Kissinger told a meeting of White House staff: 'What has been started in China can be a turning point in diplomatic history.'

CHAPTER 24

Arson and Politics

A curious thing happened in the wake of the court of inquiry's report into the destruction of the *Queen Elizabeth*. The wreck loomed large in the harbour for a long time. The ship had always attracted attention and she continued to fascinate, but for the wrong reasons. She was a felled giant. Her tortured appearance made her a magnet for tourists, with owners of small boats doing a brisk trade in ferrying out the inquisitive. But in other respects the once great Cunarder completely disappeared from view, leaving behind unanswered questions. Who had been behind the attack? And why? Questions that would produce speculation for decades.

There had been, of course, worldwide coverage of the ship's destruction, and the main Hong Kong newspapers were diligent in reporting the hearings of the court of inquiry. However, after the court gave its verdict in July 1972 few stories about the ship appeared, and those that did usually referred to oil seeping from her, or plans to remove the wreck. The Hong Kong newspapers were not noted for investigative journalism largely, one suspects, because proprietors did not wish to upset anyone with influence in a colony that could feel like a small town, despite its teeming population. It did not pay to ask questions, to make important people lose face, one of the worst things that can happen in Chinese society.

The memory of the *Queen Elizabeth* did produce the odd flourish in print. In August 1973 Derek Davies, the flamboyant editor of the *Far Eastern Economic Review*, saw it as 'one of the great unsolved mysteries'. He wrote:

> So I penned a letter to the Hong Kong police asking how their enquiries into the crime were going, 19 months later. The police replied that their enquiries were 'proceeding' and any results so far were 'confidential'. It looks very much as if the man who incinerated C. Y. Tung's dream will never be brought to justice.[1]

Davies is likely to be proved right, though he seems to be wide of the mark if he thought that one man could have started nine or more fires on what was then the world's largest liner. It is doubtful whether the investigation was even 'proceeding' in August 1973. For one reason or another, 'Kojak', Detective Chief Inspector Derek Bere, lost interest in the inquiry at an early stage. Officially, the file remains open.

According to Hong Kong observers, it was 'the inferno that launched a thousand conspiracy theories'.[2] One thousand may be an exaggeration. Certainly, four main theories have emerged. Stephen Davies, director of the Hong Kong Maritime Museum, said:

> A marine court ruled that the fires were sabotage, and there are several theories on who was behind them. The most popular seems to be that the Communists were taking revenge on C. Y. Tung. Another suggestion is an insurance scam. But I don't think anyone, really, is going to come forward to say anything about that. It was also claimed that workers were unhappy about the ship's refit coming to an end. However, there were at least nine different fires, all literally during a very short period. This was an attack to destroy the ship.

The fourth theory centres on extortion, a crime long associated with the triads.[3]

Was it an alleged insurance fraud? This seems unlikely, even though the ship was fully insured and her value had risen as the refitting progressed. Most of the insurance was placed with Lloyd's of London. By December 1972 C. Y. Tung had been paid more than £3 million but the total bill was likely to be much higher – around £12 million, 'the biggest sum in passenger ship history'.[4] It was estimated that the cost of removing the wreck would be at least £9 million. Tung had also made sure that he was fully covered in the event of his ship becoming a wreck and requiring removal. He took out this insurance with the UK P&I Club. The P&I Clubs are non-profit making mutual insurance associations for shipowners. They trace their history to the eighteenth century, and in 2010 they were covering about 90 per cent of the world's ocean-going tonnage. Tung was not left out of pocket but he had lost his dream and the blaze was a major embarrassment. He was 'a lover of ships', and he had always been in love with the *Queen Elizabeth*.

Days after the disaster Kenneth Milburn, Hong Kong's Director of Marine, commented:

> The acquisition of the ship by C. Y. Tung at the second attempt was the culmination of a long standing and seemingly altruistic desire to see her back in service and engaged in work which would benefit young people and

contribute to international goodwill. Mr Tung is a successful shipowner controlling a large fleet. He is a lover of ships and has a phenomenal grasp of many facets of this complex industry. He is an international figure with offices and business interests in many countries. He is a music lover, a patron of the arts, and seems to derive particular pleasure from the company of his worldwide circle of friends and business associates.[5]

Captain Alan Loynd, a Hong Kong marine consultant, said: 'There were rumours of an insurance fraud, but C. Y. Tung was pretty committed to the project. He had the money. Who was behind the fires remains one of the great mysteries.'[6]

Was it extortion? David Hodson, a former assistant commissioner in the Royal Hong Kong Police, said:

Rackets involving extortion, protection and labour have always been widespread in Hong Kong. People who set up in business and use labour have to live with gangs. Often they come to an accommodation. This applies to the docks. Repair of ships can be a hazardous business, and the use of labour always opens itself to problems. Disputes can be created.[7]

There were a number of rackets involving the conversion of the *Queen Elizabeth*, with sub contractors claiming wages for workers who did not exist. It will be recalled that the first alarm on 9 January 1972 was raised by police launch No. 10 under the command of Inspector Ted Ho Sze-ming. The launch did not just happen to be in the area. That morning it was taking a detective from marine CID to the liner to investigate one of the rackets.[8] Professor Harold Traver, a Hong Kong criminologist, said: 'It is absolutely true about the docks and rackets. Triads, heroin, trafficking, smuggling, theft, unions that were not really unions, and so on was the order of the day.'[9] Triad societies had long been in control of labourers and foremen in the docks. Disturbances would be created if they did not get a share of the profits. But they were not averse to fighting each other, especially in the aftermath of the Second World War:

Throughout 1946-47, frequent clashes occurred between societies seeking to gain control of the various wharves, especially in the Western district where the Wo Shing Tong, Wo Yung Yee and Wo Hop To were the main contenders for power.[10]

Theft was a huge problem and it was not confined to petty pilfering. At one time military stores were a favourite target. Barge-loads of food, building steel and marine diesels, for example, would disappear. Other thefts included 242 cases of revolver ammunition, a motor launch from an Australian destroyer and condenser tubes from the frigate HMS *Amethyst* after her famous escape down the Yangtze River. The smuggling of war materials boomed during the Korean War.[11] But would extortion, a failed attempt, have been a good enough reason to destroy the *Queen Elizabeth*? This seems unlikely.

The theory that disenchanted workers seeking to prolong work on the liner were responsible for the fires was originally put forward by a barrister, R. F. Stone, who represented the Seawise Foundation, an affiliate company of C. Y. Tung's Island Navigation Corporation, at the court of inquiry. On the last day of the hearings in April 1972, he told the court:

> It might be said with some determination that there is neither a shred of evidence nor a comprehensible motive which would suggest any planned political action behind the fire. Indeed there was, of course, no direct evidence with regard to any individual in connection with it. But such a possibility could not be excluded, particularly in a workforce of about 2,000. Many of them must have the cover of leaving the ship about the time the fire started. You have heard evidence about the condition and system in operation – a labour force whose immediate security of employment depended upon a ship which was nearing completion. Working for a sub contractor on piecework or being employed on a daily basis must be more divisive, more prone to rivalries and jealousies than a labour force regularly employed by the same employer. This is not to be alarming or speculative but these are relevant facts. Deliberate act could not be excluded as a possibility and these circumstances tend to make that possibility more probable.[12]

There are several interesting points in the QC's statement. Stone referred to 'the fire', when it was clear that there had been multiple fires. He suggested that many of the workers had the cover of leaving the ship at the time of 'the fire', and pointed the finger of suspicion at 'jealous' men employed by sub contractors. The court had heard of the curious arrangement that allowed workers to go ashore for lunch, usually at 11.30 a.m. But these men were employed by the Island Navigation Corporation. The first of the fires was reported shortly after that time. It was the men working for the sub contractors who remained on board to have lunch. So if any of them had been responsible, they risked death or injury. The court noted it was 'astonishing' that there had not been any loss of life. If it had been an attempt to prolong work, it certainly produced the opposite effect because the ship was completely destroyed.

In the weeks after the disaster many of the workers employed by sub contractors were in dispute with the Island Navigation Corporation over severance pay and compensation for lost tools. On 27 January more than

200 angry men staged a sit-in in the corridors of the company's offices. They claimed they represented most of the 1,200 workers who were told that their services were not required after 9 January. 'We will sit outside their offices daily until reasonable terms are agreed upon,' said one man.[13]

On 9 June 1972 a mysterious explosion rocked one of C. Y. Tung's tankers, the 77,648-ton *Pacific Glory*, killing three men and injuring sixteen. The ship had been in a floating dock, which was moored off Tsing Yi Island – like the *Queen Elizabeth*.[14]

After the release of the court of inquiry's report the following month the C. Y. Tung group ruled out a political motive for the attack on the liner. Such a theory was 'without foundation', said a spokesman. The company also dismissed speculation suggesting a link with the explosion on the *Pacific Glory*. The *South China Morning Post* reported:

> Last night the spokesman declined to say why the political motive theory had been discarded or to give any other possible explanation for the disaster [the liner]. He said suggestions that the deliberate acts might have been politically motivated were 'in our opinion without foundation. Nor can we think of any political motive which would support such suggestions. Some people have linked the *Seawise University* catastrophe with the accident last month on board the *Pacific Glory*. Our investigations so far suggest that the incident was entirely accidental and free of possibility of anything sinister'. The spokesman went on to refer to the court's statement that it was not prepared to assign blame or to engage in any speculation with regard to determining the identity of the person or persons responsible for causing the fires on the *Seawise University*. 'It behoves all of us therefore not to indulge in speculation,' he said. The spokesman said the group firmly believed the authorities 'are thoroughly competent in pursuing the various matters mentioned in the court's report'.[15]

The claim that disenchanted workmen were behind the fires on the *Queen Elizabeth* was still being made in 2009. M. H. Liang, a former company executive, said:

> The fires were started by workmen. It happened 10 days before the Chinese New Year, and they were worried that the work was coming to an end. They wanted to prolong the job. This was an old ship with a lot of wooden panels and varnish. When they started the fires they didn't realise how inflammable it would be.

Tellingly, he added: 'We carried out our own investigation but we didn't find the culprits.'[16]

If the police and the company were unable to find who was responsible, it is difficult to see how with certainty the explanation could be down to a group of men who simply wished to prolong a job. Let us return to part of the court statement made by the company's lawyer, R. F. Stone: 'It might be said with some determination that there is neither a shred of evidence nor a comprehensible motive which would suggest any planned political action behind the fire.'

Not a shred of evidence? In a television interview with Alan Whicker about two months before the disaster, C. Y. Tung had admitted that he was experiencing trouble with the Communist union controlling his workforce. One day in late December 1971 graffito in Chinese characters appeared on the liner's funnels, saying 'C. Y. Tung go home – you are not wanted here'. The words were painted out but they reappeared the next day in a different colour. This happened on several occasions. The graffito was done at night.[17]

But the most compelling piece of evidence emerged four days after the ship's destruction. A photographer working for the Hong Kong newspaper *China Mail* was flying over the wreck when he spotted large Chinese characters near one of the funnels. The newspaper reported:

> The characters spelled the words 'China' and 'America' – and had miraculously escaped damage by the blaze which wiped out the vessel. Government officials probing the fire think that other words may have been burned away by the flames. It is almost certain the characters were painted on the deck before the *Queen Elizabeth* caught fire on Sunday. There has been a tight guard on the vessel ever since – and no intruders have been sighted near the wreck. *Mail* photographer Raymond Tam spotted four large white Chinese characters this morning as he took pictures of firemen boarding the *Queen*. The discovery adds new weight to speculation that the *Queen* – renamed *Seawise University* – may have been sabotaged. A number of left-wing workers were employed on the renovation work. The *Queen's* millionaire owner, Mr C. Y. Tung, comes from Taiwan. Each Chinese character is about eight feet high. They were daubed on a section of the deck near the ship's rear funnel.[18]

There has been no suggestion that the words were part of a hoax. Surprisingly, little was made of this discovery. For years such Chinese characters would have suggested anti-US propaganda, but in the months leading to the *Queen Elizabeth*'s destruction a different climate had emerged. America and China might not have been the best of friends but they were no longer the great enemies, on the surface anyway. There had been a diplomatic upheaval, which would be signalled by President Nixon's arrival in China on 21 February, six weeks after the ship's demise. Perhaps those Chinese characters were an indication of the shape of things to come, the new understanding between the two countries – and Taiwan's apparently numbered days.

Two days after the *China Mail* report appeared, Hong Kong Governor Sir Murray MacLehose held a special meeting at Government House, to discuss the *Queen Elizabeth*. He was told that there had been problems with 'four left-wing unions'.[19]

In Taiwan, the English-language newspaper *China Post* carried a comment piece on 16 January. It was restrained and part of it said:

> In view of the excellent fire-fighting system, the uncontrollable fire with occasional explosions pointed to the very strong possibility of sabotage. This was confirmed by a statement by the liner's former master, Commodore Geoffrey Marr, who stated that the fire 'must have been sabotage'. In view of the infiltration of Chinese Communists in Hong Kong's labour unions, sabotage is quite likely.

Mao's spies at the Hong Kong offices of the Xinhua News Agency – run by hardline Communists, the so-called East River Gang – would almost certainly have been monitoring the work on the *Queen Elizabeth* and reporting back to Beijing. They could not have failed to notice that the world's greatest ocean liner was nearing completion and flying the Taiwanese flag. Even more provocatively, huge five-sided cherry blossoms, the national symbol of Taiwan, indicating resilience, had appeared on the funnels. The restored ship would soon be a major propaganda victory for the Nationalists, just as the Communists were wooing President Nixon, believing they were close to gaining control of Taiwan, with the blessing of the United States, the island's main ally. The ship was due to start her maiden voyage as the *Seawise University* from Vancouver on 18 April 1972, a 75-day trip around the Pacific which would take in Los Angeles, Honolulu, Suva, Sydney, Fremantle, Bali, Singapore, Hong Kong, Kobe and Yokohama. The ship was set to impress China's neighbours and boost Taiwan's supporters in the US.

China only recently had taken Taiwan's place at the United Nations, and there was another reason why the ship would be an embarrassment for the Communists – she had the support of the UN Secretary-General, U Thant. C. Y. Tung revealed that a speech by U Thant had inspired him to launch a floating university so that students of many races could meet and promote mutual dependence and cooperation. The idea was supported by a significant number of US universities.[20]

For many years Kevin Sinclair was one of the leading journalists in Hong Kong. Shortly before his death in 2007, he asked:

> Who could possibly want to see the death of a *Queen* destined to do so much good for so many? The most likely theory was political. C. Y. Tung had much

of his fleet based in Taiwan. He had fled China in 1949. On the huge funnels etched in steel was the plum blossom. As well as being the corporate sign of Tung's vast fleet, this was also the floral symbol of the breakaway island of Taiwan. In the political fury of the Cultural Revolution, was this sufficient cause for the destruction of a vessel like the *Queen Elizabeth*? To many who pondered the fate of the mighty vessel, this was the most likely explanation for its cruel fate.[21]

But why would Tung be keen to play down the theory that the destruction of the *Queen Elizabeth* had been politically inspired? Loss of face, such a crucial part of the Chinese psyche, must have been a factor, whatever the reason. There is another possible explanation: trade. Chinese politics always have been something of a contradiction. Tung was one of the most powerful shipowners in the Far East. He had a large merchant fleet and many of his ships were flying under flags of convenience. Taiwan and mainland China did not trade directly. They were enemies. But cargoes could be routed via Hong Kong. Perhaps China and Taiwan did not always adhere to the rules that hostilities had thrown up. Perhaps there was secret direct trading ...

The British scholar Michael Hoare had this observation:

This relates to a later period than the 1970s, but it may be a hint. At a gathering of specialists in London about 1992, a senior Taiwan political figure was answering questions relating to the strict rule that trade with the People's Republic of China was only allowed if the goods passed through Hong Kong. He surprised us somewhat by adding, 'Well, sometimes the ships don't always actually go into Hong Kong harbour'. This refers to a more recent period, but it indicates that things are not always quite as they seem.[22]

Secret meetings between Chinese Communist and Nationalist officials in Hong Kong apparently had been going on for many years. The view of the British Embassy in Beijing soon after Nixon's visit was that China looked on Taiwan as 'a sort of super Hong Kong for siphoning capital investments from Japan and the USA'.[23]

Despite the political setbacks, Taiwan's economy boomed between 1970 and 1990. It amassed huge trade surpluses from its earnings in international trade. In 1987 the trade surplus was a record $18.7 billion. For many years the United States, despite Nixon's concessions to China, remained Taiwan's most important trading partner. Japan was second to the US. But in 1999 – two years after China regained control of Hong Kong – the former colony replaced Japan because of the volume of goods – industrial machinery, electronics, textiles – being sent from Taiwan to mainland China. A further irony saw Taiwanese businesses investing heavily in China. In 1998 Taiwan's trade surplus with its great enemy had grown to $15.7 billion.[24] Between 1987 and 2000 the total trade between the two countries amounted to $209.63 billion. Of this, $179.49 billion accounted for exports to China, and $30.14 billion for imports to Taiwan, leaving a trade imbalance in the fortress island's favour of $149.35 billion. Money could temper a great deal of loss of face.

However, C. Y. Tung regained some prestige in respect of his plan for a floating university. Soon after the *Queen Elizabeth*'s destruction he announced that he would continue with his educational programme. His Seawise Foundation acquired the cruise ship SS *Atlantic* from American Export Lines. She was renamed SS *Universe Campus* and began her new life later that year. But the ship was only 18,000 tons and low profile. Tung could pursue his passion for education and the People's Republic of China would not be upset. The idea of a floating university proved to be a great success.

In his annual report for 1972 Sir Murray MacLehose did not mention the *Queen Elizabeth*, despite the fact that the disaster had attracted so much international attention, and he had been quick to order a major inquiry. Had Special Branch of the Royal Hong Kong Police carried out its own investigation because of the speculation suggesting a political motive? Probably. But any reports are likely to have been destroyed. Special Branch was disbanded before Hong Kong's handover to China in 1997. Some of its files ended up in The National Archives in Kew, south-west London. For example, the 1970 file is available, but there is every indication that it has been heavily pruned. The file for 1974 is listed. However, it remains closed. The files for 1971 and, crucially, 1972 are missing. The Foreign and Commonwealth Office in London had its own Hong Kong Department, keeping a close eye on the colony. Any reports on the *Queen Elizabeth* appear to have vanished from the department's files. At least one relevant file in the Hong Kong Public Records Office remains closed.

Perhaps this remarkable silence has something to do with Britain's attitude towards China at the time. Like the United States, Britain was keen on improving relations with the People's Republic of China – at the expense of Taiwan. In January 1971 the Foreign and Commonwealth Office produced a policy document on China. The main objectives: to normalise and improve bilateral contacts; to increase Britain's share of the Chinese market; to help bring China into a healthier relationship with the rest of the world; to maintain the peace and prosperity of Hong Kong; and to maintain and improve 'our presence in Peking, which gives us an exceptionally high level of specialist Chinese expertise – this is of outstanding use in the context of intelligence exchanges with our allies'.

The document added:

We have now reached a crucial point in our relations with China. Since the end of the Cultural Revolution the Chinese have adopted a more conciliatory foreign policy – in some respects even more conciliatory than before the Cultural Revolution. They are increasingly confident of admission to the United Nations, and are showing a more cooperative face to the world. We may well have to wait a long time for a more favourable moment to develop our relations.[25]

On 13 March 1972 Britain and China signed an agreement to exchange ambassadors. Britain also announced that it would close its 100-year-old consulate in Taiwan. Prime Minister Edward Heath was a strong supporter of close ties with China, and no doubt felt upstaged by President Nixon's visit the previous month. Heath would go to China for the first time in 1974 – after he had lost office. But he would make many more trips, and develop lucrative business interests.

The paucity of official documents on the *Queen Elizabeth* surprised Philip Bowring, a columnist for the *International Herald Tribune* and a former editor of the *Far Eastern Economic Review*. He wrote in 2003:

At the time the most common speculation was that the fires had been set by Communists for political reasons, to spite C. Y. Tung who was closely identified with the Nationalist government on Taiwan ... Perhaps the British were involved in a cover-up. Public exposure of Communist involvement would have obstructed delicate efforts then under way to improve relations with Beijing.[26]

There is no doubt that the attack on the *Queen Elizabeth* was well planned. It was a Sunday, the ship's refit was nearing completion, the number of workers had decreased, the fires broke out soon after many people had left to go ashore for lunch, a significant number of fire doors, shell doors and portholes were open, ensuring that flames would be fanned quickly, and the small number of firemen and security staff were soon overwhelmed by the magnitude of the task they faced.

Trevor Hollingsbee, an intelligence specialist and a former senior superintendent in the Royal Hong Kong Police, came to this conclusion: 'Organised crime – triad – would have to have been involved to carry out such an operation efficiently.'[27]

It has been noted already that triad gangs were long established in the docks, and that in the early 1970s Hong Kong was experiencing a crime wave. The Communists had ousted triad gangs from mainland China after coming to power in 1949. Mao feared that they might create political mayhem because of support for the Nationalists. Many triads ended up in Hong Kong and

Taiwan. Later it would emerge that the Communist authorities were not averse to coming to an accommodation with the gangsters. At the time of the *Queen Elizabeth* disaster one particular gang was causing major problems in the colony – the Big Circle Boys. They were not strictly triads but they knew all about loyalty to Mao and they embraced crime enthusiastically. These criminals were former Red Guards or Chinese soldiers, including commandos, who had crossed to Hong Kong illegally and used their military training to plan raids. Many of them would go on to join recognised triad gangs.

By the early 1980s Communist officials were forging significant links with triads in the colony. Wong Man-fong, a former deputy secretary-general of the Xinhua News Agency in Hong Kong, revealed that at Beijing's request he 'befriended' gang leaders. Beijing was involved in negotiations with Britain over the future of Hong Kong and it did not want any upheaval after the handover, especially in the financial markets. Too much money was at stake. If the gangs kept a reasonably low profile, then they could carry on with their activities. Wong said: 'I told them that if they did not disrupt Hong Kong's stability, we would not stop them from making money.' The main gangs involved were the 14K and the Wo On Lok, which quickly saw the benefits of cooperation, and the Sun Yee On, which needed more persuading because of its previous support for the Nationalists. 'I made the point of warning them [the triad leaders] that the Communist Party was not someone they wanted to mess with,' said Wong. Some gang members did not trust China and left Hong Kong. One of the destinations was Britain.

There are suspicions that the Xinhua News Agency and Chinese intelligence officers had become involved with triads many years earlier. Wong was a Xinhua official from 1949 to 1992, and it has been claimed that he was the main link between the Chinese government and the triads, holding regular meetings with gang leaders in the border town of Shenzhen. Wong had planned to give a detailed account of China's links with triads, but he succumbed to official pressure not to say anything further.[28] In another claim, journalist Frederic Dannen, who investigated China's links with triads, said that a former Hong Kong detective, Robert Youill, told him of a triad held on a blackmail charge. The man 'spilled his guts and admitted he was a spy for Xinhua'.[29] According to another report, the Wo On Lok triads in Hong Kong worked for China's equivalent of the CIA.[30]

Confirmation of China's dealings with triads has come from the very top. Deng Xiaoping, who became paramount leader in 1978, two years after Mao's death, said in 1984 that 'there are many good guys among them'. Several of Deng's relatives, including children, visited Hong Kong 'to be wined and dined by top triad officials'. Deng acknowledged the damage caused by the Cultural Revolution and pushed for economic reform. 'To get rich is glorious,' the great Communist declared.

Tao Siju, head of China's Public Security Bureau, suggested in 1993 that triads were 'patriots who love Hong Kong and the motherland'. Author Martin Booth claimed:

> Rumours abound that he has actually joined a triad society. If so, it will most likely have been the San Yee On [also known as Sun Yee On], which is the most active Hong Kong society in China.[31]

China has certainly paid a price for opening the door to triads. It has been estimated that on the mainland the number of people involved in organised crime increased from about 100,000 in 1986 to 1.5 million in 2000. The rise in criminal activity has seen some odd relationships. The People's Liberation Army acquired a string of nightclubs in Shanghai in partnership with the Sun Yee On triads. In the same city, the Public Security Bureau was busy running high-class brothels. The army also invested in hotels, phone networks and airlines. Other government departments took Deng's 'rich is glorious' advice and linked up with 'private enterprise'.[32] In some cases, it has been found that police were helping to run gangs. Crime – with widespread corruption in official circles – has flourished.

CHAPTER 25

Biggest Wreck in the World

The *Queen Elizabeth* had one last starring role before work began on breaking her up. During her Atlantic years many film stars had taken passage. In 1974 the ship once again caught up with Hollywood, or rather Pinewood Studios, sadly as a wreck. She appeared in the James Bond film *The Man With The Golden Gun*, with Roger Moore making his second outing as 007. Part of the ship was supposed to be the Hong Kong headquarters of MI6. There was a certain irony in this. The ship's sabotage had no doubt aroused the interest of the security service. Bond had a licence to kill and the film's makers had a licence to embark on artistic expression. There were accurate shots of the ship lying forlorn in Hong Kong harbour, but the scenes showing the interior, with Bond and M in a rather impressive HQ, albeit at an angle to account for the vessel's list, were far from the truth. In reality, the ship was largely a burnt-out mass of tangled metal, with very limited access. The interior scenes were all done in the safety of Pinewood.

Some of the world's leading salvage companies were keen to tackle the wreck. It would be the biggest marine salvage job ever attempted, and potentially lucrative. But work to remove the tens of thousands of tons of steel did not start until 15 December 1973, nearly two years after fire swept through the ship.

The police investigation, the insurance claim involving the UK P&I Club and the importance of finding an effective plan for the wreck – at the right price – all contributed to the delay. In any case, the first job was to remove more than 3,000 tons of oil, which could have caused widespread pollution, and this task fell to a Japanese company, Fukada Salvage.

In October 1972 a high-level meeting was held at the Marine Department to consider how to deal with the wreck. The meeting was attended by the acting Director of Marine, M. J. Alexander, and representatives of the UK P&I Club and the Island Navigation Corporation. Salvage experts had inspected the wreck – the parts that were accessible – and found that the vessel's condition was 'much worse than had been anticipated'. All decks and bulkheads had collapsed, the shell plating was weak and only the fuel tanks could be used for buoyancy. There were between 6,000 and 7,000 tons of mud in the ship. Salvage expert Captain Jock Anderson thought she was likely to break up during any attempt to refloat her. She could even roll over to port, blocking access to the nearby Kwai Chung container terminals. The meeting heard that six salvage proposals had been received and that removal of the wreck would probably cost US$20 million. No company had offered to do the job on a 'no cure, no pay' basis. The UK P&I Club felt that 'it may well be unwise to attempt a removal operation'. It suggested leaving the wreck in place and improving access to the Kwai Chung container terminals and the oil berths at Tsing Yi Island by dredging a channel to the west of the ship. The acting Director of Marine pointed out that the wreck remained a hazard to shipping, especially during the typhoon season, and it could also hinder future plans for port development. The Marine Department was 'under considerable pressure from the shipping community and there could well be strong public reaction if the wreck was not removed'.[1]

The UK P&I Club engaged civil engineering consultants Binnie & Partners, which suggested that it would be a good idea to have a Decca survey of the seabed around the wreck. The Club:

> We are glad we did … The Decca survey showed that amidships the ship was actually resting across a tongue of hard alluvium. Had one salvor been allowed to get the contract and raise the ship with artificial flotation and then had done anything wrong at all, we might have ended up with a skyscraper – the ship was over 1,000 feet long – because the ship would have revolved round the alluvium like a see-saw. Binnies had found by their separate investigations that the strength and resistance of the mud were not sufficient to counter the plunging weight of the ship. The ship was in a very unstable position and duly one day she lurched upright by about 20 degrees.

There was an interesting observation:

> None of the books on wreck removal and salvage or on the great liners has anything about the history of her end. The owners, the salvors and ourselves are the only people who know about it. Altogether the wreck removal took five years and cost [US] $10 million, more than the value of the ship under conversion, the majority of which was recovered from the war risks underwriters since the loss was caused by malicious damage.[2]

War risks? The *Queen Elizabeth* was seen by many as a casualty of the long-running conflict between China and Taiwan. And $10 million was considerably less than the amount that some of the major salvage companies wanted. In 2009 the UK P&I Club revealed that all its files and records on the wreck removal had been destroyed.[3]

Fukada Salvage, the company that had removed the oil from the wreck, was also interested in the main contract, and submitted a proposal in April 1972. Its experts decided that it would be 'impossible' to refloat the entire ship. The company suggested cutting away the upper decks and refloating what remained of the vessel below C Deck.

Hamburg salvors Ulrich Harms came up with a novel plan. The funnels and masts would be cut off, and 'the general idea is to sink the wreck by dredging a trench alongside the ship's hull and letting the wreck sink into this trench to the extent that it will not cause any hindrance to navigation'.[4] Soon afterwards there was a change of plan. The company decided it would be better to salvage the ship for scrap. The operation would take 65 weeks and cost US$20 million.[5]

Perhaps the most interesting hat in the ring belonged to an American company, Murphy Pacific Marine Salvage. It had taken over some of the operations of Merritt-Chapman & Scott, which salvaged the liner *Normandie*, renamed *Lafayette*, in New York. Murphy Pacific Marine Salvage pointed out:

> The two casualty conditions were very similar; both ships sank pursuant to a serious fire, almost under similar circumstances of refitting, in shallow protected waters, on their side. The *Lafayette* was righted, pumped and raised within the original US Navy cost estimate of $5 million; Merritt-Chapman & Scott received $4,777,816 for the work. The job was completed within the expected time frame and for $222,184 less than the estimated cost.

One of the offers was not without humour – an inmate at HM Prison in Maidstone, Kent, wrote to the Hong Kong Marine Department offering his services. The letter began:

> Would you please forward chart of harbour area where the old *Queen Elizabeth* is now lying, together with any relevant details and photographs. Also it would be appreciated if I could have details of tides, depth of water, quay conditions, and as to access to the area by land and water, and the availability of labour.

The prisoner offered to do the job for 'two thirds of the figures now being quoted by Lloyd's'.[6]

In the end, the contract to remove the wreck 'in its entirety' went to a South Korean company called Far East Salvage, with offices in Kowloon. It is not clear whether this company was specially set up for the task. 'Undoubtedly they were the cheapest,' said Hong Kong marine consultant Captain Alan Loynd.[7] Another Hong Kong marine consultant, Quincy Lloyd, described the salvor as 'principally a scrapper'.[8]

An Island Navigation Corporation employee, C. K. Pak, was responsible for arranging tugs and cranes and sending the recovered steel to a scrapyard in nearby Junk Bay. 'The company [Far East Salvage] was run by M. S. Lee, who was ex-South Korean navy,' said Pak, who became a marine consultant in Shanghai. 'His men called him The Admiral. He recruited a lot of retired soldiers and used them as divers.'[9]

The news that a decision had been taken on 'the world's biggest maritime task' was revealed on 14 December 1973.[10] Work began the next day. The wreck was listing 48 degrees to starboard and part of it was buried 35 feet in mud. It was decided to carry out the job in three stages, and stage one involved removing part of the superstructure. The Far East Salvage Company asked another salvor, Universal Dockyard, based in Kowloon, to do this work, which was completed on 5 July 1974. A total of 6,880 tons of steel was cut and taken away.

But in February the Marine Department had complained to the Universal Dockyard about lack of safety. 'There were no signs of safety belts or safety harnesses used in conjunction with lifelines being worn by personnel working in precarious positions,' said a letter.

Access to the wreck was considered to be most unsafe, there being no adequate gangway from the pontoon to the side of the wreck, the several rope ladders were observed to be in a dilapidated condition and many stanchions on the wooden walkway are detached, thus rendering the manropes useless as a safety device to prevent persons falling.

The company had failed to submit an operational plan and work schedules or install VHF radio. Large sections of superstructure that had been cut away were left on a sloping deck. 'Your assurance that these sections are adequately supported and prevented from falling away from the wreck is required.'[11]

When stage one was finished the Universal Dockyard dropped out of the picture and the Far East Salvage Company took over for the remaining stages. Stage two began immediately and involved the removal of the bow and stern and all metal above C Deck. A total of twenty-two South Korean divers were involved, working in shifts of four. As well as oxyacetylene equipment, the men were using gelignite to break up sections of the ship. On 18 September tragedy struck. One of the divers, 35-year-old H. A. Jung-sik, was sitting on a barge next to the wreck preparing a charge when he blew himself up. He was taken to hospital – the Queen Elizabeth Hospital, in Kowloon – and shortly afterwards died of his injuries. Another diver was injured. An investigation was carried out quickly. A report concluded:

> It is considered that the explosion was caused through unsafe working practice on the part of the deceased. It appears that the deceased attached the detonator to the detonating fuse down-line after he had connected the detonator leg-wires to the firing cable which in turn was already attached to the exploder. Safe practice would in fact require the procedure to be reversed.[12]

The use of explosives had worried bosses of the China Light & Power Company, which ran a power station on Tsing Yi Island. They wrote to the Director of Marine in October 1972 saying there had been rumours that the wreck 'might be demolished by a series of explosive charges'. Their fear: 'It is possible depending on the size of the charges that the shock waves produced would mechanically damage our equipment.' The Marine Department replied that it could not comment on the rumour because it was still waiting for detailed plans on the wreck removal.[13] In the event, the explosive charges used were relatively small – 3–5 lb – but by July 1976 the divers had managed to blast away a total of 40,380 lb. It was estimated that they would need a further 27,000 lb of gelignite to finish the job.

Stage two saw about 20,000 tons of steel removed. Some 120,000 cubic yards of mud was also dredged from around the wreck. One plan was to refloat the midship section of the vessel after removing machinery and boilers, using buoyancy in the bunkers and ballast tanks. But such an operation was considered too costly and possibly hazardous. The list of the wreck had changed from 48 degrees to 34 degrees, and this was attributed to the dredging, the removal of steel and the use of explosives. Stage three was the most dangerous part of the job – cutting away the wreck underwater. This began in February 1976 but four months later the work had produced only about 1,500 tons of steel. The deeper the divers went, the more dangerous it became. Visibility was limited and there was a great deal of mud in the vessel. The Far East Salvage Company also faced another problem – industrial stoppages. But the company said it hoped to remove the remainder of the wreck by the beginning of 1978.[14]

On 21 July 1976 the *South China Morning Post* produced a poignant picture. It showed a slab of metal in the harbour, surrounded by several small boats, with Hong Kong Island in the distance. The newspaper pointed out that the slab of metal 'is all that remains [above the water] of the once majestic pride of the Atlantic'. The report, headlined 'QE vanishes as divers work', went on:

It was 6 a.m. when this picture was taken by *Post* photographer Sunny Lee. Three hours later teams of divers from Korea were busy hacking away at the metal under the water … It is a sad story when one remembers her majestic debut in colony waters, when a flotilla of small craft and the *Alexander Grantham* [the fireboat] led her to what was supposed to be a temporary resting place between Kwai Chung and Tsing Yi. It turned out to be her last resting place. In 18 months the *Seawise University* will be simply thousands of pieces of scrap metal. Half of it is already.

Island Navigation Corporation executive M. H. Liang could see the salvage work from his office window, and he was quoted as saying: 'It's something we would rather forget, you know.'

But it was not something that Liang would be allowed to forget. By March 1977 the work on the wreck was a major concern. It had become too dangerous and it was feared that lives would be lost. Liang asked the Director of Marine if the operation could end when there was a clear depth of 60 feet above the wreck. This depth would be safe for shipping in the harbour.[15]

The divers were working to depths of up to 90 feet. Two trenches about 20ft deep had been dug alongside the wreck, and men were in complete darkness. One particular danger was highlighted by salvage consultants:

In working in depths in excess of about 60ft in that part of the wreck which comprises boiler rooms, engine rooms etc, divers will often be unavoidably forced to work underneath boilers, machinery and other overhanging projections, where even the most rigid safety procedures may prove to be ineffective, and where there will be no means of providing direct access to working areas, either for the diver himself or for his standby diver in the event of emergency.

The consultants warned:

Although we are confident that the present exceptional record of diving safety can be maintained down to a depth of about 60ft, we are of the opinion that for reasons largely beyond the control of supervisory personnel, a sharp increase in accidents to divers, with some possibly of a serious nature, can be expected as wreck removal work on the midship portion of the wreck progresses to greater depths.[16]

The Port Executive Committee and the Pilotage Advisory Committee were consulted, and M. J. Alexander, who was now the Director of Marine, asked the colony's Solicitor General for legal advice as the Island Navigation Corporation and its salvors would not be removing the entire wreck under the original deal. Alexander noted: 'All-round agreement should be aimed for, because dissension by any one party could result in adverse publicity for government in the event lives were lost.'[17]

It was agreed that work could stop when the depth of 60 feet was reached, providing the remainder of the wreck was covered with mud and the seabed levelled. On 23 February 1978 Liang wrote to the Director of Marine to tell him that the salvage work would cease on 15 March. On 9 May 1979 he sent another letter saying that the wreck had been completely buried. The whole operation took more than five years. It had been estimated at the outset that 60,000 tons of the *Queen Elizabeth* would have to be removed. In the event, only about 60 per cent of the wreck was cut up and taken to the scrapyard in Junk Bay. Some 23,000 tons, including the ship's keel, are still buried in the harbour. Recent years have seen a huge expansion of the Kwai Chung container port, using landfill. Part of the *Queen Elizabeth*'s grave ended up being covered by berth 20 of terminal nine, and the remaining part is shown on charts as an obstruction.

Much of the salvaged steel was reused to build Hong Kong skyscrapers. Brass from the propellers reappeared in the shape of Parker pens in a limited edition of 5,000 in 1977.

Rumours that many divers had died during the wreck removal were still circulating in 2009. Stephen Davies, director of the Hong Kong Maritime Museum, said:

> I was told that 17 divers had died. The ship was cut down to the keel. Eventually the company went to the government and said, 'Look, if you want us to remove everything, another seven divers are going to die'. So the government backed off, and the keel remains to this day.[18]

Marine consultant Quincy Lloyd commented:

> The bottom line is that all salvage operations are hazardous and only careful planning can minimise the chances of things going wrong. They started to lose divers in 1975 due to working in the mud, where the starboard bilge had settled.[19]

Officially, only one man died, the diver who blew himself up.

CHAPTER 26

Communists to the Rescue

It was another busy day for C. Y. Tung. On Wednesday, 14 April 1982 the morning began with a session of meditation exercises and then he went to the offices of the Island Navigation Corporation. Lunch was taken in the pleasant surroundings of the Foreign Correspondents' Club, and afterwards he headed back to work. Later he went to Kai Tak Airport to greet Prince Rainer and Princess Grace of Monaco at the start of a visit to Hong Kong. Tung knew the couple well – he was Monaco's honorary consul in the colony – and he had planned a big party for them. But at the airport he felt unwell and decided to go home. At about 11 p.m. he lost consciousness and was taken to hospital, where he died two hours later after suffering a heart attack. Tung, who did not smoke or drink, was 71. 'He chatted light-heartedly when I had lunch with him,' said company executive M. H. Liang.

> Though he always worked himself too hard and led a hectic life, we expected him to live longer. Mr Tung seldom enjoyed himself except in working. His major hobby was shipping to which he dedicated his whole life.

On 15 April the flags of some 150 ships in Tung's fleet, scattered throughout the world, flew at half mast. One of his tankers was the *Seawise Giant* – he was continuing to play on his initials, C. Y. – which weighed in at a staggering 565,763 tons.[1] Counting the number of vessels, he was the world's greatest ship owner at the time of his death.

Tributes were quick to flow in. Burton Levin, the US Consul General in Hong Kong, commented:

> Many Americans, including several of our presidents, counted him as a friend. Through his well-known contribution to international shipping he improved the welfare of millions throughout the world. A kind and compassionate man, he was particularly interested in educational work to which he devoted

considerable energy and resources. In establishing the World Campus Afloat he brought together university students from all over the world to sail and study together.

The Hong Kong General Chamber of Commerce pointed out that Tung was one of the pioneers of the shipping world who had helped to build up the colony's fleet so that it ranked after the United States in tonnage. Acknowledging that the colony was one of the world's shipping powers, the chairman of the Hong Kong Shipowners Association, David McLeod, said: 'C. Y. Tung was instrumental in starting this. He was one of the most successful and clever ship owners anywhere in the world.'[2] Inevitably, Tung's death revived stories of the loss of his 'cherished dream' ten years earlier, the *Queen Elizabeth*.

The Times of London noted: 'Despite his immense wealth, Tung lived frugally and worked extremely hard. His capacity as a linguist and his unquestioned business acumen won him widespread respect.'[3]

Instead of partying, Prince Rainer and Princess Grace found themselves joining 2,500 mourners for the Buddhist funeral on 17 April. The prince was one of the pall bearers. Among the mourners was Tung's great shipping rival, Sir Yue-kong Pao.[4]

Tung left a widow, two sons and three daughters. The sons, C. H. [Chee-hwa] Tung and C. C. [Chee-chen] Tung, had joined their father's business in the 1960s. C. Y. Tung, whose empire included banking, insurance, property and oil, had mapped out the succession some time before his death. Ship financier Cary Jackson observed: 'He leaves a legacy of a superbly managed and highly diversified company that knows its business throughout the world.'[5] The main company in the group was the Orient Overseas Container Line (OOCL), which had grown from the Orient Overseas Line when containerisation took on such importance. C. H. Tung, who had been on board the *Queen Elizabeth* when the fires broke out, took the helm of OOCL in Hong Kong and his younger brother continued to help with the international side of the business.

But ominous signs were around the corner. In the early 1980s a worldwide recession was starting to bite. Trade dropped and it became obvious that there were too many merchant ships. C. Y. Tung, of course, was an avid collector of ships. Other ship owners had been enthusiastically ordering new vessels, only to find that there was no use for them. The Tung group, for example, bought a 65,000-ton bulk carrier, costing US$25 million, from a British shipyard and sold her 18 months later for US$5.5 million. Adding to the problem were nervous banks recalling loans. In October 1982 it was estimated that more than 1,200 ships around the world had been laid up, and less than three years later *Lloyd's Register* reported that a record 1,785 vessels totalling 17.75 million gross tons had been scrapped.

In 1985 the Tung group faced a financial crisis, and in the August applied for restructuring. There were debts of US$320 million. But the recession was not the only factor.

In his book *Asian Godfathers*, Joe Studwell describes C. H. Tung as the 'less gifted son' of C. Y. Tung, and claims he was in trouble in the first place because he engaged in 'abuse' of listed companies. Studwell:

> In the early 1980s, after Tung Chee-hwa took over the family empire, he authorised and maintained hundreds of millions of US dollars of loans from his main listed vehicle, Orient Overseas (Holdings) Ltd (OOHL), to what he called the Tung Private Group, a euphemism for more than 200 private companies he controlled. These loans, which no sane minority investor in OOHL would have wanted to make, were frittered away and otherwise blown on bad investments whose returns – had there been any – would have accrued to the Tung family alone. When OOHL was restructured in late 1986, the public company wrote off US$156 million of the loans it had made to the Tungs' private businesses.

C. H. Tung admitted to shareholders that OOHL's financial position

> seriously worsened principally as a consequence of the rapid deterioration in the financial position of the Tung Private Group, with which OOHL is closely associated and from whom substantial amounts were owing.

Studwell also points out that 'unwarranted and excessive investment' had started during the last years of C. Y. Tung's reign.[6]

Who came to C. H. Tung's rescue? With the family's strong ties to Taiwan, it would not have been unreasonable to assume that the flourishing island was the best-placed candidate. In fact, the opposite happened. Remarkably, the Communists saved the 'enemy'. Chinese banks, including the Bank of China, came to Tung's aid in a US$120 million deal masterminded by a colourful Hong Kong tycoon, Henry Fok.

Fok was known as The Godfather in Hong Kong because of his political influence and close ties with Beijing, which regarded him as a 'patriotic capitalist'. He was arguably the Chinese Communist Party's most trusted person in the colony. The son of a fisherman, Fok, who once worked as a coolie, forged his links with China during the Korean War. Defying a United Nations embargo, he smuggled medical supplies, sheet iron, tyres and petrol to China. He denied rumours that he had also smuggled weapons. The Communists went on to reward him with various business monopolies. Fok developed a close relationship with Chinese leader Deng Xiaoping. He made a fortune from property in Hong Kong and casino operations in Macau after joining forces with the 'king of gambling', Stanley Ho. In 1991, a son, Thomas, was jailed in the US for conspiracy to send 15,000 assault rifles to Croatia without a licence. Fok died in Beijing in October 2006, aged 83, after a long battle with cancer.[7]

In 1996 Canada had been so worried about 'the threat posed by the acquisition and control of Canadian companies by members or associates of triads with affiliations to the Chinese Intelligence Services' that the Canadian Security Intelligence Service and the Royal Canadian Mounted Police launched a joint study, called Sidewinder. The ensuing report drew attention to Deng Xiaoping and how he had turned to wealthy Hong Kong businessmen to help his economic reforms, based on the theme 'to get rich is glorious'. Among the businessmen named in the report were Henry Fok and Stanley Ho.[8] It is worth recalling that in 1984 Deng, referring to triads in Hong Kong, said there were 'many good guys among them'. They were also seen as 'patriots who love Hong Kong and the motherland'.

In March 2010 Stanley Ho, aged 88, insisted there was 'absolutely no foundation in any suggestion' that he had been involved with triads. Ho issued a statement after a report from New Jersey's Department of Gaming Enforcement alleged that he had links with organised crime. State officials launched an investigation because of casino operator MGM Mirage's dealings with Ho's daughter Pansy. MGM Mirage had stakes in casinos in Atlantic City and Macau. Pansy Ho was deemed to be an 'unsuitable' business partner due to her close financial ties with her father.[9]

If China's 1986 bailout of C. H. Tung's inherited empire – so long linked to Taiwan – was a surprise, then there was an even greater turnaround during the next decade. When Britain handed Hong Kong back to China in 1997, the man whom Beijing 'chose' to run the former colony was one C. H. Tung, who as a child had fled from Shanghai because of the advancing Communists. To some he was seen as a businessman who would be forever in China's debt. One Hong Kong civil servant remarked: 'C. H. is a fully owned subsidiary of the PRC [People's Republic of China]. They own him and he knows it.'[10] Tung's outlook might be summed up in a comment he made in June 1997, a month before he took charge: 'Freedom is not unimportant. But the west just doesn't understand Chinese culture. It is time to reaffirm who we are. Individual rights are not as important as order in our society. That is how we are.' Tung became chief executive of Hong Kong after winning 80 per cent of a selection committee's votes. The committee had been appointed by China. His brother, C. C. Tung, took over the running of the shipping business.

Before joining the family empire C. H. Tung had gone to the University of Liverpool to read mechanical engineering. Afterwards he lived in the United States for nearly a decade, working for General Electric. The experience left a lasting impression:

I lived in America during the 1960s. I saw what happened with the slow erosion of authority, and society became more disorderly than is desirable. I certainly don't want to see this happen [in Hong Kong].[11]

Before the 1997 handover the Communist Party in Hong Kong was illegal. It was an underground movement controlled by the Xinhua News Agency. In 2010, surprisingly, it was still an underground movement, with no formal registration of members. The party is run along Leninist lines and comprises tight-knit cells. 'The role of the party in Hong Kong is as mysterious as ever,' said an *Asia Times* report. 'Few people will comment on it because it is deemed to be too sensitive, and longtime observers of Hong Kong say it is almost impossible to get anyone to say they belong.' The report quoted Jonathan Mirsky, a former correspondent of *The Times* of London, as saying: 'I covered Hong Kong for 40 years starting in 1958, and I never met anyone who would admit to being a member of the party.'[12]

Before taking office as chief executive Tung said he would consider legalising the Communist Party. But Beijing obviously prefers to keep the organisation secret in its Special Administrative Region, where democracy remains a sensitive issue. The Communist Party could not afford to lose face in any elections, and secrecy allows its spies to monitor what is going on more effectively. Christine Loh, a former Hong Kong legislator, pointed out:

Nowhere else in the world is there a system where the ruling party remains an underground organisation as it does in Hong Kong. Even more extraordinary is the fact that as China rises in global importance the ruling party should feel so uncomfortable about showing itself in the most advanced city in the nation.[13]

Tung has never commented on whether he was a party member. In 1996 he was described as being among the least pretentious of Hong Kong's tycoons. He insisted on remaining in the Victoria Peak flat he shared with his wife rather than move into Government House.

In September 1997 he invited several of the activists of the 1967 riots to a party at Government House. Two years later a number of prominent local leftists were given medals or appointed justices of the peace on his recommendation. But the greatest controversy came in 2001 when Tung awarded Hong Kong's highest honour, the Grand Bauhinia Medal, to Yeung Kwong, a former chairman of the pro-Communist Federation of Trade Unions, for helping to 'improve workers' rights'. Yeung had been one of the leaders of the 1967 riots. 'It was hard to understand why this was done,' Christine Loh reflected.

It could not have been an official attempt to reverse the verdict of the riots or the Cultural Revolution since the mainland had already discredited the excesses of that period. Perhaps it was a gesture on the part of Tung to ameliorate his pro-business image so as to gain support from the traditional left-wing hardcore of the patriotic camp. However, by honouring Yeung Kwong he reopened the whole subject of the riots, the Cultural Revolution and what Yeung Kwong represented, thereby furthering undermining his own credibility in the eyes of the community.[14]

Tung won a second term as chief executive in 2002 in an uncontested election, but he resigned in 2005, citing health reasons. There had been widespread criticism of his leadership.

And Taiwan? Despite the concessions made by Nixon and Kissinger in the early 1970s, the island fortress remains independent of the People's Republic, prosperous, an outcast from the United Nations and ever wary of military action by its giant neighbour.

Epilogue: Long Live the Queen

At Southampton on 11 October 2010, Queen Elizabeth II named a new Cunard ship. Looking up at the 92,000-ton giant, she told the dockside crowd of around 2,000: 'I name this ship *Queen Elizabeth*. God bless her and all who sail in her.' So the famous name would live on. Interestingly, Cunard had chosen not to name the ship Queen Elizabeth 3, even though a large part of the original liner remains buried in Hong Kong harbour. Cunard bosses were opening a new chapter in the shipping line's history, but there would always be the memories, as the Queen must have been aware. Seventy-two years earlier, aged 12, she had been at the launch of the *Queen Elizabeth* in Clydebank, when her mother performed the ceremony. Queen Elizabeth II was also in Clydebank in 1967 for the launch of the *Queen Elizabeth 2*. As Cunard president Peter Shanks pointed out on 11 October 2010: 'There is only one person here who can claim presence at all three Elizabeth namings, and that person is Her Majesty the Queen.'

The new ship had certainly caught the imagination of the public. Her maiden voyage, a 13-day trip taking in Lisbon, Cadiz and the Canary Islands starting the day after the ceremony, had sold out in just 29 minutes and 14 seconds. But will she achieve the fame of her loved predecessors? Time will tell. The first *Queen Elizabeth* and the QE2 were thoroughbred ocean liners and unmistakably had the stamp of Great Britain. The latest addition to Cunard's fleet was built by Fincantieri Cantieri Navali at Monfalcone, northern Italy, an 'assembly line model' of the Vista class, though she has been strengthened to cope with the challenges of Atlantic crossings. True ocean liners cost a lot more to build than cruise ships.

But Cunard was keen to emphasise 'the rich heritage of the first Cunarder to bear the name' and the 'new golden age of ocean travel'. A brochure enthused:

The harmony of classic and contemporary strikes an elegant chord throughout this magnificent ship. Images and features from her predecessors,

Queen Elizabeth and *QE2*, sit comfortably alongside her modern charm. Entertainment ranges from lavish high-tech musical productions to the timeless refinement of garden parties, Ivor Novello-style evenings around the piano and grand balls at sea. Opportunities for relaxation stretch from the simple pleasures of a 6,000-book library to state-of-the-art spa treatments, films from the golden era, or viewing the unique collection linking Cunard with royalty and British maritime heritage.

The new ship cost £350 million and can carry 2,092 passengers. The bill for the original *Queen Elizabeth* was £5 million and although she weighed in at some 8,000 tons less, her passenger capacity was 2,260. At 1,031 feet, she was 67 feet longer. Her top speed was more than 30 knots against the new ship's 23.7 knots, a reflection of these fuel-economy times. The *QE2* has a remarkable top speed of 34.6 knots.

At the time of writing a huge question mark hangs over the future of the *QE2*. In 2007 Cunard announced that it was selling the liner to the Dubai investment company Istithmar for £65 milllion. The *QE2* left Southampton for Port Rashid on 11 November 2008, arriving on 26 November, when ownership passed to Nakheel Properties, a company of Dubai World. To the dismay of many of the liner's admirers, plans to turn her into a floating hotel were revealed, with extensive changes to the ship's appearance inside and out, even removing the iconic funnel. But Dubai's financial crisis intervened, and the ship remains in port unchanged, with a skeleton crew looking after her.

It is to be hoped that the *QE2* does not suffer a fate as sad as that of the first *Queen Elizabeth*.

Appendix 1

Cunard produced a superb programme for the launch of the *Queen Elizabeth* at Clydebank on 27 September 1938. The last page was headed 'The World's Largest Liner – Some Features Of The Queen Elizabeth', and it emphasised the magnificence of the ship that was being created. There were nine key points:

Dimensions

Length ... 1,031 feet.
Length of Promenade Deck ... 724 feet.
Breadth ... 118 feet.
Depth (to top of Lounge structure) ... 120 feet.
Number of decks ... 14.
Gross tonnage (approx) ... 85,000.

Comparison with *Queen Mary*

In the *Queen Elizabeth* there are only two funnels, compared with three in her sister ship. This will mean a much more generous allowance of deck space and promenades, as well as an increase in passenger accommodation.

Three anchors will be provided, as compared with two in the *Queen Mary*. The additional anchor will be placed in the centre of the stem.

The bow itself will be shaped with a greater rake than the *Queen Mary*'s. As a result, the *Queen Elizabeth* will be 13 feet longer than her sister ship. Another new feature in the *Queen Elizabeth* is the absence of a break in the forward part of the hull. The flush main deck produces remarkably graceful lines from bow to bridge.

Giant Castings

Some of the largest castings ever used in the construction of a liner have been forged for the *Queen Elizabeth*, including:
Shaft brackets (outer propellers) ... 180 tons
Shaft brackets (inner propellers) ... 120 tons
Rudder and stock ... 120 tons
Stern frame ... 190 tons
Stem casting ... 60
Total ... 670 tons

Propelling Machinery

The *Queen Elizabeth* will be a quadruple-screw vessel driven by Parson's single reduction geared turbines. Each of the propellers weighs 32 tons and will be driven by an independent set of machinery comprising a large gear wheel operated by four turbines.

Each of the massive gear wheels will be about 14 feet in diameter, and the total weight of the four gear wheels amounts to nearly 320 tons.

Boilers and Engine Rooms

Two separate engine rooms will be required for the *Queen Elizabeth*'s propelling machinery. Steam will be supplied to the sixteen turbines by twelve high-pressure watertube boilers. These are the largest boilers ever constructed for a ship and contain 71,000 tubes. Oil fuel will be distributed in about forty bunkers, from which 4,000 feet of piping will lead to the furnaces.

Electrical Equipment

The electrical services of the *Queen Elizabeth* will be on a most elaborate scale. The four immense turbo-generators installed in her tremendous power station will be capable of supplying sufficient electrical energy to meet the lighting and heating requirements of a town with the population of nearly 200,000. Four thousand miles of cable will be required and about 30,000 lamps will be installed.

Air-Conditioned Rooms

In the three classes of accommodation – cabin, tourist and third class, the *Queen Elizabeth* will have no fewer than twenty-nine public rooms, many of which are to have the latest system of air-conditioning. A specially equipped theatre and a garden lounge will be included in the magnificent range of rooms for cabin passengers on the Promenade Deck.

Another innovation will be the introduction of a special Restaurant Deck which, as its name implies, will provide accommodation for the three impressive cabin, tourist and third class restaurants, as well as all the spacious kitchens, service rooms and pantries.

Exercise and Recreation

Never before have opportunities for the cult of physical fitness been so carefully studied as in the *Queen Elizabeth*. Not only will there be a gymnasium, squash racquets court, swimming pool and Turkish and electric ray baths for cabin passengers, but tourist passengers are also to have their own gymnasium and swimming pool. A separate gymnasium is being introduced for third class passengers.

In addition, the Sports Deck for all classes and the wide terraced decks at the aft end of the vessel will provide magnificent open-air 'playing fields'.

Maiden Voyage

The contract for the construction of the *Queen Elizabeth* was signed on October 6th, 1936, and the keel was laid three months later, in December. She will be ready to make her maiden voyage from Southampton and Cherbourg to New York in 1940.

Appendix 2

The marine court of inquiry into the loss of the *Queen Elizabeth/Seawise University* on 9 January 1972 wanted answers to sixty-three questions. This is an edited version of the set of questions and answers:

Q1 Who were the owners of the *Seawise University* on 9 January?
A1 The Seawise Foundation, an affiliate company of the Island Navigation Corporation and one of the C. Y. Tung group of companies.

Q2 How long had the ship been under these owners?
A2 Since her purchase by C. Y. Tung in September 1970.

Q3 Was the *Seawise University* a British ship on 9 January?
A3 Yes.

Q4 When, where and by whom was the ship built?
A4 By John Brown and Company; Clydebank in 1940 [construction of the liner actually began on 4 December 1936 and she started her first voyage, the wartime dash across the Atlantic, on 2 March 1940].

Q5 On 9 January was the *Seawise University* undergoing renovations at anchor in Hong Kong harbour?
A5 Yes.

Q6 If the answer to the preceding question is Yes, what was the nature of the renovations and to what ends were they being carried out?
A6 The vessel was being extensively refitted for re-commissioning as a passenger vessel. The work of renovation was very extensive and included the creation of vertical fireproof zones and other changes in her fabric and equipment ...

Q7 If the answer to question 5 is Yes, who was in charge of the renovation work?
A7 The Island Navigation Corporation.

Q8 Who was in command of the ship on 9 January?
A8 Commodore Chen Ching-yien.

Q9 What was the approximate number of crew on board when fire broke out?
A9 250.

Q10 How many workmen were on board when fire broke out?
A10 294.

Q11 By whom were they employed?
A11 Thirty-one were employed by the Island Navigation Corporation and 263 by sub-contractors.

Q12 What were their working hours?
A12 Generally 8 a.m. to 11 a.m. and 1 p.m. to 4.30 p.m., plus overtime.

Q13 Where did the workmen normally take their midday meal?
A13 Most of the Island Navigation Corporation's ordinary workmen went ashore for lunch. Those employed by sub-contractors normally ate in the first-class restaurant on R Deck.

Q14 How many visitors were on board when fire broke out?
A14 About 60.

Q15 What gangway or gangways were in position on 9 January?
A15 Gangways were at shell doors on R Deck, port and starboard, and they led down to pontoons on both sides.

Q16 Were there any other means of entry and exit?
A16 There were six shell doors open on C Deck, which had rope ladders for emergency exit, and a further ten doors were open on C Deck with welding barges and rubbish barges afloat below.

Q17 Were there any guards at the points of entry or exit on 9 January?
A17 Security guards were at both the R Deck shell doors and one guard was on C Deck at a shell door aft on the starboard side of the vessel.

Q18 What was the state of the weather in Hong Kong harbour on 9 January?
A18 It was a fine, cool, dry day.

Q19 What was the direction and force of the wind?
A19 The wind was blowing from the north west on the port bow at about 12 knots.

Q20 What was the condition of the sea?
A20 Slight to moderate.

Q21 Were fire patrols and/or fire-fighting crews provided for the *Seawise University* on 9 January?
A21 Yes.

Q22 If the answer to the preceding question is Yes, what was the nature and strength of the fire patrols and/or fire-fighting crews? Was the strength adequate for a ship of this size?
A22 Four fire patrolmen and four professional firemen formed the nucleus of the

fire-fighting crew on 9 January. It is not considered that the strength of these two groups was adequate in view of the size of the ship and her location.

Q23 Were the fire patrols trained and instructed on the course of action to take in the event of fire?

A23 Most of the members of the fire patrol, which consisted of 12 men in three shifts of four, had received some instructions. A number had also received training from the fire service at Sek Kong, but some were only very recently recruited and would have been given only the most general instruction and training over a few days from the fire officer on board the ship.

Q24 Were the fire patrols and fire-fighting crews familiar with the positions of the fire-fighting appliances and alarms?

A24 Yes.

Q25 As at 9 January, had the crew members been properly instructed on what to do in the event fire?

A25 Up to 23 November 1971, 102 officers and ratings had attended a two-day fire-fighting course at Sek Kong. No more could be taken on for instruction up until the time of the fire. Apart from this there was a 'fire and emergency station bill in port', which laid down duties for officers and crew, including firemen and fire patrolmen, up to a number of 25. Duties were not nominated and there were obvious difficulties in the way of such nominations, including the fact that recruiting was going on and of those members already recruited there would be a turnover as a result of leave of absence. The only way, therefore, for each man to discover his precise duties at a time of fire would be to muster with the others at the appointed fire control centre so that the senior officer on duty could tell them of it and explain their duties. There is no evidence that this was done. A high proportion of the newly recruited crew were hotel staff, most of whom had never been to sea. They knew little about the fire-fighting equipment on board and topography of this very large and complicated ship.

Q26 What fire-fighting appliances, fire alarms, fire detector systems and fire sprinkler systems did the ship have?

A26 Fire appliances: there were 367 hydrants with hoses and nozzles, 184 soda acid extinguishers, 98 CO_2 extinguishers, 59 foam extinguishers, 37 dry-powder extinguishers and 480 sand buckets. Firemen also had access to sets of breathing apparatus and spare extinguishers.
Fire alarms: a manual system covered all accommodation areas.
Smoke detectors: these were fitted in the holds.
Sprinklers: a system with detectors and alarms covered all accommodation areas, public rooms and galleys.

Q27 Were these appliances and systems in full working order on 9 January?
A27 Yes.

Q28 Did the ship have a working public address system?
A28 A temporary public address system had been installed. It ceased to work after the first fire alert.

Q29 Where and at what time were signs of fire first observed?

A29 At approximately 11.28 a.m. at an alleyway on the port side of A Deck. But this may not have been the first fire.

Q30 Who spotted that fire?
A30 Three cabin boys who saw flames coming from a pile of rubbish.

Q31 What action did they take?
A31 They ran shouting 'fire!' and came across a fire patrol, which went to the scene with extinguishers.

Q32 At what other places and times was fire observed?
A32 At about the same time fires were reported on B Deck and Sun Deck. Later there were reports of fire on a main stairway between A and B decks, on R Deck and D Deck. Further fires broke out on B, R and Sun decks. These separate sites of fire eventually combined in one conflagration covering the ship from stem to stern.

Q33 Who spotted the other fires?
A33 The evidence does not show who first saw these other sites of fire.

Q34 What action was taken?
A34 Attempts were made to fight the fires as and when they were observed.

Q35 Was the assistance of the Hong Kong Fire Services Department called to the *Seawise University*?
Q35 Yes.

Q36 If the answer to the preceding question is Yes, at what time was the assistance called and by what means?
A36 A call was made by VHF from a police launch under the command of Inspector Ho Sze-min, who recorded a time of 11.35 a.m. as his first sighting of smoke. He sent a message to harbour control at 11.45 a.m., which was received by the fire control centre at 11.52 a.m.

Q37 At what time were fireboats alongside the *Seawise University* and ready for action?
A37 Fireboat No. 2 arrived at 12.27 p.m. followed shortly afterwards by several other fireboats.

Q38 At what time did they start fire-fighting operations?
A38 At about 12.30 p.m. fireboat No. 2 was playing hoses on the port side superstructure. Firefighters boarded the vessel at about 12.55 p.m.

Q39 What fire-resisting bulkheads and/or fire doors were in the ship and were the doors open or closed when fire broke out?
A39 Fire-resisting bulkheads divided the ship into eight main vertical zones. A large number of fireproof doors had been fitted but some remained to be completed. Very few, if any, of these doors were closed when fire broke out.

Q40 What type and system of electrical wiring was installed in the ship and was it satisfactory?

A40 Normal marine cables suitable for DC supply at 225v. There had been considerable re-wiring and it was found to be satisfactory.

Q41 Did any of the lights go out shortly after the discovery of fire? If so, what was the explanation.
A41 Yes. The accommodation lights were switched off on the order of the chief engineer to prevent further fires through shorting of cables.

Q42 Were any open fires, burning or welding operations going on prior to the emergency?
A42 Yes. There were burning and welding operations during the earlier part of the morning on 9 January.

Q43 If the answer to the preceding questions is Yes, what were they, where were they and what precautions were taken to safeguard such operations?
A43 On the morning of the fire there were 60 welders working on funnels and various sites on P, M, A, B, C, D and R decks, and many of them in machinery spaces, mainly dealing with fireproof doors and pipe work. Nineteen fire-watchers were employed at vulnerable points.

Q44 What inflammable material was on board and how and where was it stored?
A44 Apart from inflammable parts of the ship's own fabric, materials were stored at various points: a) paint b) gas cylinders c) some carpeting in an area of the swimming pool [which one?] d) several hundred wooden deck chairs on Promenade Deck e) some mattresses and sheets of plywood on B Deck.

Q45 What amount of fuel oil was on board and how was it distributed?
A45 There were 3,070 tons of oil in double-bottom tanks.

Q46 What shell doors were open when fire broke out?
A46 Thirty-two shell doors were open, 16 of them on C Deck. Reasons were given for this unusual situation but the court is not satisfied that it was necessary to have had so many doors open. Only one of these doors was subsequently partially closed.

Q47 What precautions were taken to control smoking?
A47 'No smoking' notices were posted at various places on the ship. Security guards checked on these areas. There were daily announcements on the public address system concerning the danger of smoking.

Q48 At a certain stage of the fire-fighting operations was it found necessary to stop putting water into the *Seawise University*?
A48 Yes.

Q49 If the answer to the preceding question is Yes, at what time was this and what was the angle of the list?
A49 At 3.28 p.m. when the list was between 12 to 15 degrees to starboard.

Q50 Was any water subsequently directed at the ship? If so, at what time, by what authority and for what reason.
A50 At about 5.30 p.m., when the list appeared to have decreased, the playing of

water from the fireboats was resumed sporadically at perceived sites of fire and in order to cool the hull and superstructure, and this went on until about 8 p.m. Operations continued during the following two days on such parts of the vessel that were visible.

Q51 Did the *Seawise University* eventually capsize and founder. If so, what was the probable cause?

A51 Yes. At noon on 10 January the ship capsized due to complete loss of stability because of the inflow of water through open shell doors.

Q52 Were the outbreaks of fire associated?

A52 The evidence suggests that there were at least three independent outbreaks of fire at roughly the same time – one on A Deck or B Deck, one at A Deck at a different location and one in the officers' accommodation at the fore-end of Boat Deck. Later several fires were observed on R Deck.

Q53 What was the cause?

A53 The probable cause of these outbreaks was, in each case, a deliberate act on the part of a person or persons unknown.

Q54 At what time was the *Seawise University* evacuated?

A54 Evacuation began shortly after the outbreak of the fires. It was completed at 3.27 p.m. on 9 January.

Q55 Was there any loss of life or injury?

A55 There were no deaths. Several people broke legs and ribs. There were numerous rope burns and minor injuries such as cuts to hands.

Q56 At what notice could the ship have been able to use her propulsion?

A56 At least six hours.

Q57 At what notice could the anchors have been weighed?

A57 Immediately if electric power was available.

Q58 Was controlled beaching a feasible proposition?

A58 No.

Q59 If the answer to the preceding question is Yes, would beaching have permitted the fire-fighting operations to continue? If so, would there have been any likelihood of fire being brought under control?

A59 Does not arise.

Q60 Was any advice on fire precautions given to the owners of the *Seawise University*?

A60 Yes.

Q61 If the answer to the preceding question is Yes, by whom was it given?

A61 By officers of the Marine Department in consultation with officers of the Fire Services Department.

Q62 Did any government department have any statutory responsibilities in respect of the *Seawise University*?

A62 The legislative position in relation to hazards arising from work being carried out aboard ships at anchor in the harbour is somewhat obscure and unsatisfactory. It is doubtful that any government department had unequivocal statutory powers to control the working methods employed in the operations aboard the *Seawise University*.

Q63 If the answer to the preceding question is Yes, what was the nature of such responsibilities and were they discharged?

A63 Does not arise.

Appendix 3: A diagram showing the various decks and features of the *Queen Elizabeth* during her golden years of Atlantic travel. The numbers not given in the key above are as follows: 31. First Class Games Deck; 32. Tourist Games Deck; 33. Radar Equipment; 34. Navigating Bridge; 35. Crow's Nest; 36. Foremast; 37. No. 2 Hatch; 38. Cargo Derricks; 39. No. 1 Hatch; 40. Anchor Gear; 41. Electric Cargo Winches;

KEY TO INTERIOR STRUCTURE

D DECK
1. Tourist Accommodation

C DECK
2. Tourist Accommodation
3. Cabin Class Rooms
4. Swimming Bath, 1st. Class
5. Curative Baths

RESTAURANT DECK
6. Tourist Accommodation
7. Tourist Dining Saloon
8. Restaurant, entrance
9. Main Restaurant
10. Kitchens

B DECK
11. Tourist Cinema
12. Tourist Accommodation
13. First Class Rooms

A DECK
14. Tourist Smoking Room
15. First Class Cabins
16. Purser's Bureau
17. Air Conditioning Plant
18. First Class Rooms

MAIN DECK
19. First Class entrance
20. Barber's Shop
21. First Class Rooms

PROMENADE DECK
22. First Class Lifts
23. First Class Lounge
24. Pantry
25. First Class Writing Room
26. Salon

BOAT DECK
27. Lift Machinery
28. Air Conditioning Plant

SUN DECK
29. Squash Court
30. Engineers' Accommodation

42. Cargo Stowage Space; 43. Baggage Space; 44. Cargo; 45. Mails; 46. Linen Store; 47. No. 2 Boiler Room; 48; Turbo-generator Room; 49. Oil Fuel Tanks; 50. No. 3 Boiler Room; 51. No. 4 Boiler Room; 52. Forward Engine Room; 53. Aft Engine Room. (*J. & C. McCutcheon*)

Appendix 4

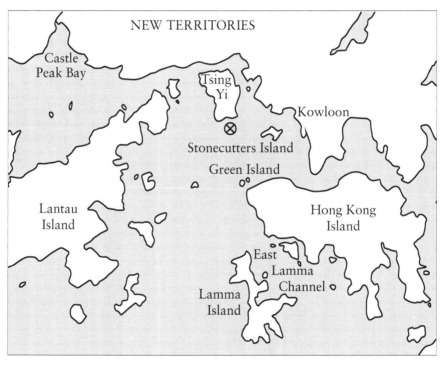

NEW TERRITORIES

Castle
Peak Bay

Tsing
Yi

Kowloon

Stonecutters Island

Green Island

Lantau
Island

Hong Kong
Island

East
Lamma
Channel

Lamma
Island

The approximate position (X) of the *Queen Elizabeth* (*Seawise University*) in Hong Kong harbour on 9 January 1972. (*Map illustration by User Design, www.userdesign.co.uk*)

Notes and Sources

Chapter 1

1. Launch of the *Queen Elizabeth*: *The Times* and *The Daily Telegraph*, 28 September 1938.
2. *Normandie* and the grocer: *RMS Queen Elizabeth, From Victory To Valhalla* by David Hutchings, chapter 2.
3. Air raids: Southampton City Council and Glasgow City Council archives. Learning and Teaching Scotland.
4. *The New York Times*, 8 March 1940.
5. Fighting on the *Queen Elizabeth*: *Warrior Queens* by Daniel Butler, chapter 4.
6. Rumour of the loss of the *Queen Elizabeth*: *Captain of the Queens* by Captain Harry Grattidge, chapter 13.
7. General Marshall's concern: *The Second World War, The Grand Alliance* by Winston Churchill, chapter 37.
8. Churchill's complaint: personal minute of Churchill dated 23 March 1941.
9. Churchill's broadcast: *RMS Queen Elizabeth, From Victory To Valhalla*, by David Hutchings, chapter 7.

Chapter 2

1. *The Queens And I* by Commodore Geoffrey Marr, chapter 8.
2. Ibid, chapter 8.
3. *I Captained The Big Ships* by Robert Thelwell.

Chapter 3

1. *American Notes* by Charles Dickens, chapter 2.
2. Cunard Eagle and BOAC-Cunard: *Of Comets And Queens* by Sir Basil Smallpeice, chapters 13 and 14.
3. *The Queens And I* by Commodore Geoffrey Marr, chapter 13.
4. Ibid.
5. Cunard press release, 10 January 1964.
6. Confidential monthly sales bulletin for October 1965.
7. *Of Comets And Queens* by Sir Basil Smallpeice, chapters 1 and 2; obituary, *The Independent* 17 July 1992.
8. *Of Comets And Queens* by Sir Basil Smallpeice, chapter 17.

9. Cunard board minute, 25 January 1967.
10. Ibid, 26 April 1967.

Chapter 4

1. *The Queens And I* by Commodore Geoffrey Marr, chapter 14.
2. *The Elizabeth: Passage Of A Queen* by Leonard Stevens.
3. *The Queens And I* by Commodore Geoffrey Marr, chapter 14.
4. Letter from Roger Dawe to Ben Meynell at the Board of Trade, dated 10 May 1967.
5. Document titled 'Future Use Of The *Queens*', Board of Trade, Shipping Policy Division, 23 May 1967.
6. Document titled 'Future Use Of The Liners *Queen Mary* And *Queen Elizabeth*', Board of Trade, Shipping Policy Division, 19 June 1967.
7. Cunard board minute, 26 July 1967.
8. Ibid, 30 August 1967.
9. Ibid, 25 October and 29 November 1967.
10. Ibid, 28 February 1968.
11. Ibid, 27 March, 24 April 1968.
12. *Philadelphia* magazine, June 1968.
13. Ibid.
14. Ibid.
15. *Philadelphia* magazine, July 1968.
16. Cunard board minute, 31 July 1968.
17. Cunard board minutes, 28 August, 11 September, 22 October, 21 November and 4 December 1968.
18. *The Queens And I* by Commodore Geoffrey Marr, chapter 15.

Chapter 5

1. *The Queens And I* by Commodore Geoffrey Marr, chapter 15.
2. *The Miami News* and *The Miami Herald*, 9 December 1968.
3. *Life* magazine, 11 September 1970, *Destiny's Daughter* by Russell Galbraith, chapter 29.
4. *The Miami Herald*, 26 April 1970.
5. *The Queens And I* by Commodore Geoffrey Marr, chapter 16.
6. *The Miami Herald*, 29 May 1969.
7. Cunard board minutes, 30 April and 28 May 1969.
8. *The Miami Herald*, 6 September 1970, *Life* magazine, 11 September 1970.
9. *St Petersburg Times*, 6 April 1970.
10. *Fort Lauderdale News*, 24 May 1970, *The Miami News*, 8 September 1970.

Chapter 6

1. Cunard board minute, 26 August 1970.
2. *Philadelphia* magazine, June 1968.
3. Ibid.
4. *Life* magazine, 11 September 1970.
5. *The Miami Herald*, 11 May 1969.
6. *The Miami Herald*, 29 November 1970, US Treasury Department handbook on the Mafia.
7. *The Miami Herald*, 23 June 1971.

8. Information supplied to the author by the Federal Court in Miami.

Chapter 7

1. *The Miami Herald*, 5 May 1969.
2. Ibid, 22 November 1972.
3. *Miami Daily News*, 19 June 1951, and *The Miami Herald*, 22 November 1972.
4. *The Miami News*, 3 February 1973.

Chapter 8

1. *The Queens And I* by Commodore Geoffrey Marr, chapter 17.
2. *The Miami Herald*, 11 February 1971.
3. *The Queens And I* by Commodore Geoffrey Marr, chapter 17.
4. Ibid.
5. *The Miami Herald*, 7 March 1971.
6. *The Queens And I* by Commodore Geoffrey Marr, chapter 18.
7. *South China Morning Post*, 16 and 17 July 1971.
8. *The Queens And I* by Commodore Geoffrey Marr, chapter 18.
9. *South China Morning Post*, 16 July 1971.
10. Letter from the Director of Marine to Captain T. Lam, Port Captain, Hong Kong Export Line, dated 19 July 1971. Leonard Warrallo's evidence to the Marine Court of Inquiry, reported by the *Hongkong Standard*, 23 March 1972.
11. Letter from the Director of Marine to the Hong Kong Export Line, dated 31 August 1971.
12. Letter from the Director of Marine to Captain T. Lam, Port Captain, Hong Kong Export Line, dated 13 September 1971.
13. 'Boat People Of Hong Kong', an episode of *Wicker's Orient*, a Yorkshire Television production.

Chapter 9

1. Background of C. Y. Tung: *Changing Places, The Remarkable Story Of The Hong Kong Shipowners* by Stephanie Zarach, chapters 1, 2, 3 and 6; *Hong Kong! Hong Kong!* by Dick Wilson, chapter 2; confidential report by Kenneth Milburn, Director of the Hong Kong Marine Department, 18 January 1972; *China Post* (Taiwan), 18 January 1972; *South China Morning Post*, 16 April 1982; and *The Times*, 16 April 1982.

Chapter 10

1. Various sources.
2. *The New York Times*, 12 December 1988.
3. *Triad Societies In Hong Kong* by W. P. Morgan, chapter 4.
4. Preface of *Triad Societies In Hong Kong* by W. P. Morgan.
5. Commissioner of Police Review 1978.
6. Annual police report for 1970–71.
7. Article by Professor Harold Traver in the *Hong Kong Journal*, 4 January 2009.
8. *The Triads As Business* by Yiu Kong Chu, chapter 1.
9. *South China Morning Post*, 19 September 1992.

10. *The Chinese Mafia* by Fenton Bresler, chapter 11.
11. *South China Morning Post*, 18 August 1973.
12. Speech by Superintendent Norman Temple to the Rotary Club of Kowloon, 28 February 1974.

Chapter 11

1. Obituary of Charles Sutcliffe by Kevin Sinclair, 27 September 2005, publication unknown.
2. Various sources, including *Hard Graft In Hong Kong* by H. J. Lethbridge, chapter 5, and *The Standard* (Hong Kong), 1 June 2006.
3. *The Standard* (Hong Kong), 30 May and 1 June 2006.
4. *The Daily Telegraph*, 20 April 2006, and *Asian Pacific Post*, 6 September 2006.
5. *Hard Graft In Hong Kong* by H. J. Lethbridge, chapter 5.
6. Statement by Walter Easey, November 1975.
7. Obituary of Sir Jack Cater, 28 April 2006.
8. *Hard Graft In Hong Kong* by H. J. Lethbridge, chapter 6.
9. Annual reports of the commissioner of police.

Chapter 12

1. *Far Eastern Economic Review*, 13 July 1995, and *Target Zhou Enlai: The Kashmir Princess Incident of 1955* by Steve Tsang.
2. *South China Morning Post*, 17 July 1971.
3. Ibid, 3 July 1971.
4. *MAO, The Unknown Story* by Jung Chang and Jon Halliday, chapter 43.
5. Ibid, chapter 40.
6. Report, marked 'secret', prepared by John Morgan, head of the Far Eastern Department, Foreign and Commonwealth Office, dated 17 May 1971.
7. Letter sent by Hong Kong Defence Secretary Peter Lloyd to John Morgan, head of the Far Eastern Department, Foreign and Commonwealth Office, dated 5 October 1971.
8. *South China Morning Post*, page 1 story headlined 'Police smash Soviet spy ring in colony', 25 August 1972. *Where Empires Collided* by Michael Share, chapter 6.
9. *Daily Express* story headlined 'Hong Kong saves Reds from letter bombs', 15 December 1972.
10. Telegram marked 'confidential' from Sir Murray MacLehose, dated 13 December 1972.
11. Telegram marked 'secret' from Sir Murray MacLehose, dated 7 December 1972.
12. Telegram marked 'confidential' from Sir Murray MacLehose, dated 8 December 1972.

Chapter 13

1. Article in *The Correspondent*, June/July 2008, magazine of the Foreign Correspondents' Club, Hong Kong.
2. Comments by John Hudson, undated, on Cruise.Page.com
3. Evidence to the Marine Court of Inquiry into the ship's loss, 1972, *Hongkong Standard*, 22 March 1972.
4. *Mariners: The Hong Kong Marine Police 1948-1997* by Iain Ward, chapter 11.
5. Comments to the author by Colin Reigate in June 2009.

6. Written witness statement dated 17 January 1972.
7. Main account of the fire and rescue: various sources, including the report of the Marine Court of Inquiry into the ship's loss, 1972; *Mariners: The Hong Kong Marine Police 1948–1997* by Iain Ward, chapter 11; and interview with Iain Ward in Hong Kong in November 2009.
8. *South China Morning Post*, 10 January 1972.
9. Reports in the *Hongkong Standard*, *Lloyd's List* and *The Times*, all dated 10 January 1972.
10. *The Queens And I* by Commodore Geoffrey Marr, chapter 19.
11. *South China Morning Post*, 11 and 13 January 1972, *Lloyd's List*, 13 January.
12. *South China Morning Post*, 11 January 1972.
13. Confidential report by Kenneth Milburn, dated 17 January 1972.
14. *Of Comets And Queens* by Sir Basil Smallpeice, chapter 20.

Chapter 14

1. Confidential report prepared by Kenneth Milburn for the Governor of Hong Kong, Sir Murray MacLehose, dated 17 January 1972.
2. Evidence to the Marine Court of Inquiry, reported in the *South China Morning Post*, 25 March 1972.
3. *No Cure No Pay* by William Worrall and Kevin Sinclair, chapter 22.
4. *South China Morning Post*, 2 July 1979.
5. Account of the loss of the *Normandie*: various sources including *Normandie* by John Maxtone-Graham, chapter 11; *Time* magazine, 27 April 1942; and 'The Normandie Fire' by Paul Hashagen, *Firehouse* magazine, April 1993.

Chapter 15

1. Report of the Marine Court of Inquiry, paragraph 5.
2. Ibid, paragraph 6.
3. Ibid, paragraph 38.
4. Ibid, paragraph 40.
5. Ibid, paragraphs 34 and 35.
6. Ibid, paragraph 39.
7. Ibid, paragraphs 31, 32 and 33.
8. Ibid, paragraph 26.
9. Ibid, paragraphs 26, 27 and 28.

Chapter 16

1. *Hongkong Standard*, 23 February 1972.
2. Ibid, and written witness statement.
3. *Hongkong Standard*, 23 February 1972.
4. Ibid.
5. Report of the Marine Court of Inquiry, paragraph 41.
6. *Hongkong Standard*, 19 February 1972.

Chapter 17

1. *Hongkong Standard*, 22 February 1972.
2. Report of the Marine Court of Inquiry, paragraph 67.
3. Ibid, paragraph 72.

4. Ibid, paragraph 79.
5. Ibid, paragraph 80.
6. *Hongkong Standard*, 24 February 1972.
7. Ibid, 25 February 1972.
8. Ibid, 26 February 1972.
9. Ibid, 3 March 1972.
10. Ibid, 4 March 1972.
11. Ibid, 7 March 1972.
12. *South China Morning Post*, 11 March 1972.
13. *Hongkong Standard*, 15 March 1972.
14. *Hongkong Standard* and *South China Morning Post*, 18 March 1972.

Chapter 18

1. Report of the Marine Court of Inquiry, paragraphs 101–108.
2. Ibid, paragraphs 98–100.
3. Ibid, paragraph 109.
4. Ibid, paragraphs 110–112, 114.
5. Ibid, paragraphs 117 and 118.
6. Ibid, paragraphs 119–122.
7. Ibid, paragraphs 128 and 129.
8. Ibid, paragraphs 130 and 131.
9. Ibid, paragraphs 132–134.
10. Ibid, paragraphs 166 and 167.
11. Ibid, paragraph 169.
12. Ibid, paragraphs 173 and 174.

Chapter 19

1. *Hongkong Standard* and *Lloyd's List*, 13 January 1972.
2. *South China Morning Post*, 20 January 1972.
3. Report of the Marine Court of Inquiry, paragraph 173.
4. *South China Morning Post*, 20 July 1972.
5. Interview with Iain Ward at the Hullett House Hotel, Kowloon, the former headquarters of the marine police, November 2009. *Mariners: The Hong Kong Marine Police 1948–1997* by Iain Ward, chapter 11.
6. Conversation with the author, October 2009.
7. Comments to the author, June 2009.
8. Letters to the author from the Hong Kong Police dated 10 July 2009 and 8 September 2009.
9. *Hong Kong Murders* by Kate Whitehead.
10. Comments to the author, March 2010.
11. Obituary of Bere, *South China Morning Post*, 15 February 2002.
12. *OffBeat*, newspaper of the Hong Kong Police, 1997.
13. Comments to the author, March 2010.

Chapter 20

1. Report by Maynard Parker, *The Atlantic Monthly*, November 1967.
2. Report, marked secret, for the Secretary of State for Commonwealth Affairs, dated 23 June 1967, paragraph 7.
3. Report by Maynard Parker, *The Atlantic Monthly*, November 1967.

4. Report by Special Branch, 'The Communist Challenge', dated 15 May 1967, paragraphs 2, 3 and 5.
5. Ibid, paragraph 16.
6. Ibid, paragraphs 17 and 18.
7. Report, marked secret, for the Secretary of State for Commonwealth Affairs, dated 23 June 1967, paragraphs 17 and 20.
8. Telegram, marked confidential, dated 25 May 1967.
9. Report by the Secretary of State for Commonwealth Affairs, marked secret, dated 24 May 1967.
10. Articles in the *People's Daily*, *Ta Kung Pao* and *Wen Wei Pao*, all dated 29 May 1967.
11. *MAO, The Unkown Story* by Jung Chang and Jon Halliday, chapter 53.
12. Report, marked secret, by E. Bolland, head of the Far Eastern Department, Foreign Office.
13. CIA Intelligence Memorandum, 'The Situation In Hong Kong', dated 11 July 1967, paragraph 18.
14. CIA Intelligence Memorandum, 'The Outlook For Hong Kong', dated 25 August 1967, summary and paragraph 18.
15. Report by Maynard Parker, *The Atlantic Monthly*, November 1967.
16. *South China Morning Post*, 16 August 1972.
17. Comments by the *Kung Sheung Daily News*, 19 August 1972.

Chapter 21

1. White House memorandum, marked top secret/sensitive, 25 October 1970.
2. Draft letter to Chou En-lai, undated but probably written about 10 December 1970.
3. Memorandum for Nixon from Kissinger, marked top secret/sensitive, 12 January 1971.
4. State Department intelligence briefing, 14 April 1971.
5. Message from Chou En-lai dated 21 April 1971 but received by Kissinger on 27 April.
6. Record of Nixon–Kissinger telephone conversation, 27 April 1971.
7. White House memorandum marked top secret/sensitive/exclusively eyes only, 1 July 1971.
8. White House memorandum on meeting of 10 July 1971, marked top secret/sensitive/exclusively eyes only, 6 August 1971.
9. Briefing for Nixon by Kissinger, 'My talks with Chou En-lai', 14 July 1971, marked top secret/sensitive/exclusively eyes only.
10. White House memorandum for the president's files, 19 July 1971.
11. *South China Morning Post*, 17 July 1971.

Chapter 22

1. Statement by ambassador George Bush to the United Nations, in plenary, on Chinese representation, 18 October 1971.
2. Article by William Rogers, 'The case for dual Chinese seating in the UN', United States Information Service, 20 October 1971.
3. Confidential telegram from the British Embassy in Washington to the Foreign and Commonwealth Office, 26 October 1971.
4. Enver Hoxha's *Selected Works: 1966–1975*, vol. 4, and *Reflections On China*, vol. 2.

5. Memorandum of conversation, New York City, East Side, 10 December 1971.
6. *The Kissinger Transcripts*, edited by William Burr, chapter 1.
7. *Nixon And Kissinger, Partners In Power* by Robert Dallek, chapter 4.

Chapter 23

1. *Hongkong Standard*, 22 February 1972.
2. *The Kissinger Transcripts*, edited by William Burr, chapter 1.
3. White House memorandum of conversation, 21 February 1972, marked top secret/sensitive/exclusive eyes only.
4. *Hongkong Standard*, 22 February 1972.
5. Jack Anderson, syndicated columnist, *Florence Times* (Alabama) 3 February 1972.
6. *China Post*, 'the only English language morning paper in free China', 23 February 1972.

Chapter 24

1. 'Traveller's Tales' by Derek Davies, *Far Eastern Economic Review*, 6 August 1973.
2. Magazine of the Foreign Correspondents' Club, Hong Kong, June/July 2008.
3. Conversation with the author in Hong Kong, June 2009.
4. London *Sunday Express*, 31 December 1972.
5. Report for the Governor of Hong Kong, 18 January 1972.
6. Conversation with the author, August 2009.
7. Conversation with the author, October 2009.
8. *Mariners: The Hong Kong Marine Police 1948–1997* by Iain Ward, chapter 11.
9. Comments to the author, September 2009.
10. *Triad Societies In Hong Kong* by W. P. Morgan, chapter 4.
11. *Mariners: The Hong Kong Marine Police 1948–1997* by Iain Ward, chapter 5.
12. *South China Morning Post*, 5 April 1972.
13. Ibid, 28 January 1972.
14. Ibid, 10 June 1972.
15. Ibid, 21 July 1972.
16. Conversation with the author, June 2009.
17. *RMS Queen Elizabeth, The Ultimate Ship* by Clive Harvey, chapter 11.
18. *China Mail*, 12 January 1972.
19. Hong Kong Public Records Office, HKRS 545-1-294.
20. *South China Morning Post*, 20 July 1972.
21. *Tell Me A Story* by Kevin Sinclair, chapter 25.
22. Comments to the author, October 2009.
23. Letter from John Addis, British Embassy, Beijing, to John Morgan, head of the Far Eastern Department, Foreign and Commonwealth Office, 18 March 1972.
24. International Monetary Fund.
25. FCO policy document, January 1971. National Archives, London, FCO 21/831.
26. *International Herald Tribune*, 31 December 2003.
27. Comments to the author, June 2009.
28. Report by Stephen Vines, *The Independent*, 12 May 1997.
29. 'Partners In Crime', a report by Frederic Dannen, *The New Republic* magazine, July 1997.
30. *The Dragon Syndicates* by Martin Booth, part 5, chapter 5.
31. Ibid.
32. 'Partners In Crime', a report by Frederic Dannen, *The New Republic* magazine, July 1997.

Chapter 25

1. Notes of meeting held at the Marine Department on 31 October 1972. Marked 'not for circulation'.
2. *Mutuality: The Story Of The UK P&I Club* by Peter Young, chapter 11.
3. Letter to the author from the UK P&I Club's London agents, Thomas Miller, dated 29 July 2009.
4. Letter from Ulrich Harms to the Island Navigation Corporation, dated 10 March 1972.
5. Ibid, 9 May 1972.
6. Letter dated 2 January 1973.
7. Conversation with the author, August 2009.
8. Comments to the author, August 2009.
9. Conversation with the author, July 2009.
10. *South China Morning Post*, 14 December 1973.
11. Letter to the Universal Dockyard from the Marine Department, dated 5 February 1974.
12. Report by C. Ranson, Chief Explosives Officer, Mines Department.
13. China Light & Power Company letter dated 27 October 1972. Marine Department reply dated 31 October 1972.
14. Letter from C. Y. Chen, manager, Far East Salvage Company to the Director of Marine, dated 16 June 1976.
15. Letter from M. H. Liang, assistant general manager, Island Navigation Corporation, 1 March 1977.
16. Progress report up to 1 February 1977, prepared by M. J. Anderson for J. P. Williams and Associates (Hong Kong).
17. Memo dated 26 July 1977.
18. Conversation with the author, June 2009.
19. Comments to the author, August 2009.

Chapter 26

1. *South China Morning Post*, 16 April 1982.
2. Ibid.
3. *The Times*, 16 April 1982.
4. *South China Morning Post*, 18 April 1982.
5. Ibid, 16 April 1982.
6. *Asian Godfathers* by Joe Studwell, chapter 5.
7. *South China Morning Post*, 29 October 2006, *The Times*, 31 October 2006.
8. Sidewinder report dated 24 June 1997.
9. *Wall Street Journal*, 19 March 2010.
10. *The Independent*, 24 November 1996.
11. BBC Politics 1997 website.
12. 'Hong Kong's Red Shadows' by Lin Neumann, *Asia Times*, 10 June 2004.
13. Introduction to *Underground Front, The Chinese Communist Party in Hong Kong* by Christine Loh.
14. Ibid, chapter 10.

Bibliography

Aitken, Jonathan, *Nixon, A Life* (Weidenfeld & Nicolson, 1993).

Anastasia, George, *Blood And Honor, Inside The Scarfo Mob – The Mafia's Most Violent Family* (Camino Books, 1991).

Andrew, Christopher, *The Defence Of The Realm, The Authorized History Of MI5* (Allen Lane, 2009).

Arnott, Robert, *Captain Of The Queen* (New English Library, 1982).

Booth, Martin, *The Dragon Syndicates, The Gobal Phenomenon Of The Triads* (Doubleday, 1999).

Bresler, Fenton, *The Chinese Mafia* (Weidenfeld & Nicolson, 1980).

Bundy, William, *A Tangled Web: The Making Of Foreign Policy In The Nixon Presidency* (IB Tauris, 1998).

Burr, William, editor, *The Kissinger Transcripts, The Top Secret Talks With Beijing And Moscow* (The New Press, 1999).

Butler, Daniel, *Warrior Queens, The Queen Mary And Queen Elizabeth In World War II* (Leo Cooper, 2002).

Cameron, Nigel, *Hong Kong: The Cultured Pearl* (Oxford University Press, 1978).

Chang, Jung, with Halliday, Jon, *Mao, The Unknown Story* (Vintage, 2007).

Churchill, Winston, *The Second World War*, six volumes (Cassell & Co., 1949).

Dallek, Robert, *Nixon And Kissinger, Partners In Power* (Allen Lane, 2007).

Davies, Philip, *MI6 And The Machinery Of Spying* (Frank Cass Publishers, 2004).

Deng, Xiaoping, *Selected Works* (Foreign Languages Press, Beijing, 1984).

Elliott, Elsie, *Crusade For Justice: An Autobiography* (Heinemann Asia, 1981).

Endacott, G. B., and Birch, Alan, *Hong Kong Eclipse* (Oxford University Press, 1978).

Faligot, Roger, and Kauffer, Remi, *The Chinese Secret Service* (Headline Book Publishing, 1989).

Fenby, Jonathan, *The Penguin History Of Modern China, The Fall And Rise Of A Great Power, 1850–2009* (Penguin Books, 2009).

Fox, Stephen, *The Ocean Railway: Isambard Kingdom Brunel, Samuel Cunard And The Revolutionary World Of The Great Atlantic Steamships* (HarperCollins, 2003).

Galbraith, Russell, *Destiny's Daughter, The Tragedy of RMS Queen Elizabeth* (Mainstream Publishing, 1988).

Goodstadt, Leo, *Uneasy Partners: The Conflict Between Public Interest And Private Profit In Hong Kong* (Hong Kong University Press, 2005).

Grant, Kay, *Samuel Cunard – Pioneer Of The Atlantic Steamship* (Abelard-Schuman, 1967).

Grattidge Harry, *Captain Of The Queens* (Oldbourne Press, no date but early 1950s).

Hanhimaki, Jussi, *The Flawed Architect: Henry Kissinger And American Foreign Policy* (Oxford University Press, 2004).

Harvey, Clive, *RMS Queen Elizabeth, The Ultimate Ship* (Carmania Press, 2008).

Heath, Edward, *The Course Of My Life* (Hodder & Stoughton, 1998).

Hersh, Seymour, *The Price Of Power: Kissinger In The Nixon White House* (Summit Books, 1983).

Hollingworth, Clare, *Mao And The Men Against Him* (Jonathan Cape, 1985).

Hoxha, Enver, *Reflections On China*, vol. 2 (8 Nentori, Tirana, 1979).

Hutchings, David, *RMS Queen Elizabeth, From Victory To Valhalla*, (Kingfisher Publications, 1990).

Hyde, Francis, *Cunard And The North Atlantic 1840–1973* (Macmillan, 1975).

Johnson, Howard, *The Cunard Story* (Whittet Books, 1987).

Kim, Samuel, *China, The United Nations And World Order* (Princeton University Press, 1979).

Kissinger, Henry, *The White House Years, 1968–72* (Weidenfeld & Nicolson, 1979).

Lacy, Robert, *The Queens Of The North Atlantic* (Sidwick & Jackson, 1973).

Lethbridge, H. J., *Hard Graft In Hong Kong, Scandal, Corruption, The ICAC* (Oxford University Press, 1985).

Loh, Christine, *Underground Front, The Chinese Communist Party In Hong Kong* (Hong Kong University Press, 2010).

Marr, Geoffrey, *The Queens And I, The Autobiography Of The Captain Of The Queen Mary And The Last Captain Of The Queen Elizabeth* (Adlard Coles, 1973).

Melson, P. J., editor, *White Ensign – Red Dragon, The History Of The Royal Navy In Hong Kong 1841–1997* (Edinburgh Financial Publishing, 1997).

Miners, Norman, *The Government And Politics Of Hong Kong* (Oxford University Press, 1982).

Morgan, W. P., *Triad Societies In Hong Kong* (Government Press, Hong Kong, 1960).

Nixon, Richard, *The Memoirs Of Richard Nixon* (Arrow Books, 1979).

Patten, Chris, *East And West* (Macmillan, 1998).

Robertson, Frank, *Triangle Of Death, The Inside Story Of The Triads – The Chinese Mafia* (Routledge & Kegan Paul, 1977).

Share, Michael, *Where Empires Collided, Russian And Soviet Relations With Hong Kong, Taiwan And Macao* (Chinese University Press, 2007).

Shirk, Susan, *China, Fragile Superpower* (Oxford University Press, 2007).

Sinclair, Kevin, *Asia's Finest: An Illustrated Account Of The Royal Hong Kong Police* (Unicorn Books, 1981).

Sinclair, Kevin, *Tell Me A Story, Forty Years Newspapering In Hong Kong* (published by the *South China Morning Post*, 2007).

Smallpeice, Basil, *Of Comets And Queens, An Autobiography* (Airlife Publishing, 1981).

Snow, Philip, *The Fall Of Hong Kong: Britain, China And The Japanese Occupation* (Yale University Press, 2003).

Stevens, Leonard, *The Elizabeth: Passage Of A Queen* (George Allen & Unwin, 1969).

Steele, James, *Queen Mary* (Phaidon Press,1993).

Studwell, Joe, *Asian Godfathers, Money And Power In Hong Kong And South-East Asia* (Profile Books, 2007).

Summers, Anthony, *The Arrogance Of Power, The Secret World Of Richard Nixon* (Victor Gollancz, 2000).

Thelwell, Robert, *I Captained The Big Ships* (Barker, 1961).

Thomas, David, and Holmes, Patrick, *Queen Mary And The Cruiser, The Curacoa Disaster* (Leo Cooper, 1997).

Tsang, Steve, editor, *In The Shadow Of China, Political Developments In Taiwan Since 1949* (Hurst & Co, 1993).

Tsang, Steve, editor, *Government And Politics, A Documentary History Of Hong Kong* (Hong Kong University Press, 1995).

Tucker, Nancy Bernkopf, *Taiwan, Hong Kong, And The United States, 1945–1992* (Twayne Publishers, 1994).

Tucker, Nancy Bernkopf, *Dangerous Strait, The US–Taiwan–China Crisis* (Columbia University Press, 2005).

Walker, Colin, *Memory Of A Queen: RMS Queen Elizabeth* (Oxford Publishing Co, 1972).

Ward, Iain, *Mariners: The Hong Kong Marine Police 1948–1997* (IEW Publications, 1999).

Warwick, Ronald, *QE2, The Cunard Line Flagship, Queen Elizabeth 2* (WW Norton & Co, 1985).

Watton, Ross, *The Cunard Liner Queen Mary* (Conway Maritime Press, 1989).

Welsh, Frank, *A History Of Hong Kong* (HarperCollins, 1997).

West, Nigel, *The Friends: British Post-War Secret Intelligence Operations* (Weidenfeld & Nicolson, 1988).

Whitehead, Kate, *Hong Kong Murders* (Oxford University Press, 2001).

Williams, David, *Glory Days, Cunard* (Ian Allan, 1998).

Wilson, Dick, *Chou, The Story Of Zhou Enlai 1898–1976* (Hutchinson & Co, 1984).

Wilson, Dick, *Hong Kong! Hong Kong!* (Unwin Hyman, 1990).

Worrall, William, with Sinclair, Kevin, *No Cure No Pay, Memoirs Of A China Sea Salvage Captain* (published by the *South China Morning Post*, 1981).

Yiu, Kong Chu, *The Triads As Business* (Routledge, 2000).

Zarach, Stephanie, *Changing Places, The Remarkable Story Of The Hong Kong Shipowners* (Hong Kong Shipowners Association, 2007).

Acknowledgements

I would like to thank the following for their help: Lieutenant Alberto Borges, Special Investigations Section, Miami Police; the British Library, St Pancras, London; the British Library (Newspapers), Colindale, London; Broward County Library, Fort Lauderdale, Florida; Allan Brunton-Reed, managing director, The ABR Company; Stephen Davies, director of the Hong Kong Maritime Museum; Scott Deitche; Kathleen Dickson, British Film Institute; Susan Falken, US Department of Justice, Eastern District of Pennsylvania; Dr Dafydd Fell, Centre of Taiwan Studies, School of Oriental and African Studies, London; John Fox, historian, Federal Bureau of Investigation; Peter Halliday, former assistant commissioner, Royal Hong Kong Police; David Hardy, Records Management Division, Federal Bureau of Investigation, Washington DC; Terry Helmers, University of Miami; Michael Hoare; David Hodson, former assistant commissioner, Royal Hong Kong Police; Mark Hoey; Trevor Hollingsbee, former senior superintendent, Royal Hong Kong Police (Marine); Bernard Hui, senior assistant archivist, Hong Kong Public Records Office; the Imperial War Museum Photograph Archive; the Independent Commission Against Corruption, Hong Kong; the Investigation Bureau, Ministry of Justice, Taiwan; Dr Kam-yuen Lam, curator of the Hong Kong Police Museum; M. H. Liang, former executive of the Island Navigation Corporation; Mick Lidbury; Quincy Lloyd; Christine Loh; Keith Lomas, former deputy commissioner, Royal Hong Kong Police; Captain Alan Loynd, Branscombe Marine Consultants; John Lui, Hong Kong Marine Department; Sir John Morgan, former head of the Far Eastern Department, Foreign Office, London; the National Maritime Museum, Greenwich, London; Mark Nelson; C. K. Pak, Shanghai marine consultant; Philadelphia Library; Colin Reigate, former chief inspector, Royal Hong Kong Police (Marine); Keith Rusby, chief salvage officer, Group Ocean; John Shipley, Miami Library; Mark Tam, editor of *OffBeat*, magazine of the Hong Kong Police Force; The National Archives, Kew, London; Professor Harold Traver, Hong Kong criminologist; John Turner, former chief superintendent, Royal Hong Kong Police (Marine); the UK P&I Club; the University of Liverpool Library; James Walker; Iain Ward, former superintendent, Royal Hong Kong Police (Marine); Major Timothy Wheadon; Dave Woodward, picture archivist, ITV; Jorge Zamanillo, HistoryMiami.

I am grateful for the reminiscences and observations of Captain Harry Grattidge and Commodore Geoffrey Marr, and the reports of Greg Walter of *Philadelphia* magazine.

Finally, my thanks to Duncan McAra and Amberley's Campbell McCutcheon and Louis Archard for their guidance.

Brian Izzard
March 2012

Index